JEWISH PARTISANS:

A DOCUMENTARY OF JEWISH RESISTANCE IN THE SOVIET UNION DURING WORLD WAR II

VOLUME I

Edited, and with an Introduction
by
Jack Nusan Porter

Translated from the Hebrew by the
Magal Translation Institute, Ltd.
Based on Original Russian, Polish, and Yiddish Sources

Hebrew Version: Binyamin West (ed.)
Heym Hayu Rabim: Partizanim Yehudim B'brit
Ha-moatzot B'milchemet Ha-olam Ha-shniya
Tel Aviv: Archives for the Committee of Russian Jewry,
Hapoel Hatzair Publishing Cooperative, 1968
in cooperation with the
Yad Vashem Memorial Institute, Jerusalem

Library of Congress Catalog Card Number: **81-40258**

Dedicated to my parents

Irving Porter (1906-1979) and

Faye (Merin) Porter

My father died before this book was published.

May his memory be a blessing.

Do not judge your fellowman
until you have stood in his place.

> --Hillel the Sage, <u>Pirke Avot</u>
> (<u>Sayings of the Fathers</u>)

I believe

I believe in the sun even when it is not shining.

I believe in love even when feeling it not.

I believe in God even when He is silent.

> --Inscription on the walls of
> a cellar in Cologne, Germany,
> where Jews hid from the Nazis

TABLE OF CONTENTS

ACKNOWLEDGEMENTS

My thanks must first go to the Russian army for liberating my parents' home and to the Russian partisan movement for allowing my parents to fight with dignity and to avenge the deaths of my two sisters and the twenty-five members of my family who died a lonely death on a dark Sabbath eve in September 1942. Despite my personal disgust at what the Soviet leaders and bureaucrats are doing to Jews in the Soviet Union today, we must give credit where it is deserved, and it was deserved by the Russian people and the Russian army during World War II.

A special note of thanks must also go to the late Binyamin West, editor of the Hebrew version of this book, (They Were Many: Jewish Partisans in the Soviet Union During World War II), published in 1968 by the Labor Archives Press of the Hapoel Hatzair Publishing Cooperative in Tel Aviv, in cooperation with the Yad Vashem Memorial Institute of Jerusalem this present book owes a great deal to West's support and encouragement. I am sorry he did not live to see the English version.

Acknowledgements must also go to my cousin Yehudah Merin of Tel Aviv who first showed me a copy of these memoirs and encouraged me to have them translated and published. I am especially grateful to Morris U. Schappes, Erich Goldhagen, and Joshua Rothenberg for reading the introduction and offering their critical advice. For various degrees of moral and intellectual support and advice, I wish to thank Leni Yahil; Shlomo Noble of the YIVO Institute of New York; Vladka Meed of the Jewish Labor Committee; Eli Zborowski of the American Federation of Jewish Fighters, Camp Inmates, and Nazi Victims; Moshe Kaganovitch of Tel Aviv; Yuri Suhl of New York; and Elie Weisel of Boston University.

I should also mention the many partisan friends of my parents who were so generous with their encouragement and support: Moishe Flash (Montreal); Abraham Lerer (Cleveland); Jack Melamedik (Montreal); Morris (Moishe) Kramer (Philadelphia); Avrum Puchtik (Tel Aviv) as well as Chunek Wolper, Sasha (Charlie) Zarutski, Itzik Kuperberg, Berl Avruch, Yehudah Wolper, Joseph Zweibel, Vova Verbe, Jacob and Berl Bronstein, Jacob Karsh, Abba Klurman, Isaac Avruch, Joseph Blaustein, Sender Lande, and finally Berl Lorber, a commander in the Kruk Partisan Detachment who fought under the <u>nom de guerre</u> "Malenka" and now resides in Seattle, Washington. The others live in Israel for the most part; some in New York; a few in Milwaukee, Denver, and in the Soviet Union.

Many of the people, however, who worked on this book with me were born after the war. I'd like to thank Laurie Smith and Danny Matt for help with some Hebrew translation; Morey Schapira for advice on "grantsmanship"; Seymour Rossel for helping rearrange the order of articles; and Doris Gold for suggesting the title.

My thanks also to Miriam Magal and the Magal Translation Institute, Ltd. of Tel Aviv, who undertook the translation of the book from the Hebrew into English. They must be quite relieved to see it in print, as am I. This book took nearly eight years to see the light of day!

Finally, no words can adequately express my gratitude to my family: to my wife Miriam, our son Gabriel Alexander, to the Almuly's, my in-laws, to my sister Bella and her husband, Mitchell Smith, and my brother Reb Shloime and his wife, Shushi, and, finally, to my parents. My parents were informal editors throughout. I am only sorry that my father did not live to see this book, but he knew it would be published one day.

Jack Nusan Porter
Boston, Massachusetts
May 1, 1981

PREFACE

As he was being carried away in an ox-cart to his death, Simon Dubnow, the great historian of Eastern European Jewry, shouted out to the people: "Yidn, farshraybt" (Jews, remember! Jews, record!). And the Jews have been doing that ever since. The Nazis attempted to exterminate two entire people--Jews and the Gypsies. The Gypsies had no written tradition (though they have a very rich oral one) and, consequently, one can find very little written on or by Gypsies. The Jews, on the other hand, follow the Eleventh Commandment: Thou Shalt Write.

Hiroshima and Auschwitz. These are the two touchstones of our generation. Not enough can be written on either one, yet there remains much ignorance, much ambivalence, and much callousness. The world is still puzzled by its perception that the Jews "allowed" themselves to go to their deaths without a struggle. Young people, especially young Blacks, are especially perturbed. They tell me that "if it ever happens here", they will get themselves a gun and fight. Their bravado exposes a deep ignorance of the Nazi era.

This book is an attempt to set the record straight. Though it can be read on various levels, it should be seen first and foremost as a document, an historical document gathered by Russian-Jewish intellectuals in 1948 at the height of anti-Semitic hysteria, but written mainly by non-Jewish Soviet partisan commanders recounting the deeds of the Jewish fighters in their units. Furthermore, the original version of this collection was written in Russian, not Yiddish, despite the fact that it was a Yiddish publishing house that first produced it. Why was this book written ... and why in Russian ... and why, in most cases, by non-Jews?

In order to answer these questions, a brief history is necessary. The major portion of this book first appeared in Moscow in 1948 under its Russian title, Partizanska Druzhba (roughly Partisan Brotherhood), and was compiled by the editors of the Moscow-based Der Emes (in Yiddish, "The Truth") Publishing House and the Jewish Anti-Fascist Committee (JAFC). This committee, composed of the cream of Jewish writers, poets, and intellectuals, had as its primary duty the task of gaining worldwide support for the

Soviet Union during the early days of the war when Russia stood almost alone against the Nazi onslaught.

There is a fascinating tale about this committee. In 1943 two of its leaders, the poet Itzik Feffer and the renowned Yiddish actor and director Solomon Mikhoels, went abroad on an official mission to the Jewish communities of the United States, Canada, Mexico, and Britain. This mission was decided on at the very highest Soviet governmental level. Stalin himself not only authorized it, but attached great political significance to it. Mikhoels and Feffer remained abroad for about seven months; they toured forty-six cities in the United States and addressed audiences totaling over half a million people. From all accounts, it was an extremely successful tour. There is an apocryphal story that before leaving America, Mikhoels and Feffer were given a tank bought with money donated by the Jewish community, a tank with a large Jewish star on it. This tank was used by the Soviet Army during World War II.

In any event, Jewish trust in the Soviet leadership was high, but after the war, Stalin, for reasons not yet fully understood, no longer needed Jewish support and during the final six years of his life, the USSR was gripped by political terror and a series of purges. The Jewish Anti-Fascist Committee tried in its own way to disseminate information on the vital role Jews played during World War II. This task was not easy: Jews were made to appear as traitors to the state and collaborators with the Nazis. The original editors of Partisan Brotherhood moved quickly to gather material in order to show the truth, that Jews were active citizens in the resistance and in the Red Army. This book was therefore addressed to a non-Jewish audience.

Jewish war veterans, some crippled, were mocked in the streets: "Where did you win those medals, kike? In a crap game? Did you buy them on the black market?" It was during such a time that the editors of the Der Emes Publishing House and the JAFC worked feverishly to collect these memoirs and to present them to the Russian-speaking public. The purpose of these memoirs was twofold: first, of course, it was to be a chronicle of Jewish participation in the resistance, but there was a more important reason--the JAFC had to prove that the Jews were not traitors and cowards during the war, but brave and loyal fighters for the "motherland"; Jewish patriotism, in other words, had to be documented--not by Jews, but by non-Jewish army and partisan officers (some of them national heroes). This would give credence to the Jewish cause, a credence for Stalin to accept, and a credence for the Soviet people to honor.

The JAFC served as an important documentation center for the events and problems of Russian Jewish life during the war and for a few years afterwards. It also fulfilled an important mission by publishing the Yiddish newspaper Einekeit ("Unity"), which brought to the Jewish population much information about the Holocaust, especially news of the murder of Jews and the destruction of Jewish communities. Einekeit also printed authentic material about Jewish soldiers and officers who excelled in battle against the Nazis, whether in the front line of the Red Army or in the partisan movement.

The collection Partisan Brotherhood was prepared for print in Moscow on October 9, 1948. Apparently, there was not enough time to issue the book before all Yiddish cultural projects in the Soviet Union were abolished. Stalin began the purges of Jewish leaders and intellectuals; he closed Jewish schools and cultural centers; he threatened mass pogroms against the Jews. Many of the most active members of the Jewish Anti-Fascist Committee, including Mikhoels and Feffer, were later killed. The Der Emes Publishing House was closed in late 1948, but the book Partisan Brotherhood did appear in print in a limited edition.

Ironically, a few copies of the Russian manuscript were preserved by the Lenin Library in Moscow, and fifteen years later, an Israeli journalist, Binyamin West, heard about the book and was allowed to purchase a microfiche copy from the library's archives. In 1968 West's Hebrew translation of the book appeared in Israel. My cousin Yehudah Merin of Tel Aviv saw a copy and noticed that it contained a rare photograph of my father in a pose with his commander. Both my mother and father were active in a partisan group which fought in the vicinity of Rovno, Volynhia, in the western Ukraine from 1942 to 1944. In 1974 I wrote to the Lenin library and received a copy of Partizanska Druzhba. The English translation made by the Magal Translation Institute, Ltd. of Tel Aviv was done from the Hebrew version and checked against the Russian original. Additional material on partisan life was translated from other sources by the same institute.

So one sees that this book has both a personal as well as a professional interest to the editor.

Jewish Partisans is a sociological account of the Jewish partisan movement in the Soviet Union. It is broken down into five parts, plus an introduction. The first part, "Prologue," consists of fiction, the stories of Shmuel Persov, a Russian-Jewish writer, but it is fiction that is so lifelike that it is difficult to differentiate it from the true accounts that follow. Part Two, "Initiatives," begins with two versions of the partisan oath and continues with personal accounts of initiation into partisan warfare. Part Three, "Partisan Society," consists of memoirs written by non-Jewish Russian commanders and deals with the sociological structure of partisan life, including civilian camps guarded by such partisans. It also contains rare insights into two aspects of the underground: the role of women and the role of media (partisan filmmaking). Part Four, "Partisan Warfare," is composed of straight-forward accounts of battle conditions and missions against the Germans. It also contains accounts of partisan warfare in the ghettos of Kovna (Lithuania) and Odessa (USSR). The book concludes with summary statements about Jews awarded medals of honor from the government written by L. Singer and a stirring conclusion by the great Russian writer and journalist, Ilya Ehrenburg.

The book also contains maps of the region, several partisan documents, organizational charts of the partisan command, and the structure of an individual partisan group as well as a sources section, glossary, and an annotated bibliography on Jewish resistance and related topics. The order of articles has been rearranged for this volume.

This collection is both a literary document and an historical account. When these memoirs first appeared, they were used for propaganda, hence the somewhat "heroic" style of writing. Today these same memoirs are historical documents. I have tried, both in my introduction and in my notes, to point out any errors and to explain any excesses in the text. Corroborated by interviews with partisan survivors in America, Canada, and Israel, this book is not exaggeration, but, in fact, only touches the surface of heroism that took place during the war among Jewish partisans. I have attempted to be objective. I do not claim to be detached.

This book, <u>Partisan Brotherhood</u>, offered for the reader's attention, tells of the struggle of the Soviet people during the Great War for the Fatherland which our country fought against fascist Germany. This was a war engaged in behind enemy lines, in territories temporarily conquered by Hitler's soldiers.

Basically, <u>Partisan Brotherhood</u> contains material about the military activities of Jewish partisans, and was collected by the Jewish Anti-Fascist Committee of the USSR. The collection consists of memoirs of former commanders and commissars of partisan units as well as testimonies written by Soviet writers. They tell of various events in the "partisan war" and give individual profiles of partisan heroes and heroines. Despite its varied sources, <u>Partisan Brotherhood</u> is a unified work. All the accounts included in this book are concerned with a single subject: namely, the friendship and unity of the Soviet people, a friendship which took shape at the very beginning of the 1917 October Revolution, was strengthened during the terrible days of the Civil War following the revolution, and which found its fullest expression in the Great War for the Fatherland against the German conquerors.

At the start of the war, during the first difficult days for our country, Comrade Stalin, in his historic Moscow speech of November 6, 1941 at a gathering of the Council of Workers Delegates, said:

> The Germans built their war plans on the instability of the Soviet rear guard, and on the assumption that, following the first failure of the Red Army, conflict would break out between the workers and the farmers, and a division would take place among the peoples of the USSR. They thought that rebellion would spread and that the state would be split into factions. This would have facilitated the advance of the German conquerors up to the Ural Mountain passes. But the Germans made a grave error! The failures of the Red Army did not weaken, on the contrary, they strengthened the bond between the workers and the farmers, and intensified the friendship among the peoples of the USSR. Furthermore, they transformed the family of the peoples of

the USSR into one strong camp which supported its Red Army and Red Navy with devotion.

The unity of the Soviet people was expressed with extraordinary courage during the war against the Nazis. Soviet people from all nationalities fought in partisan units, as well as within the lines of the Red Army. Those Soviet patriots who were left in territory conquered by the enemy, and who were able to take up arms, joined the partisans and fought bravely and devotedly for the honor, freedom, and independence of their homeland. In the front lines, these "avengers of the people" included, together with the Russians: Ukrainians, Beylorussians, Jews, Georgians (Gruzim), Armenians, Latvians, Uzbekians, and members of other Soviet nationalities. All of them saw themselves as belonging to a single fighting partisan force.

These "avengers of the people" fought against the enemy and presented a model of brotherhood and friendship, of spiritual and ideological unity, among people who felt themselves as equals within their Soviet homeland. The struggle of the Jewish partisans against the Nazis is presented in this book as part of the overall struggle of all the Soviet people, who rose as one to defend their country.

Shoulder-to-shoulder with partisans of other nationalities, the Jewish partisans fought against the Germans. They blew up bridges, destroyed military transports, wiped out reinforcements of the German Army, killed its officers and soldiers, and, with unyielding hatred, swept away the Nazi filth.

This book reveals only a few pages of the partisan struggle of the Soviet people. In this close-knit Soviet family, the Soviet Jews were loyal members, helping to protect the achievements of the Socialist Revolution.

October 9, 1948

Editor's Note

It is important to make a few comments regarding the style and rhetoric of this introduction. There is no question that the Soviet people engaged in a heroic struggle against the Nazis. They fought bravely and endured great losses; however, the Soviet peoples were not always the "close-knit family" they are portrayed as; they did not always present a "model of brotherhood and friendship, of spiritual and ideological unity." This was especially true during the early phases of the war when some Soviet nationalities, the Ukrainians and Latvians, for example, openly welcomed the Nazis, hoping that a German victory would liberate them from Soviet rule. However, the German occupation was often so brutal that it pushed these nationalities back into the waiting arms of the USSR. The role of the Jews within the partisan and regular army units is accurate; Jews placed fourth in the number of participants within these units, behind the Russians, Ukrainians, and Beylorussians. Despite occasional anti-Semitism within the partisan groups, Jews did play a significant role in the war. To demonstrate this fact is the true intent of this book, despite the rhetoric that appears.

ПАРТИЗАНСКАЯ
ДРУЖБА

ВОСПОМИНАНИЯ О БОЕВЫХ
ДЕЛАХ ПАРТИЗАН-ЕВРЕЕВ,
УЧАСТНИКОВ ВЕЛИКОЙ
ОТЕЧЕСТВЕННОЙ ВОЙНЫ

ОГИЗ
Государственное издательство «Дер Эмес»
Москва 1948

Facsimile of Russian original of the book,
Partizanska Druzhba. Source: Lenin Library-Moscow.
(Taken from microfilm copy.)

INTRODUCTION:

JEWISH RESISTANCE IN THE SOVIET UNION

Jack Nusan Porter

The Myth of Jewish Cowardice

World War II cost four trillion dollars and the lives of over fifty million men, women, and children, including not only six million Jews, but eight million Chinese and twenty million Russians![1] When scholars attempt to describe such a Holocaust, words often fail.

There are many myths, falsehoods, and half-truths still associated with the Holocaust. One of the most controversial of these is that the Jews were "cowards" and that they walked passively to their deaths like "sheep to slaughter" to use a popular and by now tiresome phrase. The confusion, the accusations, the ambivalences, still exist, especially among young people.

William Helmreich, a sociologist at City College in New York (CCNY), recently completed a preliminary study of forty-two Jewish undergraduates from several Eastern universities and found that the Holocaust was a subject very much on the minds of these students. Their reactions to the behavior of European Jews during the war are expressed in the following quotes:[2]

> How did the Jews let themselves be led to the camps? Why didn't they fight back? If I was going to a camp, I think I would have fought back and refused to go.
> ---a 20-year-old junior at CCNY

> The Jews sort of accepted it and went off to the concentration camps like sheep.
> ---an 18-year-old freshman at Yale

> Why didn't they fight? Some did, but not enough. No one really had the courage to stand up. Not even the American Jews.
> ---a 19-year-old sophomore at Brooklyn College

European Jews made the mistake of believing
so strongly in their religion that they could
not see beyond it. And so they behaved like
a bunch of .....
                        ---a 20-year-old senior at Yale

The question of cowardice is a value-laden one and
a very difficult one to answer. The quotes above
clearly reflect a generation of young people who cannot
empathize with a situation that remains imponderable
even to those who experienced it, even those who did
fight back.   Soon after the Eichmann trial in 1961
(which most of these undergraduates may not even
remember), a number of books and articles appeared.
Some blamed the victims; some defended them.   Today,
fifteen years later, the debate is still not settled.
The victims are still being judged as cowards, even
though more and more research has appeared to make this
debate futile.

Raul Hilberg in his important book The Destruction
of the European Jews notes an almost complete lack of
resistance on the part of the Jews.[3] Social historian
Hannah Arendt in her book Eichmann in Jerusalem has a
theory of complicity, that the Jews aided the Nazis in
their own destruction.   Furthermore, she describes
Jewish resistance as "pitifully small, incredibly weak,
and essentially harmless".[4] Psychiatrist Bruno Bettelheim also agrees with the "complicity theory" and in
his book The Informed Heart, almost pleadingly asks:
"Did no one of those destined to die fight back? ...
Only a very few did."[5]

Ruth Kunzer, in a very perceptive piece on the
literature of the Holocaust, has this to say in
response to Bettelheim, Arendt, and Hilberg:[6]

    (Bettelheim's) thesis, as fashionable today
    as Arendt's on the failure of thousands of
    methodically starved, systematically brutal-
    ized and dehumanized human beings to revolt
    without weapons and cooperation from the
    outside, suffers, in George Steiner's percep-
    tive words, 'from a failure of imagining.'

This "failure of imagination" is a failure to
understand that the real question is not why there was
so little revolt, but why, amidst the death and the
destruction, there was so much resistance.   One reason
why the myths and obfuscations are perpetuated is

because the actual role of the Jews was suppressed, especially by the Russians and Ukrainians. Not only was Jewish participation in the resistance and the Russian army suppressed, but it was often portrayed as collaboration with the Nazis.[7] That is why this book, when it appeared, was so important--and why it too was suppressed.

It is also interesting to note that Arendt, Bettelheim, and Hilberg are all German or Austrian Jews. Russian or Polish Jews were rarely prone to label themselves and their compatriots "cowards." Jewish theologian Eliezer Berkovits explains such accusations as examples of Jews alienated from Judaism who therefore defame the martyrs of their people in order to find themselves a more emotionally comfortable spot in the midst of a disintegrating Western society.[8] In other words, when such Jewish scholars as the three mentioned above talk of "cowardly victims," or of a "Jewish death instinct," or of "Jewish complicity in their own deaths," they in essence find an ingenious way out of facing a bitter truth: Auschwitz ushered in a final chapter in the moral disintegration of Western civilization. For these Western intellectuals, devoted as they were to the ideals of Western (and German) rationalism, this dissonance is too much to handle. So they find a scapegoat--the Jew--but, in reality, the label is turned inward because they too are Jews.

Bettelheim has written that the resisters were "very few" in number, and Arendt called Jewish resistance "pitifully small" and "essentially harmless".

Yet it was these "very few" who in the Warsaw Ghetto held off SS General Jurgen Stroop and his command of 1000 SS-tank grenadiers, 1000 men of the SS-Calvary, two units of artillery, one unit of army engineers, plus armed units of the Latvian and Lithuanian SS, for nearly four months from April 19, 1943 to late August, 1943, with only a few rifles, a handful of grenades, and numerous homemade "molotov cocktails."

It was the "essentially harmless" nature of Jewish resistance that forced even Goebbels to admit that "now we know what Jews can do if they have arms"[9] and in a letter to Reichkommisar Lohse in Riga, Wehrmacht-kommisar Bremmer, on November 20, 1941, emphasized that:[10]

-3-

...the Jewish population is in the forefront of propaganda, resistance, and sabotage against the Germans in Beylorussia.

...in the cities of White Russia the Jews constitute the largest part of the population and the driving force of the resistance movement ... and everywhere, where reports about sabotage, incitement of the population, resistance, etc. have forced us to take measures, Jews were found to be the originators and instigators, and in most instances, even the perpetrators.

In another report to Reichkommisar Lohse, on August 31, 1942, Generalkommisar Wilhelm Kube, the Gauleiter (administrator) of White Russia (Beylorussia), made similar remarks:[11]

In all the clashes with the partisans in White Russia, it has become clear that, both in the general commissariate territory which was previously part of Poland and that which was Russian, the Jews--along with the Polish rebel movement in the west and the forces of the Red Army in the east--have been the main leaders of the partisan movement.

We thus have documented proof that the Germans were both amazed and disturbed about armed Jews. In fact, in some ways the Germans were also delighted because Jewish resistance would clear the Nazi conscience of killing "innocent civilians" while giving them the excuse to accelerate their program of "solving the Jewish problem."

There were, however, many forms of resistance, and resistance took place under many guises and within different circumstances. It was both armed and unarmed, organized and disorganized, planned and spontaneous, passive and active, offensive and defensive as well as moral, spiritual, and psychological--and each form involved risk of life.

Passive resistance, known as the "white resistance," took many forms: escaping from ghettos, writing a diary, conducting Hebrew classes, praying, singing Jewish songs, studying the Bible, wearing one's payis (earlocks) and beard publicly, and carrying on a Jewish cultural and artistic life. Under freedom these acts are taken for granted, but living in the hell of Europe, these same acts were raised to the level of heroism.

Many people refuse to acknowledge the many forms of resistance. For example, there exists a special type of resistance based on a religious or moral principle (such as a belief in nonviolence) in which one could not and would not engage in armed resistance, preferring instead to suffer, or even to die, rather than comply with the demands of the enemy. The father and mother who walked calmly to their deaths, hand in hand with their little children, all the while believing in God's trust, in <u>Kiddush ha-shem</u> (the holiness of martyrdom), but up to the end, still maintaining <u>kiddush ha-hayyim</u> (the sanctification of life)--their family together, their spiritual belief intact--this too was a heroic act.[12]

However, people have become hardened from watching too much violence and too many Westerns and war movies. They wish to hear only of <u>armed</u> resistance, the only <u>real</u> kind of resistance to them. Armed resistance took place on four major "fronts".

Ghetto Revolts

There were armed revolts within the major Jewish ghettos of Europe: Warsaw, Vilna, Bialystok, Lachwa, Minsk, Czestochowa, Slonim, Kleck, Bedzin, Nieswiez, Braslaw, Glubokie, and several other places. We know of organized Jewish undergrounds in Kovna (Kaunas, Lithuania), Cracow, Riga, Rome, Odessa, Paris, and Brussels as well as throughout Czechoslovakia, Hungary, Italy, France, Belgium, Holland, Greece, and Poland.

Not all were able to carry out their plans--some groups were discovered and killed by the Nazis before they could accomplish their tasks. The urban underground and the armed revolts were essentially an extension of the general partisan movement--in this case, the partisans can be seen as <u>urban</u> guerrillas instead of <u>rural</u> guerrillas. There was a link between them but quite often, and the Warsaw Ghetto uprising of 1943 was a tragic example, the Jewish rebels were isolated from the general non-Jewish resistance.

But generalizations about Jewish-Gentile animosity within the partisan movement cannot be made. An investigation of the particular circumstances surrounding each case must be undertaken. What held true in Warsaw between Polish and Jewish resistance groups would not apply to Paris, for example, where there was a great deal more cooperation. In Paris, Jewish underground groups managed to ambush and murder several high-ranking German officers; and in Cracow, Poland they succeeded in blowing up a cafe where several German officials were killed. One could go into more detail about the uprisings in the Jewish ghettos, but many books have been written on the subject and I direct the reader to them. (See the bibliography.) However, one final example of "urban partisans" must be mentioned.

There was even Jewish resistance within Berlin itself. Yuri Suhl in his anthology They Fought Back: The Story of Jewish Resistance in Nazi Europe devotes an entire chapter to the Herbert Baum Group, a youthful band of thirty German Jews (nearly all of them were about the age of 22), who conducted underground acts of rebellion during the years 1937-1942. They were eventually infiltrated, discovered, and executed, and a monument to them stands in the Weissensee Cemetery in East Berlin today.[13]

Uprisings in the Concentration Camps

A second stage of resistance took place within the extermination camps themselves. Unlike the partisan resistance in the forests, resistance in the "death camps" and within the sealed-off Jewish ghettos were, in the words of Erich Goldhagen, a revolt on death row, a last gasp effort against eventual extermination. There was no hope for success in overcoming the enemy and little in even surviving the revolt. Still, organized uprisings took place in the concentration camps of Auschwitz, Treblinka, Sobibor, Koldczewo, in the camp at Janowska Street in Lvov (Lemberg, Poland), and in several other smaller camps.

One could say that to survive in these camps at all could be considered an act of resistance. However, in addition to the many acts of passive (spiritual and psychological) resistance, there were many acts of active Jewish courage. Sobibor is a good example. There, on October 14, 1943, a revolt took place that involved 350 people. Ten SS men were killed and thirty-eight Ukrainian guards were either killed or wounded. About 400 to 600 inmates escaped; nearly half of them died in the mined fields surrounding the camp, but the rest were able to survive and enter the forest to join the partisan groups already there.

Among the leaders of the Auschwitz underground which blew up a crematoria during the final days of the war, were Jozef Cyrankiewicz, later to become Premier of Poland, and a young Jewish woman, Rosa Robota--one of many Jewish women who played an essential, though limited, role in the Jewish resistance.[14]

Jewish Participation in Allied Military Forces

Resistance in the ghettos and in the concentration camps were two relatively minor and ineffectual staging areas. Many more times effective, of course, was the Jewish role in national military forces and in the partisan groups which were often absorbed into the regular army units as the war continued. Wherever the Jews were permitted to take part in the general struggle within their own national armed forces, they engaged in them in great numbers.

In the allied regular armies and navies, some one and a half million Jewish soldiers and officers took part. Even the tiny Palestinian Jewish community contributed 26,000 soldiers to the allied cause. In the United States alone, a total of 550,000 Jews took part; of these more than 8,000 fell in battle and another 10,000 died of wounds. Great Britain contributed 62,000 Jews to the British Army--in addition to some 25,000 from other parts of the British Commonwealth, with Canada contributing 17,000 Jews in its army.[15]

As for eastern Europe, according to official sources, slightly over 32,000 Jews fell in battle in the first few days of the September, 1939 Blitzkreig--about 15 percent of the total casualties; and 61,000 Jews were taken prisoner--about 14 percent of the total of 420,000 Polish soldiers taken prisoner, which in turn was 52 percent of the total number of 800,000 Polish armed forces. Overall, some 150,000 Jews were in active service in the Polish army at the outbreak of the war.

In the Soviet Union, it is estimated that more than half a million Jews fought in the Red Army. Many of them fell in battle, while more than 100,000 were decorated for valor and devotion to duty. More than one hundred Jews (figures range from 105 to 147) were named "Hero of the Soviet Union," one of the highest designations.[16]   Abraham H. Foxman in his chapter on Jewish resistance in the excellent textbook The Jewish Catastrophe in Europe cites two examples.

A Russian-Jewish lieutenant Moshe Berkovitch was twice awarded the "Order of the Red Star" for heroism. In hand-to-hand combat, he killed three German soldiers with his bayonet, choked two with his bare hands, and brought back alive a German officer as prisoner.   And one of the greatest acts of courage was undertaken by three Jewish soldiers (Papernik, Ocheret, and Rinesky), all "Heroes of the Soviet Union," who tied bundles of hand grenades around their bodies and threw themselves under advancing German tanks, one of many desperate attempts to repulse the Germans in the early stages of fighting on the Russian front.[17]

Jews also participated in the national armies of France, Greece, and other occupied countries. Palestine not only contributed officers, soldiers, and doctors to the Allied forces, but engaged in numerous, though ineffective, underground activities.   Hannah Senesh was an example of a halutza (Israeli pioneer) who died at the hands of the Nazis.   Palestinian underground members were also active in the illegal immigration to Israel of European refugees both during and after the war.[18]

Jewish Participation in the Partisan Movement

It was among the partisans that the Jews could be most effective, not only in engaging the Germans but in saving families and individuals from the embattled ghettos. Escape from the ghettos and the concentration camps led directly to joining forces in the forests, though, as will be shown, most Jewish undergrounds decided to stay within the ghetto and not abandon their fellow Jews until the very last minute. Jewish participation as partisans took place in every country that had a resistance movement. This introduction, however, will deal mainly with resistance in the Soviet Union, which had the largest partisan organization in the war and the largest number of Jewish partisans.

In partisan warfare on Soviet, Polish, Slovak, Yugoslavian, French, Greek, Belgian, Dutch, Bulgarian, and Italian territory, one estimate of over 100,000 Jewish fighters has been made, but this figure is greatly exaggerated.[19] A closer approximation to the truth is a maximum of 50,000, with 25,000 Jewish partisans in the Soviet Union; 10,000 in Poland; 10,000 in France, Holland, and Belgium; 2,000 in Yugoslavia; 2,500 in Slovakia; and over 1,000 in Greece, Italy, and Bulgaria. It is still an impressive figure and could go slightly higher given the fact that the Jewish identity of some partisans was never made known to their comrades or commanders. The Jewish role should not be exaggerated, but neither should it be underestimated or disparaged.

Military warfare is only one aspect of resistance movements; other actions include clandestine political organization, intelligence gathering, propaganda and proselytizing campaigns, and diplomatic efforts to obtain outside assistance. Partisan warfare during World War II was geared for small-scale ground combat operations designed more to harass the enemy than to destroy him. Guerrillas can operate in almost any environment--deep in tropical jungles, within highly urbanized centers, or in dense forests and mountains. Some of the most effective partisan action of the war took place in the mountainous regions of Yugoslavia, Italy, and Greece and within the heavily forested and marshy regions of western Russia, the Ukraine, and Beylorussia.

Partisan warfare is rarely decisive in and by itself--its major goal is to badger and slow down the enemy and to engage in counter-propaganda and intimidation until regular army units are strong enough to engage the opponent. Normally, guerrilla warfare is employed by societies and groups too weak to defend themselves in open combat, but major combatants have often supplemented their conventional military encounters with elaborate guerrilla campaigns. This was the case especially among Russian partisans.[20]

Partisan organizations tend to be highly flexible and decentralized, and their tactics are usually confined to small-scale, hit-and-run forays against supply lines, police and military installations, small outposts, fuel depots, railroad lines, and other poorly defended targets. Because of their small size and limited military objectives, guerrilla units are often able to avoid open engagements with conventional armed forces and can thus occupy a disproportionate share of the adversary's military strength. In any study of resistance, the social and political context must be taken into account along with the usual military analysis.

Partisan Warfare in the Soviet Union

The Soviet partisan movement was established in the wake of the German invasion of the USSR on June 22, 1941 (Operation Barbarossa), and was, in both conception and scope, the greatest irregular resistance movement in the history of warfare.[21] It combined all the classic elements of resistance movements of the past with modern means of communication, transportation, and modern weapons and, at its peak, involved a far greater number of people than had ever before been drawn into an irregular force. The exact total strength of the Soviet partisan movement will never be known, but the best evidence indicates that it reached a total of 30,000 men by January 1, 1942, rose to 150,000 by the summer of 1942, to 200,000 by the summer of 1943, and then declined slightly to 150,000 to 175,000 by June 1944 as partisan territory was retaken by Soviet forces. The partisan turnover resulting from casualties, sickness, and desertions over a three-year period, brought the total number who participated in the Soviet movement to about 400,000 or 500,000. These figures only include the partisans enrolled in regular, permanently organized combat units. They do not include a host of agents, saboteurs, demolition teams, as well as doctors, nurses, cooks, and other support personnel. Of the former, some operated independently, and, at other times, worked together with the combat detachments.[22]

Reuben Ainsztein maintains that at least 20,000, and possibly 25,000, Jews took part in the Soviet movement. He notes that this is an impressive figure when calculated on a population basis in comparison to other Soviet nationalities and, furthermore, when one takes into account the fact that the Soviet partisan movement became an integrating force capable of absorbing tens of thousands of fighters in the occupied territories only after the Nazis had destroyed most of the Jews of Eastern Europe.[23]

In order to explain this phenomenon better, it would be beneficial to describe the stages the partisan movement underwent and the shifts in composition among its fighters.[24]   The movement was in a constant state of flux.   In its first stage, almost immediately after the Germans attacked Russia, that is, in June, 1941, a partisan movement was established behind German lines, partly through the independent activity of Communist party members, Red Army officers, and Soviet non-commissioned officers.   It depended heavily on party members, who comprised as much as 80 percent of individual units, while units averaging between 25 and 40 percent Communist party membership were not unusual. Up until the end of 1941 and continuing until the spring of 1942, the partisan movement could be characterized as a volunteer organization.   The early bands were quite small; morale was low; leadership, too often political, left a great deal to be desired; and, consequently, little impact was made on the German army. Though they did not materially hinder the German offensive operations, they did make it difficult for the smooth functioning of the German occupation to take place and they were successful, at least in some areas of Beylorussia and the Ukraine, in gaining the passive support of the inhabitants, while throwing considerable doubt into the minds of others as to the wisdom of collaborating with or supporting the Nazis.   The number of Jews joining the partisans during this stage was small and insignificant.

The second major stage occurred in the spring of 1942 when the partisans began drafting men.   The percentage of Communist party membership declined rapidly, though members were still quite important as instruments of Soviet control, as political officers (politruks) and as commissars.   The number of Red Army stragglers increased greatly and, together with the drafting of peasants, would make these two groups account for about 80 percent of the total strength of the movement.   The Central Partisan Staff was created on May 30, 1942, and Soviet officers were parachuted behind German lines to organize the growing number of partisans.   Forming part of Stalin's Supreme Headquarters, this central staff would take another year or so to coordinate and impose a centralized system of control and command over the immense territory stretching from the front lines westard to Poland.

Most of the Jews who became partisans did so in 1942 and in the first half of 1943.   Though the Germans were still very powerful and the partisans were still fighting for a foothold, morale was high.   The partisan movement had come to life.   The influx of Red Army officers and stragglers (some of whom had been fighting in small groups since July and August, 1941) professionalized the partisans to a great degree. The draft gained momentum and continued until 1944. The most decisive and discernible shift followed the great losses the Germans suffered during their first encounter with the notorious Russian winter of December, 1941 and January, 1942, which weakened the underclothed Germans, until like a monstrous elephant attacked by jackals, the German army bogged down to wait for the warmth of spring.

The last stage of the partisan movement was also the turning point of the war: the Battle of Kursk in July, 1943. From this point on, the Russians were on the offensive, and, after two brutal years of fighting, the Germans were pulling back. In August and September of 1943, following the failure of the Wehrmacht attempt to regain the offensive in their ill-starred "Operation Zitadelle," the Red Army launched a general assault of great force, and, at the same time, the partisans mounted their first large-scale offensive against the enemy's rear. Taken in toto, the partisan role in this offensive was not completely effective according to one analysis, but on the face of it, it seemed highly successful.[25] More than 20,000 demolitions were set off on the railway lines behind the German's Army Group Center which bore the brunt of the Soviet attack. There was also extensive sabotage of railroad installations, highways, ammunition and gas depots, and signal facilities, plus an intensive propaganda and terror campaign that resulted in widespread defection among German native auxiliary troops and police.

At the end of 1943 until the end of the war, as a result of the Red Army's victories and the massive supply of arms by the Beylorussian and Ukrainian partisan staffs, it became relatively easy to join the partisans, but by then there were hardly any Jews left to take advantage of these changed circumstances.[26] Furthermore, the composition of the ranks had changed. In 1943 there was a new wave of volunteers. Many of these people were of doubtful quality; military and political collaborators plus managers and professional people who had tried to carry out their peacetime occupations under German occupation. Others either decided "to get on the bandwagon" or joined because they found life between the partisans and the Germans intolerable. The exact number of such people cannot be estimated, but it is likely that, especially in the Ukraine and in

Lithuania, they became a significant element. Combined with the peasants who were drafted earlier in the spring of 1942, these new elements made discipline even more difficult. It was lucky that, by this time, the Russian army was on the offensive and the Germans were being turned back. Consequently, the ineffectiveness of the partisans at this stage was not a crucial factor in the outcome of the war.

Composition of the Soviet Partisan Movement

The major distinctive component groups within the partisan movement were the peasants, the Red Army stragglers, and the escaped POWs, all three of which comprised the largest segment of the ranks; these were followed by the urban contingent, the intelligentsia, Communist party members, collaborators, and, finally, women.[27]. The Jews fell within the categories of the urban contingent and the intelligentsia, with a smaller number being Red Army soldiers.

The Peasants

The peasants probably furnished between 40 and 60 percent of the total partisan recruits, and virtually all of them were drafted, many against their will. Since the partisans were able to move freely throughout most of the rural districts, it was relatively easy to enter the villages, select the men, and march them off as partisans. Though they wanted to be neutral, the peasants saw no other choice but to join the partisans, especially after the Germans began relinquishing their hold on the occupied territories. They remained a distinct group--passive, unenthusiastic, and untrust-worthy. They were practical-minded opportunists with one overwhelming desire--to have the collective farm system abolished. Thus, at the beginning of the war, they were willing to tolerate the German regime if they could extract economic advantage from it. They disliked turning over their produce to the Germans, but they liked even less turning it over to both the Germans and the partisans. They were caught in a dilemma between German brutality on the one hand and Russian collectivization on the other.

The Urban Contingent

While there were very few peasants who were convinced Communists, the urban working population was, on
the other hand, strongly influenced by Communism. The
Soviet program of industrialization had impressed the
workers. Nevertheless, there were certain urban
classes, such as the formerly rich and other declasse
bourgeoise, who were hidden sympathizers with the
Nazis.

It is impossible to estimate the number that left
the urban areas to join the partisans. Their numbers
were small in relation to those of the peasants and
former Red Army soldiers. Generally speaking, though,
the urban contingents were sympathetic to the
partisans.

The Intelligentsia

The term as used here refers less to the upper
intelligentsia (professors, writers, editors, journalists), most of whom were evacuated and who, in any
case, were few in number, than to the broad, lower
reaches of the class (local doctors, teachers, admini-
strators, and the subprofessional people--clerks,
bookkeepers, and others). These men and women, because
they thought in terms of their careers, were likely to
believe that they had to choose one side or the other.
From the partisan's point of view, they were valuable
additions to the units. Their skills were useful; they
were persons whose attitudes generally influenced
others; and the Germans would in turn be deprived of
their talents. A good many Jews, especially doctors,
came out of these ranks.

The intelligentsia formed a sizeable group in the
early stages of the partisan movement, comprising most
of the officer contingent and a segment of the rank and
file as well. As the movement grew, this group
declined in number, although it remained an important
element in the partisans throughout the war.

Red Army Stragglers and Soviet POWs

The German army took over three million prisoners
in the first six months of the war; this figure grew to
five million by the end of the war. Of these, about

two million died in the POW camps. If, as can probably be estimated, one in ten avoided capture, then the total would come to more than 300,000 stragglers. To this, one must add the thousands more that the Germans released, chiefly Ukrainian and others who were considered anti-Communist. Wretched POW conditions forced many thousands more to try to save their lives by escaping. By January, 1942, these former Soviet soldiers at large in the occupied territory probably totaled between 300,000 and 400,000.

The massive upswing of the partisan movement which followed the successful Soviet winter offensive of 1941-42 brought thousands of former army men into the movement, until, by the summer of 1942, they formed the largest single increment. In July, 1942, at the onset of the second stage, the Germans estimated that they made up 60 percent of the total partisan strength. These men became the backbone of the partisan movement. They had military training and experience; for the most part, they had neither family nor property ties in the occupied territory; they had definite moral and legal obligations to the Soviet Union; and their previous experiences in the POW camps led them to prefer partisan activity to life under the German occupation.

Communist Party Members

As was mentioned earlier, during the first stage of fighting, the partisans were overwhelmingly composed of Communist party members. After the spring of 1942, when drafting recruits began on a mass scale, the Party contingent dropped sharply in relative numbers. The Party men, however, remained an elite group in the partisan movement throughout the war and were the most influential. At the same time, the Party segment was important chiefly as an instrument of Soviet control, especially as political advisors and ideological indoctrinators. There is no indication that Party members acted on their own as an independent, spontaneous, creative, guiding force. Because of strict Party discipline, such independent action was out of the question.

Collaborators

The taint of collaboration fell on a great many people in the occupied areas. By definition, anyone who did not actively fight the Germans was capable of being suspected of at least being a passive collaborator. To nearly everyone, then, participation in the partisan movement was valuable as an alibi, a means of avoiding persecution as a collaborator. It gave one the proper credentials, but also gave credence to the belief that, at least in the final years of the war, all partisan groups were a crew of former collaborators, hiding in the woods in order to save their skins and putting up a feeble show of resistance.

The most significant group of collaborators were former policemen, army auxiliaries, and members of German-organized indigenous military units. These men had acted as the main antipartisan forces in the past. Estimates of their numbers ranged from 800,000 to 2,000,000. Once it became clear that Russia was winning the war, the situation of these people became desperate. The partisans, in order to complete their demoralization, promised amnesty to all who would desert and join them. These efforts were very successful. Occasionally, entire collaborator units would desert en masse. Every German defeat, every German withdrawal, led to more desertions. And, in general, the promised amnesty was honored. The collaborators made useful recruits; they had military experience; they knew the terrain well; and they had important strategic and military information. By mid-1943, when the collaborators were prepared to desert in significant numbers, manpower was no longer a problem for the partisans. In the last year of the war, these men composed between 10 and 20 percent of the movement.

Women Partisans

Women made significant contributions in all areas of rebellion against the Nazis--in the ghettos, concentration camps, and forests, and as support personnel in the regular armies. To the Germans, who summed up their conception of the role of women in society with the slogan Kirche, Kueche, und Kinder (church, kitchen, and children), the enlistment of women for combat duty was an outright abomination (although they were used for intelligence gathering in occupied zones). The Soviet government, as well as many other European states, was quite active, however, in recruiting women in various aspects of the armed forces. The USSR moreover publicized the participation of its women in partisan activity as evidence of superior dedication and resolution. Furthermore, with the loss of so many men, women were crucial in many areas of defense.

In almost every partisan detachment in the Soviet Union, there were some women members, although they usually numbered no more than 2 or 3 percent of the total unit and hardly ever more than 5 percent. They were used chiefly as scouts and intelligence agents. Soviet intelligence tended to rely heavily on women agents, particularly in partisan-infested territory where women made the best agents, since men of military age were liable to arrest on sight.

Some of the women had training as radio operators and nurses, and a large proportion of the doctors assigned to the partisan units were women. The doctors had officer status. Sometimes the women were assigned to combat missions along with the men, but it appears that aside from intelligence missions, they were more often used as medical personnel, cooks, and washerwomen.

Sexism abounded within the partisan ranks. Women served in service capacities in the majority of cases, and even for those women who did go out on missions to either engage the enemy or to blow up bridges, lay mines along train tracks, or gather food and clothing from local peasants, there were many times that the male partisans would ask the female partisans to wash the dishes or mend the socks after returning to the base camp! Then, as now, women had "double-duty" and were first seen as women, not as soldiers.

Few women were drafted. For the most part, they were volunteers, motivated by either political convictions (some were staunch Communists), a desire for adventure, or the wish to achieve some form of personal achievement in a society where satisfying personal success outside of the role of mother and wife was limited. Some women "draftees" were trained in espionage or radio communication on the Soviet side of the front, but these were usually Komsomol Youth members and were therefore politically reliable.

Earl Ziemke, in his chapter on the "Composition and Morale of the Partisan Movement" in John A. Armstrong (ed.) Soviet Partisans in World War II, maintains that the principal reason for including women in nearly every partisan detachment was that "a woman became one of the prerequisites of every major partisan officer ... along with his Nagan pistol and leather windbreaker!"[28]   It was not unusual for the officers, from the brigade commander down to the battalion commanders, to "marry" the women enlisted in their unit. Needless to say, their wives, and most of them had wives who were worried sick over them, rarely knew of those affairs. The "lowly" rank-and-file partisans had to contend themselves with less convenient arrangements.

This resulted in a cynical attitude toward the women in the partisan unit. Jealousy was common. Fights, some even leading to death, often broke out over the "possession" of a woman. Women became the property of the commanders, which by implication gave them officer status, and thus the commander's "wife" often lorded over the other women and the low-ranking men. This led to trouble.

For example, if the commander's wife wanted a blanket that belonged to another man's woman, she could incite a fight and if that man rushed to his lover's defense, it could lead to insubordination and the man being shot--especially if the commander happened to be very drunk at the time.

In conclusion, one cannot minimize the heroic efforts of many women during the war. The Germans, though sexists in the extreme, nevertheless were quite happy to capture a woman partisan, because they were often exceptionally well-informed and had valuable military information. Many a woman died a courageous and painful death rather than divulge her secrets.

The Organization of the Partisan Group

The popular image of the partisan unit is a small isolated group hiding in the forest or jungle. Actually, the partisan movement became highly complex. Starting with the Central Staff of the Partisan Movement in Moscow with its liaison officer to the Supreme Command of the Red Army, it contained subdivisions for political security, propaganda, cryptography, signal corps, cartography, finance, and transportation. From there it connected to various territorial command posts and on to operations groups in the enemy rear.

These operations groups were also composed of various subsections: security, signal corps, medical corps, propaganda, and finance. Operations groups had military subunits as well, which I will describe shortly, but they also had their political counterpart, the Area or Party Center, in which Communist party work was carried out under the aegis of the Commissar. These would include Party "extension" work, illegal press, rumor mongering, and various liaison with the partisans. Under each Party or Area Center, would be one or more District Committees, which in turn would contain one or more Party Cells and Blocks. The political Commissar was sometimes more powerful than the military Chief of Staff. At times, one man held both positions. (See appendix for charts.)

The basic fighting unit of the partisans was the otryad (detachment) which consisted of anywhere from 50 to 400 personnel each (counting actual fighters plus supporting troops). The otryad was further broken down into smaller units--platoons and companies, depending on the size of the otryad. In the spring of 1942, the partisans grew to the point where the detachments combined into brigades (brigada); that is, three, four, or more otryads made up one brigada, and within each otryad could be from two to eight platoons. Later in the war, in 1943, brigades were usually organized into a soyedineniye, a brigade group, with no American equivalent, though it comes close to a division.[29] Some of these partisan detachments contained large numbers of civilians. This was often a bone of contention between partisan commanders--whether to care for these civilians or not; Jewish commanders, of course, saw it as a duty to save as many lives as possible even if the large number of civilians increased the danger of discovery. The Soviet Central Staff, furthermore, did not approve of the existence of separate Jewish partisan units and obligated the Jews and their commanders to integrate into the multinational partisan framework. Thus, such famous Jewish groups as those of Misha Gildenman, the Belsky brothers, Yehezkel Atlas, Yechiel Grynszpan, Berl Lorber, and Nicholai Kanishchuk, all had to eventually merge into the greater all-partisan central command and lose their distinctiveness as Jewish fighting forces.

Anti-Semitism in the Partisan Movement

Anti-Semitism is tenacious. It reared its ugly head even when Jews were no longer "sheep to slaughter" but valiant fighters. German propaganda followed the

Jews into the forests and mountains. This propaganda had a considerable influence; it was directed at guerrilla units in general and at what the Nazis called groups of Jewish "bandits who stand at the head of the partisan leadership, direct its activities, and leave their Jewish mark on all its doings."[30] The Germans, of course, exaggerated the role of Jewish leadership in the movement, but not by much--Jews were at the head of approximately 200 bands of partisans and participated in all the underground Russian organizations, though not always as Jews. Quite often, their Jewish identity was kept hidden.[31]

One effect of the German propaganda against the Jewish partisans was that the Soviet Central Partisan Command decided on a quick intermingling of nationalities for fear that anti-Semitic farmers situated near the partisan bases would not consent to supply food and clothing to fighting groups made up of all Jews or led by Jews. But this was not always the case. Jewish partisan groups were sometimes aided by the population, but to be on the safe side, it was not long before most of these Jewish units, forced by the Central Command, ceased to exist as separate groups.

A good example is the Kruk Detachment mentioned in this book, which fought in western Ukraine, in the state of Volyn, from late 1942 to late 1944. This detachment consisted of over 200 Jewish fighters but was led by a Ukrainian Communist, Nikolai Konishchuk. He was allowed to lead, not only because he was a respected commander and knew the territory well, but because it was better "public relations" to have a non-Jew as the head, even though all his assistant commanders were Jewish. (There is a sad footnote to this story: Konishchuk, who went under the nom de guerre of "Kruk," was killed by Ukrainian nationalists after the war.)

Anti-Semitism among fellow partisans also existed, but it must not be exaggerated. There were many more philo-Semites, especially among the leftist partisan groups. Israeli researcher Israel Gutman had this to say about the issue:[32]

> The partisan movement was not free of anti-Semitism. The extreme right-wing factions of the Polish underground viewed the Jews as "bandits" prowling around the forests. They took arms away from the Jews and even mur-

dered many of them. The leftist groups took
a less hostile stand toward the Jews. In
Lithuania, Beylorussia, and the Ukraine,
anti-Semitism was somewhat restrained after
permanent contact had been established between the partisan areas and the Soviet high
command.

For the Jew, no place was safe, but the forests
were safer than the ghettos and the death camps.
Still, the act of leaving the ghetto, especially with a
family or the remnant of a family, was a difficult one.
The environment was hostile, and Jews were often caught
or informed upon and turned over to Germans for a
reward. There were the exceptional few who risked
their lives to save Jewish lives, but they were a small
and brave minority.

Not all Jews and not all non-Jews were immediately
accepted by the partisans. Women, children, the elderly, the invalid, and the sick were often rejected.
Being accepted into the partisan movement depended
first and foremost on one's physical strength and military experience, but if either of these was lacking,
then the possession of a gun or rifle was sufficient.
Yet here too, it was difficult for Jews to acquire
arms; they had to resort to illegal purchase, robbery,
or acquisition in battle. Many non-Jews would not sell
guns to a Jew, or if they did, it was for exorbitant
sums. This situation was especially grim in those
ghettos that revolted and tried to find arms.

One of the greatest of all dangers to the partisans, to Jew and non-Jew alike, were the roving bands
of extreme right-wing Ukrainian nationalists. At the
head of these groups stood the nameless "Ottomanim" who
fought against Poles and Jews, as well as against
partisans. A more politicized group was the Banderovtsy, Ukrainian fascists who took on the name of
Ukrainian nationalist leader Stepan Bandera. Under the
standard of "Semastina Ukraina" ("An Independent
Ukraine!"), he attracted many Ukrainians to his bands.
The Germans offered the pledge of independence for a
"free" Ukrainian nation at the beginning of the war,
but they soon reneged after their initial victories
against the Russians.

Extremely anti-Communist and anti-Semitic, the
Banderovtsy killed their victims with fiendish cruelty
--not with rifles or guns, but with axes and knives.

Their motto was "Against the Poles! the Jews! and the Red Partisans!" It is no wonder that they were dreaded by the populations of Beylorussia and the Ukraine, and became at times the number one enemy of the partisans. In fact, the Germans caused fewer losses than these Ukrainian nationalists. Unarmed families were especially vulnerable to these bands, and the Germans paid large bonuses for the head of every Jew killed: a pud (a Russian measure of 16 kilograms, or about 40 pounds) of salt, a liter of kerosene, and twenty boxes of matches. Many Jews who had escaped from the urban ghettos or village round-ups, fell into the hands of the Banderovtsy.[33]

Therefore, it was often a serious bone of contention between Jewish and non-Jewish partisans and their commanders (and at times between two non-Jewish leaders) whether or not to offer help (food, clothing, and/or protection) to these Jewish families. It is one of the sad and ironic chronicles of the war that even in the midst of battle against a common enemy, there was such division and hatred among the partisans and against the partisans. It required the greatest of patience, self-control, and forbearance for the Jewish partisan to succeed in his mission.

Obstacles to Resistance

The major arenas of resistance, as well as the social structure of the Russian partisan movement, have been described, and now we come to the question that still exists in many readers' minds: Why didn't more Jews resist? Why didn't they resist physically and militarily?

The reader must put aside emotional and intellectual arrogance for a moment and ask the question with a certain reverence for both the living and the dead. Those who were not there will never fully understand what happened, and those who were have no answers. As Jewish novelist Elie Weisel so eloquently tells us: "Those who know do not speak and those who speak do not know."

What were the obstacles to resistance? There were many, and these obstacles held true for non-Jews as well as Jews. They held true, in some cases, for entire nations as well as entire families. First, it is obvious that resistance is an option not available to everyone. Physical resistance by its very nature is undertaken by only a small minority. Other forms of resistance are open to a far larger segment of the population, but here again, what of the very young, the very old, the lame, the sick, and those who were executed so quickly they had no time to resist? Are they to be labeled as "cowards" as well?

The major barrier to resistance was simply the incomprehensibility and the enormity of the crime. The magnitude and audacity of the killings psychologically overwhelmed the world, let alone the Jews themselves. Who would have believed that a culture that had produced a Mozart, a Beethoven, and a Goethe, could commit such acts? One's first reaction was to dismiss the entire idea as a cruel joke. Most of the Allied armies and their governments also rejected early reports as simply "propaganda."

Greuelpropaganda

Bruno Bettelheim describes three separate psychological mechanisms that were most frequently used for dealing with the horrors of genocide.[34] They are based on the belief that a supposedly civilized nation on a supposedly civilized planet could not stoop to such inhumane acts. The implication that modern man had such inadequate control over his cruelty was perceived as a threat to the individual psyche.

The following defense mechanisms were used: first, applicability to mankind in general was denied by asserting that such horrible acts (if in fact they did exist) were committed by a small group of insane or perverted persons. The Eichmann trial in 1961 clearly showed just the opposite: these acts were carried out with scientific and bureaucratic precision by thousands of quite ordinary people. Social psychologist Stanley Milgram has verified this phenomenon in his research: most people will harm their fellow human beings rather than disobey an authority.[35]

Second, the truths of the reports were further denied by ascribing them to deliberate propaganda; in fact the Germans themselves, masters of the art, called it greuelpropaganda (horror propaganda) and were quite aware that the more outrageous the atrocity, the more difficult it was for the world to believe, and the bigger the lie, the more likely it would be believed, but such lies had to exist in the realm of possibility and had to be based on already manifested myths and prejudices.

Third, the reports were believed, but this knowledge was repressed as soon as possible. In addition to the individual's psychological mechanisms, the Germans were experts in unnerving their victims, in bewildering them, in thwarting any plans for escape. The ploys they used are well-known: they used code words which camouflaged their real intent--"relocation," "Jewish problem," "final solution;" they made people believe that the death camps were work camps; the victims were met by an orchestra at the train station; they were given bars of "soap" when they entered the gas chambers; and, moreover, the Nazis sent postcards to the victims' friends and relatives describing how "wonderful" the situation was and how well they were doing. In short, it was a time where morality was stood on its head: right was wrong, wrong was right, true was false, and false was true. This same thought was echoed by the French partisan leader Dominique Ponchardier:[36]

> ...It was by definition the era of the false: the false combatant, the false decent man, the false patriot, the false lover, the false brother, the false false. In a world of false noses, I was one of those whose nose was real and it seemed to me, as it did to all the "reals," that in reality we were all real cons.

This sense of existential unreality and dubious authenticity still plagues us today.

Collective Retaliation

The principle of collective responsibility baffled the Jews, prevented their escape from the ghettos, and helped suppress resistance. For example, in many ghettos when an escaped fighter was caught, not only he but his entire family, his neighbors, and even his work unit were killed. When a man or woman decided to resist, he or she knew that it would endanger not only his or her life, but that of parents, children, spouse, brother, sister, and acquaintances. Resistance could, of course, include escape, either from ghetto or concentration camp. Leon Wells, in his memoir The Janowska Road tells the following tale:[37]

Now the Untersturmfuhrer (SS officer) begins his speech, directing it at us: "One of you escaped. Because of him these people will be shot. From now on for anyone who tries to do the same, I will shoot twenty of you. If I find out that you are planning an escape, all of you will be shot." After his speech, he turns to the chosen six, and shoots one after another ... when he finishes, he calls for four of us to pick up the corpses and toss them into the fire.

The Jews in the ghetto faced a great dilemma. If they left the ghetto to fight, they might save themselves but leave their families behind. If many fighters left the ghetto, the remaining population would be vulnerable. But if they did not resist in some way, they were denied the privilege of avenging themselves. The late historian of the Holocaust, Philip Friedman, succinctly summarized this dilemma in the following quote:[38]

In the Jewish underground of Warsaw, Bialystok, and other ghettos, a passionate discussion was going on. What were they to do? Stay in the ghetto or leave it for the woods? It was primarily a moral issue: Were they entitled to leave the ghetto populace to face the enemy alone, or did they have to stay on and to take the lead in the fight when the crucial moment of the extermination actions arrived? After heated debates, the opinion prevailed to stay in the ghetto as long as possible despite the disadvantages of the position, and to leave only at the last moment when there was no longer any chance to fight or to protect the ghetto populace.

The Germans understood the Jewish psyche very well and knew very well where the Jew was most vulnerable. Closely connected to the principle of collective retaliation was the strong family ties among the Jews, and here the Jews were vulnerable. Ironically, what had been a great strength to the Jewish people now became a pernicious trap. The close-knit family structure made it difficult for one or two members to leave the rest behind, since it was extremely difficult for an entire family to escape the ghetto together. A decision to leave the village or escape from the ghetto or camp in the hope of reaching the partisans required a painful decision to leave a wife, mother, father, and child.

In interviews that the author has had with his father, this theme is continually emphasized, and it is permeated with guilt, even if leavetaking meant the opportunity to take nekumah (Yiddish for "revenge") for the family:

> Am I no different from my parents or my daughters that I lived and they died? No, we were the same. Why, then, did I remain alive? I may not have been able to help them if I had stayed, but at least we would have been together to the end.

The Hope of Survival

As has been discussed, over and beyond all the concealed tricks, the half-truths, the devious ploys used by the Nazis to entrap the Jews (and the world), the most effective tool was the utter magnitude of their own evil. This led, as was shown, to numerous ways of adapting to the incomprehensibility of the time. One of the most elemental drives of the human being is to survive. Hope springs eternal. Many Jews felt they were not going to be killed; that they were too valuable; that the Germans "needed" their labor, their talents, or even their money. They would not risk the chance. They believed if they obeyed the law, then they would be spared. In short, resistance meant suicide; not to resist meant life, and why risk it? Hold onto life as long as possible.[39]

Orthodox Jews in many cases refused to take part in military resistance. Resistance to them was contrary to God's law; it was equivalent to a suicide mission, and suicide was considered a sin. Better that one trusted in God and His judgment. To the very end, they felt, one must do God's bidding, stay alive, and not risk death. One's only objectives should be Kevod Hashem (Hebrew term for "religious honor") and Kiddush Hashem ("sanctification of God's name," "religious self-sacrifice").

This form of nonviolent resistance (almost Gandhian in certain ways) has become a very controversial topic. Some readers will say that this form of passive resistance is not resistance at all--it is cowardice and human weakness, and, furthermore, it led to the deaths of many Jews who might have saved themselves (or died in active revolt) if they had not listened to the rabbis. A partisan, Moshe Flash, whom the author has interviewed, echoed these same sentiments:

> Because of God and the religiously orthodox, many Jews died because it kept the people from fighting. The rabbis had a strong hold on the people. Because of that, I had to kind of leave my religion for a while and fight.

Nonviolent resistance took many forms: there were prayer groups and Hebrew classes that would congregate in ghettos and camps in spite of heavy penalties; there were attempts to rescue Torah scrolls from burning synagogues although many people were killed in the attempt; there were stories of Hasidim <u>who prayed and danced in religious ecstasy</u> until the last minute of their lives!

Are these acts of bravery or cowardice?

Lack of Arms, Lack of Trust

Among the most serious obstacles to resistance, once the psychological, theological, and family barriers were overcome, were, first and foremost, the lack of arms, and, subsequently, the lack of communication between Jews and the outside world, and the lack of trained leadership. Yet it came down to basics: in any revolt, only a small minority are able to resist, and these few must have something to fight back with, and here the Jews were not always successful.

As Philip Friedman states in his article "Jewish Resistance to the Nazis":[40]

> A steady, uninterrupted supply of arms is a condition <u>sine qua non</u> for resistance operations. Most of the non-Jewish underground movements had received vast supplies of arms and other material from their governments-in-exile and from the Allied governments. But in no country was the Jewish underground treated on an equal footing with the recognized national underground organization.

Whatever the Jewish underground was to receive had to pass through unfriendly National channels, and often the requests were refused outright, as in the Vilna and Bialystok ghettos, or came too late and in ridiculously small quantities, as in the Warsaw ghetto. During the Warsaw ghetto revolt, led by Mordechai Anilewicz, after prolonged and maddening negotiations with the Polish underground, the Jewish partisans finally received only fifty revolvers, fifty hand grenades, and four kilograms of explosives. All this had to be used to fight off entire artillery regiments and air attacks-- and some of the revolvers were defective and useless. One of the major reasons why the Jews received so little aid from the Armia Krajowa, the Polish Land Army, the largest underground movement in Poland, was because its leadership was permeated with anti-Semites.[41]

Each gun, each grenade, and each rifle, was worth its weight in gold--because quite often each piece had to be purchased in gold on the black market from illegal arms dealers and army deserters, or had to be stolen from guards, soldiers, and peasants, or made in small clandestine factories and repair shops.[42]

Aside from the lack of arms, there was often a lack of trust and communication between Jews and the surrounding communities. Some of this was due to anti-Semitism, and some to outright fear of the Germans who would retaliate for collaborating with the enemy (Jews, Communists, and partisans). In the words of Erich Goldhagen, Jews lived not only like fish in a hostile sea, but like fish upon a hostile land. All this hampered the effective coordination between Jewish and non-Jewish fighting groups.

Added to all this was a lack of competent Jewish leadership. Seasoned and established community leaders had been ruthlessly deported and eliminated in the early round-ups. Jewish intellectuals, professionals, political and trade union leaders, former Jewish officers and soldiers, and religious heads, were among the first to be sent to labor camps or immediately killed under various pretenses.

Fortunately, the Nazis did not, in the first years of the war, pay too much attention to the young people and the women, and thus both the leadership and rank-and-file of the youth organizations (for example, Betar, Hechalutz, Dror, Hashomer Hatzair, and Zionist youth movements) survived and formed the cradle of the Jewish underground in the ghettos and, later, in the forests.

Evaluation and Conclusion

After the Eichmann Trial some fifteen years ago, a myth emerged: the Jew as cowardly sheep. Will we soon have another myth to replace it: the Jew as mighty supermen? The truth, like life itself, like the war itself, is vastly more complex.

How should we evaluate the partisans themselves? Should we exaggerate their role during World War II? They are such a romantic group. Should we overestimate their importance? Should we glorify them? The answers, of course, depend on our purpose and on our role. Religious and political leaders utilize the glory of the past to bolster their belief system or maintain adherence to their regime to teach their people the lessons of the past and to give them inspiration for the future. But the role of the historian and social scientist is more difficult and much less grandiose: to tell the story as truthfully as possible. In the past, the Jewish role in the resistance was suppressed either out of ignorance or outright prejudice. Many western historians were not fluent in those languages (Hebrew and Yiddish) which told the Jewish side and many eastern historians were motivated by political pressures or anti-Semitism. In either case, the true story never emerged. It was left to Jewish writers to make sure that the vital role of the Jewish fighters was not omitted.

But what of the evaluation of these fighters? From a strictly military point of view, the Soviet partisan movement had a certain measure of success, as much as any resistance movement can have when opposed by a first-class military power, but the success was sorely limited by several factors, some of which have been described earlier. The partisans suffered from three major problems--irregularity, ineffectuality, and control.[43]

The problem of control was an important factor. A company or battalion of fighters is often extremely difficult to control from a distance of no more than several hundred yards. In comparison, the problem of effectively ordering 60,000 to 80,000 partisans in a given sector, broken up as they were in a number of loose-knit units a hundred miles or more behind the enemy's lines and a thousand miles from the central command, even with dependable communications, is almost insurmountable.

Second, there was the problem of ineffectuality. The partisans were never able to stand up to the crack regiments of the German army face-to-face even in those areas and circumstances of their own choosing, and, furthermore, they were able to "deny" only that terrain which was tactically unimportant to the Germans at a particular time or which, because of manpower limitations, the Germans were unable or unwilling to occupy or clear. In those areas that the Germans wished to avoid, they would simply go around that particular sector. Despite the fact that the partisan bands were often extremely difficult to combat, still, the Germans, when they saw the need to clean up a sector of the rear and were not too committed at the front, were nearly always equal to the task.

Third, there was the problem of inexperience. Such inexperience, according to U.S. Army historian Edgar Howell, is the great weakness of most resistance movements, and the Soviet movement was no exception. The partisans were "irregular" in every sense of the word. They could never be equipped, trained, and controlled like a regular army or approach a regular army in effectiveness and strength. Too often, the fighters were unenthusiastic and undisciplined. Leadership was often poor. Given these factors, it is no wonder that some military experts felt that the partisans were, by and large, a "third-rate militia."[44]

To say all this is not to gainsay the strengths of the partisan movement, most notably in the years 1943-44. It had a large pool of manpower on which to rely, manpower that was innately tough, frugal, inured to hardship, and often intimately familiar with the area in which it operated. Furthermore, the partisans bruised the enemy, even if they could not vanquish it. Every rail break, every piece of rolling stock damaged or destroyed, every German soldier killed, wounded, or diverted, and every delay in the supply trains hurt. From a geopolitical point of view, the partisans were much more successful in preventing the Germans from ever fully going ahead with their occupation and economic administration of the conquered territory. The Soviet partisans and their political commissars were also a factor in spreading and maintaining Communist control over areas that were either hostile or neutral to the Russians. And, finally, the partisans permitted those people who joined them the dignity and the honor of retaliating against the Germans.

So, despite its many weaknesses, the partisan movement and the Jews within it, played an important role. It was not simply that they allowed one to die but to live with dignity.

* * * * *

Footnotes

1. Martha Byrd Hoyle, <u>A World in Flames: A History of World War II</u>, New York: Atheneum, 1970, pp. 323-324. These figures reflect civilian deaths with regard to the Chinese and the Jews. For the Russians, approximately seven million out of the twenty million dead were civilians; the rest, thirteen million, were Soviet soldiers.

2. These quotes were taken from William B. Helmreich, "How Jewish Students View the Holocaust: A Preliminary Appraisal," <u>Response: A Contemporary Jewish Review</u>, Vol. IX, No. 1 (25), Spring 1975, p. 104.

3. Raul Hilberg, <u>The Destruction of the European Jews</u>, Chicago: Quadrangle Books, 1961, pp. 662-669. See also Yuri Suhl (ed.) <u>They Fought Back: The Story of the Jewish Resistance in Nazi Europe</u>, New York: Schocken Books, 1975 pp. 3-4. (Originally published by Crown Publishers.)

4. Hannah Arendt, <u>Eichmann in Jerusalem: A Report on the Banality of Evil</u>, New York: Viking Press, 1963, p. 108. See also Jacob Robinson, <u>And the Crooked Shall Be Made Straight: The Eichmann Trial, the Jewish Catastrophe, and Hannah Arendt's Narrative</u>, Philadelphia: Jewish Publication Society, 1965, pp. 213-223; and Morris U. Schappes, "The Strange World of Hannah Arendt," <u>Jewish Currents</u>, July-August, September and October 1963. Available also in pamphlet form.

5. Bruno Bettelheim, <u>The Informed Heart: Autonomy in a Mass Age</u>, New York: The Free Press, 1960, p. 263. See also Jacob Robinson, <u>Psychoanalysis in a Vacuum: Bruno Bettelheim and the Holocaust</u>, New York: YIVO Institute of Jewish Research, A Yad Vashem Documentary Project, 1970, 36 pages.

6. Ruth Kunzer, "Teaching Literature of theHolo caust," <u>Davka</u> (a student review of the UCLA Hillel Foundation), Vol. V, No. 2, Summer 1975, p. 6. George Steiner's quote is from his book <u>Language and Silence</u>, New York; Atheneum, 1970.

7. Reuben Ainsztein, <u>Jewish Resistance in Nazi-Occupied Eastern Europe</u>, New York: Harper and Row (Barnes and Noble), 1974, pp. 394 and 396. See

also Binyamin Eliav, "Soviet Russia and the Holocaust" in <u>Israel Pocket Library</u>: <u>Holocaust</u>, Jerusalem: Keter Publishing House, 1974, pp. 177-179.

8. Eliezer Berkovits, <u>Faith After the Holocaust</u>, New York: KTAV, 1973, p. 36.

9. See Suhl, op. cit. p. 6.   Joseph Goebbels, Hitler's Minister of Propaganda, made these remarks in his diary and thereby paid a grudging tribute to the Warsaw Ghetto uprising of April, 1943.

10. Suhl, op. cit. pp. 239-240.

11. Quoted in the introduction to the Hebrew version of this book by Binyamin West, <u>Heym Hayu Rabim</u>, Tel Aviv: Labor Archives Press, 1968, p. 11.   This letter also appeared in Dr. Y. Karmish, "Enemy Sources Tell of Jewish Bravery" (English translation of original Hebrew), <u>Yediot Ya-Va-Shem</u> (Yad Vashem Newsletter) No. 6-7, Teveth 5727, January 1957.

12. For further discussion on this theme, see Shaul Esh, "The Dignity of the Destroyed: Towards a Definition of the Period of the Holocaust," <u>Judaism</u>, Vol. II, No. 2, Spring 1962.

13. See Ber Mark, "The Herbert Baum Group: Jewish Resistance in Germany in the Years 1937-1942" in Yuri Suhl, op. cit. pp. 55-68.

14. See Abraham Foxman, "Resistance: The Few Against the Many" in Judah Pilch (ed.) <u>The Jewish Catastrophe in Europe</u>, New York: American Association for Jewish Education, 1968, pp. 117-119; and especially, Suhl, op, cit., pp. 189-195 and 219-225.

15. The figures in this section are taken from Foxman, op. cit., pp. 122-123.

16. Again, the figures are from Foxman, op. cit., 121.   Foxman has quoted from Reuben Ainsztein, "The War Record of Soviet Jewry," <u>Jewish Social Studies</u>, January, 1966, p. 8.   See also Binyamin West, op. cit., p. 9.   Some may question the authenticity of these awards because so many were

given out by the Russian command both to its
soldiers and its partisans in order to boost
morale. This may be true, but great acts of
heroism still abounded and these medals reflect
that, even though a great many of them were
eventually distributed.

17. See Reuben Ainsztein, "The War Record of Soviet
    Jewry," p. 14.

18. For further information on Hannah Senesh, see
    Marie Syrkin, Blessed is the Match, New York:
    Alfred Knopf, 1947.

19. These are, of course, very rough estimates. See
    Foxman, op. cit., p. 123; Reuben Ainsztein,
    Jewish Resistance in Nazi-Occupied Eastern Europe,
    pp. 393-396; Israel Gutman, "Partisans" in
    Israel Pocket Library: Holocaust, Jerusalem:
    Keter Publishing House, 1974, pp. 114-116.

20. See Franklin H. Osanka (ed.), Modern Guerrilla
    Warfare, New York: The Free Press, 1962 and his
    extensive bibliography, pp. 475-508. See also his
    article "Internal Warfare: Guerrilla Warfare" in
    International Encyclopedia of the Social Sciences,
    New York: Macmillan Company, 1968, pp. 503-507;
    Otto Heilbrunn, Partisan Warfare, New York:
    Praeger, 1962. For an analysis of the Soviet
    partisan movement, see Edgar M. Howell,
    The Soviet Partisan Movement, 1941-1944,
    Washington, D.C. Department of the Army (Pamphlet
    20-244), August 1956.

21. This is the evaluation of a United States Army
    officer and historian, Edgar M. Howell, ibid., p.
    203.

22. These figures were compiled from official German
    sources and can be found in the chapter by Earl
    Ziemke, "Composition and Morale of the Partisan
    Movement" in John A. Armstrong (ed.), Soviet
    Partisans in World War II, Madison, Wisconsin:
    University of Wisconsin Press, 1964, p. 151.

23. Reuben Ainsztein, Jewish Resistance in Nazi-
    Occupied Eastern Europe, p. 280. The emphasis is
    from the original. For a fuller treatment, see
    his subchapter, "The Size of the Jewish
    Participation," pp. 393-396.

24. The background information on these three stages were acquired from three sources: Ainsztein, Jewish Resistance in Nazi-Occupied Eastern Europe, pp. 280-281; Howell, op. cit., pp. 204-205; and Ziemke, op. cit., pp. 148-150 and 194-196.

25. Howell, op. cit., p. 205

26. This is the opinion of Ainsztein, Jewish Resistance in Nazi-Occupied Eastern Europe, p. 394.

27. This description of the partisan composition is based on Ziemke, op. cit., pp. 141-146.

28. Ziemke, op. cit., pp. 147-148.

29. Ainsztein, Jewish Resistance in Nazi-Occupied Eastern Europe, p. 280.

30. Quoted from Binyamin West's introduction to Heym Hayu Rabim, p. 10.

31. From an interview with Israeli Holocaust researcher and professor at the Bar Ilan University, Dr. M. Diburzchki, Maariv (an Israeli newspaper), July 28, 1964. Quoted in West, op. cit., p. 10.

32. Israel Gutman, op. cit., p. 109. The material in this book was first published in the Encyclo pedia Judaica.

33. West, op. cit., pp. 11-12.

34. Bruno Bettelheim, The Informed Heart, op. cit., pp. 252-254.

35. See Stanley Milgram, Obedience to Authority, New York: Harper and Row, 1973 and his article, "The Perils of Obedience," Harpers Magazine, December, 1973.

36. Ponchardier is talking of the postwar liberation of France, but his words also apply to the war years themselves. The quote is from Blake Ehrlich, Resistance; France 1940-1945, Boston: Little Brown, 1965, p. 272.

37. Leon Wells, The Janowska Road, New York: Macmillan, 1963, p. 190. For further discussion

of collective responsibility, see Abraham Foxman's excellent discussion upon which I have elaborated, op. cit., pp. 94-95.

38. Philip Friedman, "Jewish Resistance to Nazism: Its Various Forms and Aspects" in Jacob Glatstein et al. (eds.), Anthology of Holocaust Literature, New York: Atheneum, 1973, p. 276.

39. This dilemma is graphically portrayed in a play by Arthur Miller, Incident at Vichy in The Portable Arthur Miller, New York: Viking Press, 1971, pp. 283-342.

40. Philip Friedman, op. cit., p. 277. This section on lack of arms and lack of trust relies heavily on Foxman's discussion, op. cit., pp. 123-24.

41. See Yuri Suhl, op. cit., p. 6.

42. Friedman, op. cit., p. 277.

43. For a more intensive discussion of this point and others that follow, see Howell, op. cit., pp. 209-213 and Kenneth Macksey, The Partisans of Europe in the Second World War, New York: Stein and Day, 1975.

44. Howell, op. cit., p. 210. However, Howell is not completely correct since partisan groups play an important role outside of military matters too, but even so, a few partisan movements were quite effective. The most notable was General Tito's partisans in Yugoslavia. About 2,000 Jews took part in his ranks and Tito's first and closest comrade-in-arms was Moshe Piade, a Jew. Also, the Russian partisan movement played an extremely important role in keeping pressure on the Germans and its allies as the USSR was rebuilding its strength to continue the struggle.

Portions of this essay, the parts dealing with obstacles to resistance, appeared in Byron Sherwin and Susan Ament (eds.), Encountering the Holocaust, New York: Impact Press. Distributed by Hebrew Publishing Company, 1979, pp. 190-195. Reprinted by permission of the editors.

PART ONE:

PROLOGUE

THE PARTISAN TALES OF SHMUEL PERSOV

Introduction

Literature on the Holocaust abounds but still there are serious gaps. We have military chronicles and political histories; memoirs of generals and of statesmen; theological essays and survivor diaries; firsthand and secondhand accounts of various stripes; bibliographies and surveys--yet with all the frenzied publishing, there are literally millions of non-Jews who do not know what the Holocaust is and thousands of Jews who do not know what it means.

One such gap is the role of Jewish resistance to attempted genocide and, in particular, partisan resistance. We know a great deal about resistance in the ghettos (especially the Warsaw Ghetto) and the concentration camps (especially Treblinka and Auschwitz) and about the role of Jews in Allied military units. However, the important Jewish contribution to guerilla warfare is only now coming to light. Some books, such as John A. Armstrong's Soviet Partisans in World War II, contain only scattered references to Jews. It has been left to a very few (and of these, most are not scholars, but journalists and novelists) to compile and present the scope of armed resistance.

Four Jews who have attempted to do so are Moshe Kaganovitch in his The Wars of the Jewish Partisans in Eastern Europe (in Hebrew and in Yiddish); Yuri Suhl in They Fought Back: The Story of Jewish Resistance in Nazi Europe; Binyamin West in They Were Many: Jewish Partisans in the Soviet Union During World War II (in Hebrew); and Reuben Ainsztein, in his 1000-page magnum opus Jewish Resistance in Nazi-Occupied Eastern Europe, the most comprehensive history of Jewish defiance written in the English language.

Still, there is much more to be done. For example, there are movies, novels, and plays that deal with the Holocaust, but the majority of these do not use the partisans as background. Yet, there is a large body of literature based on personal memoirs, written by Jew and non-Jew, most of it in Russian, Polish, Yiddish, and Hebrew waiting to be translated into English and published.

What follows are several tales by the Russian-Jewish writer Shmuel Persov (1890-1952). Persov was

born in Putshef in the Chernigov region of Beylorussia.
Until the age of thirteen, he studied in a yeshiva and
later did "post-graduate" work with the help of the
author-teacher A.N. Gensine. He was active in the Bund
between 1905 and 1906 and later emigrated to the United
States. However, with the onset of the Russian
Revolution of 1917, he returned to the Soviet Union.
He was murdered on Stalin's orders on August 12, 1952,
along with twenty-five other Jewish authors and
artists, who were among the most well known of Soviet
Jewish intellectuals. Because of Stalin's paranoid
phobia about the Jewish threat to his regime, over 400
leaders of Jewish culture died by execution, torture,
or prison hardship.

Persov produced many stores on Soviet life, including "Karnivriut" and "Royter Haryn." During World War
II, he wrote a great deal about Jewish partisans in the
forests and ghettos. He devoted a book, Dine Numen is
--Folk (Your Name--A People), to this subject. It
includes twenty-one factual accounts of Jewish resistance and of partisans who sacrificed their souls for
the sanctification of the Jewish people.

Many readers may find Persov's style naive,
heroic, "propagandistic"--and it is to some degree.
During the course of the war, more than 90 Soviet
writers were engaged in serving the needs of the war-
related propaganda effort. As "troubadors" of a
national epic, their words reflected the political ends
they were called to serve. They were hemmed in by
official Soviet ideology, and approved themes had to be
handled in fresh and original ways in order to pass the
censor. Jewish writers had an additional burden--they
found it necessary to have to prove to their non-Jewish
readership that Jews were not cowards nor traitors
during the war but, in fact, loyal sons and daughters
in the fight against fascism.

In Persov's first tale "Your Name--A People," the
"people" referred to are not the Jewish but the Soviet
people. The Jew as fighter, as partisan, had to be
presented as part of an entire nation fighting for
survival. In part, this perspective was so crucial
because at least at the beginning of the war, Stalin
ordered the press and other media to omit the Nazi persecution of Jews and to emphasize the persecution of
all Soviet peoples--Ukrainians, Beylorussians, Georgians, and others. Stalin wanted the struggle to be
carried out in the name of the beloved land, the soil

and home, and not as a mission to come to the aid of the Jews. It was for this reason that so many Jewish communities were caught unaware during the early part of the Nazi invasion of the Soviet Union.

After the war the situation worsened. A complete change of line was imposed, and the true story of Jewish extermination and of Jewish resistance was suppressed. Furthermore, Jews were later to be pictured, under Krushchev, as having been collaborators with the Nazis against the Soviets!

Shmuel Persov's tales must be seen against this background, as should the memoirs of partisan leaders Orland and Linkov that follow Persov, as well as all the tales in this book. Wartime and postwar Soviet literature must also be understood in the context of these enormous constraints. We will appreciate our own freedom as writers and readers today when we understand the pressures placed upon Soviet writers, intellectuals, and common citizens. Persov perished, as did many other writers, poets, and thinkers, in the Stalin purges, but he had completed his task in portraying Jews as active fighters and devoted citizens.

Our present day attitude toward the Soviet Union must be ambivalent; while the USSR continues to suppress Jews culturally and religiously, thousands of eastern European Jews were nevertheless saved by the Soviet army and navy in its valiant victory over Nazism. For this we owe the Soviet people and their leaders a bittersweet debt of gratitude.

* * * * *

A. "YOUR NAME--A PEOPLE"

The battalion was pulling back.

The Germans were attacking without letup on all sides. There was only one way left, the river shore. But there was no bridge around, and no time to throw a military bridge over; so the only possibility was to dash straight into the water and swim across to the opposite shore, but the partisans knew that the river was turbulent and deep.

Two Red Army soldiers who were good swimmers volunteered to examine the river in order to find a place where the water was less deep and the bottom firmer because, besides infantry, it was necessary to move the entire convoy and its vehicles. The commanders looked around with impatience at what was taking place beside the river. At any moment the Germans could mount an attack, and under these unfavorable conditions, the entire battalion could be wiped out. Time was at a premium.

One of the swimmers reached the middle of the river and began to go under. At that spot the waves were very high. The other went into the water once and twice, then disappeared for a few moments. Suddenly he surfaced...

At the river shore the tension mounted. An elderly man was brought to the commander.

"We have captured him; he has no documents," the guard said.

"Who are you," asked the commander.

"I am a Jew..."

"I can see that, but I am asking you once again: Who are you and where do you come from?"

"From the town of Hachklovirt, from the Jewish section of Neue Leben, not far from here. The Germans have..." The old man burst into tears like a child. "I happened to be away from home on that day and so I survived. But the others..." he made a desperate gesture with his hands. "Even the babies were not spared by the murderers..."

"And what are you doing here at the front?"

"Do you think I know what I am doing?... I am roaming around...perhaps I could reach the partisans where I could find local peasants; they know me, and you...you seem to be Russian too, like me...you are taking me prisoner, at the point of the rifle...as if I were..."

At this point the commander was informed that the two soldiers had returned with the following information:

"This is not a river--only the devil knows what it is. The bottom is soft and full of pits."

"But to stay here is impossible," said the commander.

"Comrade...," the Jew came closer to him. "If you will allow me..."

"Don't interrupt me," answered the commander angrily.

But the Jew insisted: "I belong to this place. I was born here...I know this river like the back of my hand..."

And without waiting for an answer, he quickly began to take off his clothes. Standing there nude, the old man looked like a naughty little boy, as if he had stuck a beard to his chin to look funny. On his back were scores of sucking cup signs which looked quite fresh.* It was a dreary day and a cold wind was howling. Without hesitation he jumped into the water, struck out in the direction of the opposite shore, dived, and then surfaced at some distance. To those standing on the shore line and watching the Jew, now diving, now surfacing, it seemed as if he were doing some tricks for them. Suddenly he came to the surface and shouted with joy:

---

*   It is difficult to tell what this is: possibly "bulkis," sucking cups used for medical treatment in eastern Europe. (ed.)

"Here, this is the right spot." A soldier swam out to where the Jew was standing. "Yes, this is the place, the water is not too deep and the bottom is firm ground." The Jew swam to the opposite shore, moving in zig-zags, diving in certain places, then surfacing again and, like an experienced instructor, gave directions to the soldier swimming beside him:

"Here! Swim to the right! A little more... that's it, that's it!" The Jew took the soldier across to the opposite side of the river and then swam back to where the battalion was waiting. When he came out of the water he was blue with cold and his teeth chattered. In order to warm himself up he started jumping around. The commander took off his military coat and said:

"Here, take this, old man. Put it on to get warm!"

The battalion crossed over with all the soldiers and the vehicles. Only the commanders and some platoons stayed behind. Turning to the Jew, the commander said:

"Are you warm now? It is high time we crossed over to the opposite side."

"Are you taking me along with you?" asked the Jew. Agrily the commander answered: "What a question! Come on, old man, hurry up!"

The Jew did not have enough time to stand up. One shell after another burst around him. There were groans from the wounded. When the commander looked in the direction of the Jew, he found him dead.

Those who had already crossed over to the opposite shore fired back at the Germans. The commanders started to swim across the river as fast as they could, taking along with them the wounded and the dead Jew. When the entire battalion was out of danger, a soldier buried the Jew in the commander's military coat, which was now soaked in blood.

At the open grave the commissar said the following obituary:

"This is his blood. He has shed it for us, and for the entire nation; and this will we say to him at

-43-

our hour of parting: May your memory be blessed, old
man..."

   After a pause, the commissar asked: "What was his
name?"   Nobody knew.   They all stood there in silence,
abashed.   Suddenly the commander raised his voice and
said: "I know your name, o' murdered brother.   Your
name is--a people!"

   The battalion presented arms, fired three volleys,
and then moved on.

B. HERSCHEL, THE OVEN BUILDER

Six new men joined the partisan battalion. All were Jews. Along with them they brought Herschel Rosen, an oven builder from a Beylorussian small town on the river Sozh. No one had appointed him leader of the group, but since he alone was armed with a rifle, he was automatically accepted as the head of all six. He had found the rifle in the forest where he had been roaming around for weeks on end hiding from the Germans. The other five Jews he met by chance in the woods. All six had undergone the same disaster. They had been thrown out from their place of residence. Wherever the Germans went, Jews were murdered. Only those six had survived. They had succeeded in running away and had wandered about in the woods and on the roads until they had reached the partisan camp.

Even in the early days of their joining the partisan battalion, the commander--who had been the mayor of the town--assigned Herschel Rosen a very difficult task: to disrupt work at the factory that produced woolen boots (walikes) in his small town. This factory was known far and wide, and the small town was proud of its high quality product. Now, why should it be that those woolen boots should go to warm the feet of the Germans?...Never! Hershchel was very familiar with the factory. He often was called there to build ovens.

"All right!" was his answer to the commander. "Only make sure that all six get arms." But the company hardly had any arms at all. In addition the partisans had to go out on a combat mission on the same day, so that in the end, Rosen was to get only one more rifle.

Armed with two rifles, three bottles filled with kerosene, and packets full of chaff and a few matchboxes, the five Jews went on their first mission, with Hershcel at their head. Herschel, an excellent craftsman, had worked not only in his small town, but had also done some odd jobs in the neighboring villages. He knew all the roads and paths in the area. He led the group under cover of darkness through marshlands and sideways. The cold and strong autumn wind chilled them to the bone. Every rustle in the leaves frightened them. Slowly their eyes got used to darkness. Before long they had crossed the marshes and, far away on the peak of the mountain, lay the small town. Up there was the factory. Herschel knew that the factory was surrounded by a board fence. He even remembered the gap between the boards. When he built the ovens there, he had to bring red sand loam from the nearby pits into the factory. Here were the pits. Only now they had been filled up.

Herschel wanted to fall down to the ground and kiss them. In these pits of red sand loam were buried the Jews who had been tortured to death, Jews from the small town of his birth. To cry? No! There was no time for that now. The time has come to take revenge on the Germans. Herschel starts to crawl forward, followed by the other five. Here was the wooden fence and here the spot with the two missing boards. Now the men were in the backyard of the factory. They were trying to hide in the shadows cast by the storerooms. Here was the opening to the factory. An armed German soldier was standing guard and whistling a melancholy tune to himself. The whistling suddenly stops. They fill his mouth with chaff and he falls to the ground. A few moments later he is lying there, dead. There were no other guards in the backyard. This fact had been known to Rosen even before he had run away from his small town. He assigned to each of the men their part of the work to be done. Two were assigned to the storerooms which were full of woolen boots. The other three had to set fire to the entire factory. He himself was to take care of the attic. According to their plan, all buildings had to be set on fire at the exact same time. Here is he, Herschel on top of the attic. He smells burned-up bricks. He passes his hands over the chimney which he built with his own hands before the war, pours some kerosene on them, and lights a match. Fire bursts out at once. The wind proves to be a great help to the partisans. Sparks are carried to the adjoining buildings and the sky turns red. The Germans start to put out the fire only to be beaten back by the wind. The partisans take advantage of the pandemonium and go out the backyard through the same opening, escaping over the marshlands and back to the forest. All through the night the Germans kept firing after the escaping partisans. Some of them even reached as far as the marshes, but they did not dare to advance any further. Some of them were to flounder and die there. Only those who were familiar with every path in the area could save themselves from the marshes.

The six partisans with Herschel at their head, now armed with two rifles and one automatic rifle, came out slowly from the marshes into a forest, which became thicker and thicker the farther they moved away from the factory. The sky abvoe was now red with flames. Formerly, this plant produced about six hundred pairs of woolen boots a week. After this operation the Germans did not succeed in running it for even a single day. It was burned to the ground with all its departments and buildings.

In the course of two years, Herschel Rosen, a vivacious and cordial man, was to turn into a ruthless partisan. His comrades would sometimes remind him of the job he did at the factory.

"My job is to build ovens for people, to make them warm, but to the Hitlerites I make it very hot."

He would answer with a sad smile. He was always very sad. For two whole years he could not walk freely into the small town of his birth. All fifty years of his life this oven builder had spent in only one place, his small town. There he had seen many days of joy and also of sorrow. When the Germans attacked his country, his hair turned white and the light went out of his eyes. But his hands were strong; they knew how to hold an automatic rifle and a mortar. His soul went out to the small town of his birth; there to see his home, the nook where he had spent his entire life. But the Germans had turned the small town into a stronghold. there was no access to the place. The small town stood at the peak of a mountain, overlooking the surrounding country. The Germans kept a strong watch over it.

Now the time came for the Red Army to recapture the small town. Once again it was to be in Soviet hands. Among the first to enter it was Herschel Rosen, the former oven builder, now turned partisan. It was impossible to recognize the streets and the alleys. Everything had been destroyed. Here had stood his house, beautiful and well kept. Now there was nothing but a heap of burned trees and bricks. The Germans had ravaged the house before they left. The heap was still smoldering. Had it not been for the foundation which had survived the flames, he would not have recognized his home. He had his own method of laying the foundations for the ovens. He had often bragged: "I can recognize my handiwork even with my eyes closed."

Having seen the destruction in his small town, Herschel turned to the mayor and said: "Send me into the ranks of the Red Army." The mayor answered: "You are right, Herschel, I will send you into the army. You will build the factory once again." Herschel was astonished and said: "You have found a good time to joke..." But the mayor replied seriously: "No, we have to rebuild the factory at once. Winter is at hand, and each pair of woolen boots is worth a good automatic rifle."

And Herschel the mason "went to war," to build the ovens of the burned-down factory and to provide the soldiers of the Red Army with new woolen boots.

C. FORTY-TWO

The attack was launched late at night. The partisans surrounded the village on all sides. Soon they would crush the German battalion like a worm. The sound of bullets was deafening. In the dark, gunfire flashed like lightning. From the door of a stable, a group of people came out towards the partisans. They were unarmed and approached with their hands raised above their heads. One of them held a white handkerchief. The commissar of the partisans gave the command to get them back behind the barn and to assign men to stand guard over them. At dawn, after the partisans had finished off the Germans, the commissar came to the stable. It was difficult to describe what his eyes saw in the light of day. Even on a person like him, who had seen so much in his lifetime, the scene had a terrible impact.

One of them, who spoke poor Russian, murmured: "We are Jews"... As they couldn't speak Russian, they were unable to make themselves understood. The commissar was in need of a translator. He sent for Abramel the tinsmith and the latter spoke to them in Yiddish.

"Who are you? Speak!"

"Doctors, lawyers, engineers, artists, scientists, from Vienna and Budapest. The fascists made up a special company out of us and sent us to the Eastern Front as forced labor, to pave roads, to uproot forests, to quarry stone, to carry earth. We were a few hundred men, but the great famine and the terrible cold, the inhuman treatment, and the hard, unbearable work, illness, and epidemics--all these have taken a heavy toll on our men. We, the survivors, are still keeping on."

The commissar wanted to know where they lived. One of the learned men from Budapest smiled wryly and said: "Here, in the empty stable. The Germans forbad us to wear warm coats and to correspond with our families." "They were allowed only to die," said Abramel the translator. "What have they in mind to do?" the commissar asked Abramel the translator. To this, Abramel retorted: "Well, they have come out to meet us carrying a white flag..." The commissar wrote down their names and took them along into the forest.

Thus, were forty-two prospective partisans to join our company.

The forty-two watched with excitement the operations of the partisans. A partisan who had fallen in the latest battle was being brought for burial. At the open grave all of them vowed to avenge the blood of their comrade. They raised the partisan flag and presented arms. In the morning, during roll call, the man on duty read the names of the newcomers. Partisan Abramel had taught them what to say when their names were to be called. "Answer like the others: 'Here'." The name of the comrade who fell the previous day was then called. A partisan who stood on the right answered: "He was killed in combat against the enemy." The newcomers asked Abramel to explain why the name of the fallen comrade was also called. "You are wrong," he replied. "Such a person never really dies..."

When the newcomers were sent to the bathhouse, they asked to wash separately, but it was difficult to comply with their request. As there was no alternative, they took off their clothes in front of all the partisans. The latter now had a chance to see on their bodies the wounds which had been inflicted by the Germans. The Viennese doctor said in a low voice: "For the slightest thing they beat us with sticks, like dogs." What could Abramel the tinsmith tell them? He had no words. He could only clench his fists and teeth and express his rage to fight. His wife and children were lying there in a common pit together with thousands of other murdered Jews...

He had never seen people washing themselves with such ecstasy. For over a year their bodies had not seen a drop of hot water. They were forbidden to wash in the German bathhouse. Even their toothbrushes had been taken away from them. After the bath they once again looked like human beings.

"Do you want to be together or to be divided up among other companies," asked the commissar. Partisan Abramel answered: "Why do you have to ask them such a question?"

* * * * *

Among the partisans who operated in the woods of Bryansk, now sprang a Jewsih group composed of forty-two men. The commissar addressed Abramel the translator: "They have to take the oath; translate the oath into Yiddish for them." That was no easy task for Abramel. The oath began with the words: I, a Soviet Citizen, volunteer...But they were not Soviet Citizens. Abramel had to think hard in order to put the oath into the proper form. He turned to the commissar and said: "What do you think of an oath in this version: 'I, a free son of my tortured people, volunteer'...?"

"That is fine, extremely fine," answered the commissar. The entire battalion with all its platoons stood at attention when each and every one of the forty-two men took the oath in Yiddish. The new partisans went about as in a dream. Only yesterday they were like human refuse, always displayed, to be laughed at and caviled, and today they were equals among equals with the veteran partisans, taking part in their training, listening together to reviews of the political situation, dressing like them, eating and drinking with all of them at one table. The commander of the Jewish group was a young Russian. It was he who taught them to use firearms and other weapons. He taught them partisan tactics, especially night fighting. "The nights are our faithful ally," he would tell them on every occasion.

But it was only during the night that some of them found it hard to move about or to aim their weapons exactly. Often they would fall to the ground. The commissar was present at their training. The faces of some of them looked haggard. He gave the order to excuse them from combat operations. They were offended. The accursed Nazis had taken their eyeglasses away from them and trampled them with their heavy heels, but to withhold from them the right to strike at the Germans--would they really have to accept that?

"We will see; get on with your training," answered the commissar.

A few days later a group of ground scouts went into action. When they came back they brought along with them a few pairs of eyeglasses. The commissar handed them to those who needed them most among the Jewish group.

"They took them off dead Germans. Try them on, please." The famous scientist from Vienna turned aside and wiped a tear. Abramel the tinsmith saw that and said: "Usually, comrade professor, partisans do not shed tears, but this drop in particular is extremely precious..." In the meantime they were not sent on combat missions. They fulfilled camp duties for the company. Wearing Russian woolen boots, German military coats, and winter caps with earflaps, the doctors and artists who had come from Vienna and Budapest could not be distinguished from Abramel the tinsmith or from the peasants and woodcutters of the Bryansk forests. Equals among equals, all together they led the unique lives of partisans. They took part in Red Army celebrations, and when they gathered in the earth hut which carried the pretentious name of "Central Partisan Club," those who came from Vienna and Budapest sang their own local songs. The partisans applauded them with great enthusiasm and asked for more and more!

On the day that followed the celebrations, the order was given to wipe out a German battalion. The partisan force was alerted. "Do you have the strength to go out on an attack?" asked the commissar.

The Jewish company with its forty-two men went out on its first combat mission. The battalion, which comprised one hundred and fifty partisans, was assigned the task of wiping out two German battalions. The Jewish group, led by the Russian commander, attacked from the right. At the beginning of the fighting one of the new partisans was wounded, but he bandaged the wound and kept on fighting. The group dispersed and began to crawl in the snow. Suddenly a partisan heard a low whisper in German. The Viennese scientist answered him in his own language. The Germans decided that these were their own men and all of them rose to their feet. The Jewish partisans fired a hail of bullets at them. Some of the Hitlerites fell to the ground, six raised their hands, and one acted as if he was going to surrender but immediately opened up with his automatic rifle. Three Jewish partisans were killed on the spot. The commander dashed forward shouting: "For the blood of our comrades...for our mothers and our wives, Fire!"

The company charged at the enemy with fixed bayonets. Doctors, lawyers, scientists, artists stabbed, fired, threw hand grenades, as if they had done nothing but fighting all their lives.

After they had accomplished their mission successfully, the men of the company returned to the battle ground and brought back the three dead comrades. They buried them, as was the practice of the partisans, with a military ceremony, vowing at the open grave to take revenge on the enemy for the blood of their comrades. In the evening at roll call, the partisans on duty read the names of those who had been killed. Abramel the tinsmith, who stood on the right, answered gravely when the name of each one was called: "Fell in battle against the invaders."

Now the Jewish partisans understood that the killed were alive too, alive in the memory of their comrades and alive on the lists of the partisan avengers. Maybe some of them would fall in battle; nevertheless, the group would always number forty-two. For all forty-two had faithfully fulfilled the oath: "I, a free son of my tortured people, volunteer..."

D. REISEL AND HANNAH

Even as very young girls, Reisel and Hannah were close friends. Together they went to the same school and together they went to get their first identity cards. When the war broke out, they both went to the school for nurses in order to go to the front together.

But when the Germans came the two friends had to separate. The Jewess Reisel was forbidden to draw water from the same well Hannah drew water from. Hannah was absolutely forbidden even to look in the direction of Reisel. The Jewish girl had to carry the yellow sign on her sleeve. But that was not all. The Germans drove all the Jews into the ghetto, a few dilapidated houses beside a river. To leave the place meant death by a firing squad. To be seen in the market buying food meant death on the spot. If a non-Jew from White Russia brought to the ghetto a few potatoes or a loaf of bread, they put to death both the Jew and the Beylorussian.

Once, when the Jews were taken out for work, Reisel succeeded in escaping and, meandering through sideroads and sidepaths, reached her friend. Hannah was shocked at seeing the great change that had come upon the tall, blooming, seventeen-year-old girl.

"Hannahle," cried Reisel, "the world has collapsed upon me! I am going to hang myself...."

An idea flashed in Hannah's mind. "Reisel, we have to get to our men, behind enemy lines. We will run away together." Reisel was excited. She was ready. But she became sad immediately. Her Jewish eyes and kinky hair would give her away. Hannah calmed her: "Reisel, I will lend you my identity card."

"And you? How will you manage?" asked Reisel. "I, with my features..." Hannah wanted jokingly to lighten the load on Reisel's heart. For Hannah had the blond hair, the grey-blue eyes, and the typical face of a Beylorussian.

"But..."

"No buts," said Hannah. She removed Reisel's photograph from the identity card and glued hers in its place.

The two girlfriends then set forth on their way to the partisans. The took special pains to keep away from villages in order to avoid meeting people. On the third day they had to get some food. For this purpose they walked into a village. Here they were caught by policemen. The Starosta (village head) released Reisel immediately. She had a real Beylorussian certificate. She was free; but he detained Hannah. Hannah made a sign to Reisel: "Don't stay here!..." But Reisel did not move. How could she leave her friend behind?

The Starosta took Hannah for interrogation, and, as it was learned later, this was a grim interrogation. "Why," he shouted, "are you going about without an identity card? You must certainly be a Jewess, and what a Jewess at that!..." Hannah pointed at her outward appearance and mentioned her typical Beylorussian language. But he, the Starosta, wouldn't hear of that.

"Here, look at her," pointing at Reisel. "She looks like a real Jewess, but when you see her identity card, you know immediately who she is. And you?...How old are you?"

"Seventeen," answered Hannah.

The Germans alerted all their commanders and police stations that from the small town of N. (here they mentioned the name of the small town), a seventeen-year-old girl had escaped from the ghetto one day before all the Jews there had been killed....

Reisel stepped forward. Hannah winked at her to keep silent. Reisel's knees weakened. Nudging her in the breast, the Starosta pushed Reisel out of his office, and to Hannah he said:

"Yes, we have found you, my little bird....You are the Jewess we are looking for."

Reisel waited for her friend outside the village till the evening, but Hannah did not come. When darkness fell a group of children came out of the nearby forest. Reisel hid beside a broken tree. When it became quiet around her, the young girl fled to where her feet took her. On the next day she was again arrested, this time by two men in the forest. They asked her for her identity card. They scrutinized her face and her card.

"This is very suspicious," said one of them. You look like a Jewess and your name is Beylorussian! Come along with us!" Through hidden forest trails he led her to a place where he handed her over to another policeman. In this manner she was to pass from one policeman to another until she reached the commander of a camp in the forest. Reisel told him what had happened to her, adding through her tears: "I should have told them I was the one who had escaped and that the identity card was Hannah's, and then..."

"Then they would have put both of you to death," interrupted the commander. "Now listen! You can no longer save your friend, nor your family which has been murdered. You had better stay with us here!"

Thus was Reisel to remain at the partisan camp. They gave her a rifle and taught her how to use it. Each shot sent a shudder through her heart. In the end she asked to be transferred to the company of field nurses, for she and Hannah had studied nursing.

"Of course, of course," the commander agreed. However, without her knowing it, the guard commander had decided to put her on guard duty.

The forest was thick and tangled. Up in one of the trees, a squirrel jumped and the branch shook slightly. Fresh snow fell from the tree. Reisel was startled. She held the rifle firmly in her hands. But at once she discovered the "culprit" and calmed down. Then once again she heard rustling among the trees and she shouted firmly: "Halt!" There was no answer. A few minutes later she heard the rustling closer and more clearly. Reisel shouted:

"Who goes there?" Getting no answer, she fired. The nearby guard did not fire. She held the rifle with greater force. She was all ears. All around it was absolutely quiet. It turned out that the commander was testing the young girl. He had ordered all the guards around not to fire on hearing the girl's shots. He himself had slipped into the area assigned to her as if he were an enemy infiltrator.

"All right," he smiled to himself. "The girl has a sharp ear and she knows how to use a rifle." "Well, comrade fighter", he asked the girl when she returned from her guard duty. "Did anything happen while you were on guard?"

"Yes, something happened. I even had to shoot, but I didn't see any traces of the enemy."

Reisel kept learning the hard job of being a fighting partisan. Soon she was to finish her training. Along with the entire battalion she went out on combat duty. On the way the battalion encamped to get ready for action. Reisel looked around and saw a broken tree. This was the tree beside which she had hidden two weeks before. Nearby was the village....She went up to the commander and asked him to send her out along with a few fighters to reconnoiter the area. Perhaps she could find out where Hannah had gone....At dawn the commander assigned to a group of veteran partisans the task of "feeling the pulse" of the German battalion stationed at the village. One of them returned quickly with the important news that two weeks before, a partisan battalion had gone through the village and killed the <u>Starosta</u>.

"But what about the girl Hannah?" asked Reisel with excitment. "I don't know anything about her," answered the partisan.

The Germans detected the partisan battalion and assigned to a well-equipped company the task of wiping it out. The partisan commander stood up and said: "It won't be the Germans who will wipe <u>us</u> out, but we, the Germans." All the platoons and companies were alerted. A small partisan company advanced forward to the small and distant bridge. Reisel could not understand what a handful of people could do. She was a little confused, and everything seemed to her as if in a dream. Only two weeks before she had waited here for Hannah's return. Death had stalked her everywhere she went. Now she was standing here, armed with an automatic rifle and hand grenades, ready to meet the despicable Germans as a woman partisan. Ten German tanks were detected approaching in the snow. They were coming nearer and nearer. But why wasn't the battalion shouting its battle cry: "Death to the invaders!"? Why weren't the partisans rushing forward or shelling them? The tanks were drawing close to the small bridge. Within one monent they would be on the bridge. Then all of a sudden she heard a number of explosions. The tanks stopped in their tracks. The Germans jumped out of the tanks firing in all directions. The partisans, who had mined the bridge, sprang up from their hiding places, fired at the Germans and killed them. To Reisel this was the first and decisive lesson in the

partisan method of war. Suddenly a comrade came from
the liaison convoy with the news that, on the other
front, the Germans had succeeded in breaking up the
partisan battalion into a number of companies so that
each company now had to fight it out on its own with
the Germans. No help was to be expected. The commander ordered his men to lie down in the snow. When the
Germans appeared he gave the order: "Fire!"

Reisel fired thirty-two rounds from her automatic
rifle, replaced the clip, and once again sent bullets
into the direction of the enemy. But the Germans too
spared no ammunition. Their bullets struck close to
the girl. Bullets whizzed past her head like flies.
Whereever they hit they raised bubbles of snow. The
enemy troops began to shell the partisans. It seemed
to Reisel that a bullet would hit her soon, and then...
"What are you firing at?" a comrade disrupted her train
of thought. The girl had aimed her rifle at a spot
from which the Germans were approaching with mad persistence. They did not crawl but went upright. She
could see the ranks of the attackers were becoming more
sparse. The battleground was covered with dead and
wounded Germans. In the late afternoon hours, the
fighting became less intensive.

The Germans did not like to engage in night
fighting. But the night was the partisan's best
friend. The companies of the battalion joined each
other again, and the commander got the battalion ready
for a night attack. The Germans knew that the partisans would attack them at night. Reinforcements were
sent to them in the form of two battalions and about
one hundred policemen. They occupied all the brick
houses in the village and the entrance to the village.
The partisans threw at them a large number of hand
grenades. Reisel tossed her hand grenades with great
skill. The moon came out over the battle area. It was
easy to detect the places from which the Germans were
firing. But the moon came to aid of the Germans too.
They cut holes in the entrance walls to serve them as
battlements. They shelled the entire village incess-
antly. One machine gun mounted to the left of the
battleground was particularly effective; so the order
was given to silence it. The partisans kept on firing,
but the Germans did not hold their fire either.
Suddenly, Reisel began to crawl forward in the direction of the entrance. The Germans, who were throwing a
great number of hand grenades, almost hit the girl.
Bowing down, she ran up to the entrance fence, sped

along it, and came up near the German firing position. The partisans held their fire. No partisan bullet should hit a comrade. Reisel mustered all her strength, and knocked strongly with the handle of her automatic rifle on the protruding barrel of the German sniper. The barrel was now twisted out of shape, and the machine was silenced.

The girl crawled back. Ten or fifteen steps separated her from the partisans. Suddenly she fell down, without even uttering a word. The automatic rifle dropped from her hands. She felt a terrible pain above her knee; her fingers touched the wet and hurting spot and then looked for her automatic rifle. But her strength failed her, and she couldn't rise to her feet. She felt someone trying to lift her and recognized two comrades of the company. Bullets and shell fragments whined around them, deafening their ears. One of the comrades was hit; another one took his place. The girl began to lose all her remaining strength, and she whispered faintly: "Enough, leave me here." The partisans did not concede to her request and they carefully took her out of the fighting area saying: "You have the right to pay for our lives with yours, and we do not?"

"Once it was Hannah who did it, and now you. Enough," she pleaded with them and passed out. She came to the next day. The commander bent over her bed and said, as if he were talking to his own beloved little daughter:

"My little child, a doctor is expected to arrive at any minute now from another company. We have settled the account with the Germans...two-thirds of them were wiped out yesterday. True, we also suffered heavy losses...." He sighed. Reisel once again began to pass out, running a temperature. She was seriously wounded. She heard voices around her. She felt that people were taking care of her. She imagined that she had caught sight of Hannah, but her eyelids were heavy as lead, and she could not raise them. Then she felt someone kiss her gently. She imagined that she sensed the breathing of Hannah on her flaming lips.

"Ah, what a dream...she opened her eyes. "Hannah, is that you?" "Yes", was the reply. Hannah bent over her sick and wounded friend. Briefly she told her:

In the morning she fell into the hands of the **Starosta** and in the evening the Germans phoned him and

-59-

ordered him to transfer the Jewess to the small town of N, since the usual practice was that the murdered Jewess should be buried in one grave. The Starosta picked out two policemen to take her there, but a partisan company who passed them on the way slipped into the village in the evening. They killed the Starosta and the policemen but she, Hannah, survived. In the partisan battalion she was acting as a nurse. The doctor took her along on all the difficult operations. Reisel could not utter a single word for joy. Hannah stroked her saying: "In a month's time you will again be in good health...."

"Take your identity card back," remembered Reisel.

"That isn't necessary any longer. We are now among our own people doing together one united task. We are women partisans."

"A difficult job," the wounded girl sighed.

Both girls knew that, but they would not shirk from their task of saving the lives of partisan fighters.

REMEMBER!

H. Orland

In mid-winter he was recuperating in this sanatorium which lies in a thick forest near the Volga. Through the trees one could see a bare mountain from which was flowing water from a spa known all over the country. The sanatorium usually carried the name of the spa, but now the people call this place "The Partisan." The sanatorium receives people from behind enemy lines. Their exploits are recorded in books which are still kept under lock and key. The personal questionnaires lie there in bundles. The convalescents leave the sanatorium to resume their activities in the woods, villages, and besieged towns, where life hangs on a hair. They fight, thus avenging the sufferings of the people.

The wound in his lungs has already healed. His appetite has returned to him. After a silence which went on for two months, he can now speak a little with people and occasionally smiles to the boy with the amputated leg--a partisan ground scout from Polesye in White Russia--who is lying beside him. Only yesterday he had gone into the forest on a long walk with Horfina, an old woman from the vicinity of Bryansk. He had been leading her by the hand. During one of the bombing raids on the forest, the old woman lost her eyesight.

Today, early in the morning, the partisan spent a long time in the ward with the Ukrainians. He spoke with them animatedly and went silent when the nurse entered the ward. He then walked into the office and asked to be released, claiming that he had recovered enough to be able to leave the sanatorium. In order to get his papers ready, it was necessary to obtain the approval of the doctor in charge of him. He took the papers and went over to the white cubicle of the manager. The hospital's manager, a professor of world-wide fame, examined his heart. He offered him an aromatic cigarette, and both sat there smoking silently. At last the professor said:

"In my opinion your trip should be postponed."

The partisan inhaled the smoke deeper into his lungs, coughed for a long time, and did not answer a word.

"Your heart has weakened, and you are in need of complete rest," said the professor, who had not received an answer. The partisan looked down at his thin and smoke-stained fingers, sank deep in his thoughts, and did not hear the professor when the latter added: "The first strain on your heart may bring on complications."

The partisan kept silent. "A long time will pass before you can be of any use," said the professor seriously. Hearing this, the partisan raised his sad eyes to look at the professor. A stubborn fire was ablaze in them. He passed his thin long fingers through his grey beard. A coarse word hung on his lips, but he restrained himself and said nothing.

"I have to forbid you from leaving this place for some time," said the professor.

At this point the partisan stood up and said quietly: "Tomorrow I am leaving this place on the two o'clock bus which goes to the railway station. Doctor, will you please give me another cigarette." He lit the cigarette with the match offered him by the professor and began to talk at some length. He endeavored to pick out the right words, simple words, as people do when they are explaining things to the young.

"I would like to speak Yiddish. It will be much easier for me." The professor nodded approval.

"As you can see, I am a Jew," he smiled, wrinkling the skin of his face. He stood up and started to pace the floor nervously. He had to make a great effort in order to stand still; the professor sat in his chair and did not take his sharp dark eyes off him for a moment.

"I am not rejecting the whole idea, and I am not denying anything. Now it is clear to me that they are now after the weak, after those who give in, even those who have no horns or claws to fight back and to resist ... " He shut his eyes and opened them again because of the deluge of thoughts that overwhelmed his mind.

"What do you call it, Doctor? Do you call it martyrdom? Why don't you speak, Doctor? Whole Jewish communities have gone like sheep to the slaughterhouse seeing before them the ten <u>Harugei Malkhut</u>.* Rabbi Akiva's head has cost us a very dear price...Jews have learned from him and followed his example.

His face had become ashen. He spoke in a whisper. "I do not refuse anything; on the contrary, I have taken upon myself things which are beyond my strength ... The murderers tied me up and made me witness the massacre of the entire Constantin community. Woe to the eyes that saw such a slaughter! Afterwards at the open grave, they gave me a spade ... and then, after the burial, they left me alone in the field and mockingly told me to march ... May the Rabbi who buried our community keep marching on and on! I am a Rabbi, I am a teacher who saw ancient Constantin."

"Is it true that the people will remember only 'Thou shalt love ... '" he said with difficulty. "Well, but where is "Remember"--"Remember what Amalek hath done unto you?! In the Ukraine I met many Jews who still remember."

At this point fire flamed in his eyes, and suddenly it seemed to him that he was standing in the middle of the synagague and with clenched fists was warning and warning: "If a Jew should forget till the day of doom what Hitler has done to the Jews, may his name be obliterated from the face of the earth." Jumping up, he put his hands on the professor's shoulders and said in a commanding voice: "Doctor, sign these papers! They are waiting for me out there by the River Bug!"

---

* The ten Jewish martyrs during the time of Rabbi Akiva who gave their lives rather than desecrate the Torah. (ed.)

THE PARTISAN MINE

AND ABRAHAM HIRSCHFELD, THE WATCHMAKER

Gregory Linkov

Our mines were causing great trouble to Hitler's soldiers, but to explode them from a distance was not worthwhile. For after the railway tracks had been destroyed in the mine explosion, much repair work was still needed, and that delayed the trains for many hours. Therefore, the Germans, that is, the railway managers and the policemen, sought special ways to get rid of the mines withough having to explode them. But it wasn't always possible to find the right expert for such dangerous work. Then it happened that in the region of Mishkashibishi a mine was removed in front of one of our demolition men--a mine which was thought to defy all experts. Later we succeeded in finding out the details of this interesting story.

In the Lenin region, in the district of Pinsk, the Nazis had arrested all the Jews who were unfit for work, put them into one camp, and executed them. The Jews who could work were put into a special camp located in the city of Slonim, where they were ordered to work in workshops, each of them according to his occupation. These Jews were told that their families had been sent over to Posnan where they would be kept till the end of the war. Among the craftsmen who worked at the Slonim camp was a watchmaker by the name of Abraham Hirschfeld. He did not work, however, at his occupation but was employed in repairing railway tracks and roads.

Then one day Hirschfeld was not sent out to work. He was called to the command building. There he was accorded special treatment--they served him breakfast consisting of a slice of white bread and a cup of coffee with milk. Abraham was surprised and became uneasy, fearing that such a human breakfast indicated a trap which the Nazis were setting for him. Actually he was not mistaken. After he had finished his breakfast he was approached by a German officer accompanied by a railway guard. They asked him about his knowledge and skill in electronics. Hirschfeld replied that he knew a lot about electrical circuits and that he would be willing to offer them his services in this field if he and his family were allowed to lead normal lives.

The Hitlerites assured him that they would take his request into consideration and asked him to follow them. They led him along the railway tracks. The railway guard went first, followed by the officer. The railway guard stopped and asked the guard something. The latter pointed at the track. "Well look here," the officer told Hirschfeld. "We want you to do this: here, under this track, there is a mine which cannot be removed. The whole thing is based on an electronic principle. You have to try to remove it. If you succeed, then we will bring your family back to you soon, and you will be once again free in your own small town. But if you do not remove it, then you won't be in need of a family. Got it?!"

"Yes, I understand exactly what you mean," answered Hirschfeld, covered with cold sweat.

"Then you can get down to work; but let's get away some distance first. You see, there is a mound of earth here under the track between the sleepers." The railway guard indicated the spot with his finger. Hirschfeld nodded and didn't say a word. "This is the concealed mine we have been speaking about."

The three Hitlerites went away to watch him at some distance. Hirschfeld stayed on the spot. He stood near the mine and thought: "Who could have put the mine here if not the partisans? But they have laid it not in order that Hirschfeld should remove it."

Then, what was he to do? To come near the mine, pull the electric wire, and blow everything up, including himself? In this case the Germans would certainly shoot Adik, his mother, and his wife. "But if I remove the mine, that would be treason," Hirschfeld whispered to himself, not knowing what to do. The Hitlerites were now about fifty or sixty meters from him, watching his movements closely. "No," said the officer, "I think that nothing will come out of it, for the Jew will simply chicken out." After a short pause he added: "You have promised him too much, for his family has already been shot." "Wouldn't it be the same whether the family has been shot or not? And why not promise to someone a hundredfold of what we actually have if he has already bought a ticket to the next world?" "Do you think that if the mine is removed, it will explode?" "Almost certainly. We have already lost twelve of our best sappers removing such mines."

"Well, but the time is up, and the man is not doing anything."

"Mr. Hirschfeld, get back to work! We are waiting for you."

Abraham decided, nevertheless, to try and remove the mine. He had two arguments for that: first, the mine had already been discovered by the enemy, a fact which was sure to prevent the blowing up of a train. The Germans could actually explode the mine themselves and lay new railway tracks. In the final analysis that was not a difficult matter. Second, if he were to remove the mine, then it would not be regarded as a mine which no one could remove, and then the partisans would think that the mine was faulty and attempt to make a more elaborate mine.

Hirschfeld stepped with courage to the mine and began to study its wire connections. But no benefit could come out of that. Only the wires which had been laid on the railway track were visible. All the rest were buried in the ground. Very carefully Hirschfeld began to expose the mine. He worked a very long time at it. For two hours the Hitlerites sat at a distance, waiting for the explosion. But no explosion took place. Hirschfeld removed the mine. He had separated the electro-detonator from the explosive charge and put it aside. The danger of explosion was over.

"The mine has been removed and you can come near now. The danger of explosion is over," Hirschfeld cried out to the Hitlerites. They approached Hirschfeld gingerly.

"Well done, Hirschfeld!" the policeman said. "You will work for us as an instructor in dismantling mines."

Hirschfeld received this announcement with silence. On that evening he was given a meal like that of a German soldier. For the past two months he had not had such a human meal.

"You will work for us as an instructor in removing mines," the policeman's words came back to him. What was he to do? Hirschfeld thought. It was absolutely evident that the mine could be removed. The only thing to do was to cut one of the pipes which connected the detonator with the battery. But until you got to that, you could be blown to bits. In order to make it impossible to remove the mine, it was necessary to add one more battery and to use bigger pipes so that when one of them was pulled, the mine would explode.

Three days went by. Hirschfeld received the same meals as any ordinary Hitlerite. But they didn't bring his family back to him as they had promised. On the night of the third day, Hirschfeld stood at the door of his flat. In the nearby street Jews were being taken to work.

Suddenly he noticed that one of his old acquaintances turned his face to the other side when he saw him and did not return his greetings.

"Well, it has become known to one and all. My friends consider what I have done as treason, and as far as they are concerned, they are right," he thought to himself with some bitterness. "The instructor and mine remover." Suddenly he noticed that one of the Jews who passed by dropped something for him. A groan almost issued from his throat, but he stifled it in time. When all the Jews and their guards had gone away, Hirschfeld looked around, and his heart contracted with pain as he picked up the crushed piece of paper. He hurried back into his room and with trembling fingers straightened out the paper. It was a piece of wrapping paper and bore the following lines, written in pencil:

Dear Abraham,

It seems that you have been given a job by the Hitlerites in return for which you are being fed like a human being. But we do not envy you. This act of yours is considered by us as an act of treason. By the way, do you know that all the members of your family have been shot?

David

The piece of paper dropped from Hirschfeld's hands. A vacuum formed in his soul. A feeling of indifference to all that was around him permeated his consciousness, including his own life. He took out of his pocket a letter he had prepared some time before, added a few words in pencil and walked out ...

Next day Hirschfeld was seen once again on the railway tracks with a number of Hitlerites. He walked at the head of the group and spoke animatedly with the lieutenant of the technical troops. They were accompanied by an army man, a policeman, and two others.

Hirschfeld stopped near the mine which had been laid under the railway tracks and got down to work. The German lieutenant and two of his men proved to be men of courage. They bent down on the spot where the mine had been laid and watched every item that Hirschfeld brought out from the ground. After the mine had been completely exposed, he called the policeman to join them. At the same time a strong explosion was heard. Of the six men who had come to where Hirschfeld had been working, only one survived; it was the army man who had watched the job of removing the mine from a great distance.

These two cases were known to me quite well--that of removing the mine without the explosion and that of the Jew's death, together with the four Hitlerites, while tinkering with the mine. But I did not know the details. A week had passed from the second event when a package was delivered to me by a man I did not know. It contained a long letter written by Hirschfeld giving all the details of the tragic conditions of his life in the days of the Hitlerites. It also described the motives for removing the first mine and how he had done it at the Mishkashibishi station. In the same letter was a drawing of what had to be done so that our mines could never be dismantled. There was also a final note written in pencil which said: "The murderers will no longer succeed in forcing me to remove our own mines."

We examined Abraham Hirschfeld's diagram and found that the details were accurate exactly to the point.

PART TWO:

INITIATIVES

THE PARTISAN OATH

"I, a citizen of the Soviet Union, hereby join the ranks of the Red partisans*, the avengers of the people, in order to vindicate the blood of parents, brothers, sisters, and children who have been brutally tortured by the Nazi fascists and to fight for my homeland and native country against Hitler, the bloodhound, and his henchmen, the blood thirsty invaders, and hereby take it upon myself:

1. To be a courageous fighter, disciplined, and always ready;

2. To guard carefully the military secrets, the secrets of the state, and army property;

3. To carry out, to the letter, without hesitation, the orders of my commanders and all those who stand at the forefront of leadership;

4. Not to spare any effort, not even my life, but to devote myself to the last drop of blood to the struggle for my country;

5. And, if I happen to violate this oath, may the hand of my comrades fall upon me."

---

* According to another version, those Jewish partisans who were not Soviet citizens could begin the oath in the following manner: "I, a free son to my people, and one who has seen enough suffering, volunteer, and hereby join the ranks of the Red (Soviet) partisans. (ed.)

THE PARTISAN OATH

(A Second Version)

"I, a citizen of the Soviet Union*, a true son of the heroic Russian people, swear that I will not lay down my weapons until the Fascist serpent in our land has been destroyed.

I commit myself without reservation to carry out the orders of my commanders and superiors and to observe strict military discipline. I swear to work a terrible, merciless, and unrelenting revenge upon the enemy for the burning of our cities and villagers, for the murder of our children, and for the torture and atrocities committed against out people.

BLOOD FOR BLOOD!   DEATH FOR DEATH!

I swear to assist the Red Army by all possible means to destroy the Hitlerite dogs without regard for myself or my life.

I swear that I will die in frightful battle before I will surrender myself, my family, and the entire Russian people to the Fascist dogs.

And, if out of fear, weakness, or personal depravity, I should fail to uphold this oath and should betray the interests of my people, may I die a dishonorable death at the hands of my own comrades!

---

* For partisans who were Ukrainian or Beylorussian, the appropriate name of the Soviet state was substituted. The oath was given in the Russian or Ukrainian language depending on the nationality of the partisan. Note the special emphasis in both oaths on loyalty and discipline and its extremely propagandistic and patriotic tone. (ed.)

The following are personal accounts of partisan
initiatives:

FRIENDSHIP

D. Stonov

After an appeal made by the Soviet government on
July 3, 1941 to the Russian people, we decided to
organize a vast partisan movement behind the German
lines. Who was the man behind the idea that "those who
took part in the 1917 civil war in the past should
themselves join the partisan camp at once"?* The idea
occurred at one and the same time to friends Salai,
Negriyev, Kamyensky, and Korochenko, as it usually
happens among old friends, after each one of them had
reached the inevitable conclusion that there was no
other way out.

"Let's do it together, after we have decided on it
with one heart," said Korochenko. But suddenly he fell
ill, and it was necessary to take him to the hospital.
Later on, when his friends visited him, he reminded
them: "If together, then of course together. Tomorrow
I'll be okay. You've got to wait till I get well."

It was thus necessary to postpone the beginning of
the activities. Until Korochenko got well, his friends
called at the headquarters of the partisan movement,
found out all about the work to be done, and, when he
finally recovered, they decided upon the day, more
accurately the night, of the take-off.

The would-be partisans, along with their families,
gathered at the flat of Alexander Kamyensky. In the
evening a car arrived at the gathering place and took
them to the airfield. At night, the plane flew across
the front line and dropped the men over the woods of
Yelyensk, in the region of Chernigov, north of Kiev.

---

* Soon after "Operation Barbarossa", the German
  attack on Russia, on May 15, 1941, Stalin appealed
  to the Soviet people to organize guerilla warfare.
  Many partisan leaders had also been active in the
  post-1917 October Revolution civil wars in Russia.
  (ed.)

In the beginning, the new arrivals from Moscow joined the partisan unit of Nikolai Nikitich Popodrenko. In this unit the 1917 civil war veterans acquainted themselves with the new conditions of partisan warfare. The new arrivals had rich organizational experience and, as Popodrenko's unit was expanding fast, every one of them was put at the head of an independent company.

Alexander Kamyensky was made commander of a partisan company named after Stalin. Between the summers of 1943 and 1944, his company accounted for two thousand and thirty-five German soldiers and officers, blew up and burned about thirty tanks and forty-nine vehicles, besides derailing fourteen engines and one hundred and twenty railway carriages.

* * * * *

Michael Zuckerman, partly clad, escaped right from under the muzzle of a German rifle straight into the woods. He knew that here, in this forest, he would find Soviet people, partisans, avengers of the people. Occasionally sinking in heaps of snow, Zuckerman roamed the forest. His strength began to ebb, but his will to live kept driving him on. When he came upon a small mound on the ground, he imagined that he could find potatoes in it to fill his stomach, but not too much, for one potato too many would bring about severe pains and vomiting. This feeling alone kept him alive and going. Then one day at dawn he saw a man with a thick beard who was wearing a short fur coat and carrying a rifle in his hand. The man called out to him: "Halt! Who are you?" but before he could answer his strength ebbed, and he fell to the ground.

The man, Alexander Masko of Karikovki, the region of Chernigov, forty-five years of age, was a partisan from the "Stalin" company. He had just finished his look-out duty and been replaced by another partisan. He lifted Zuckerman onto his back and carried him to the forest, to an earth hut.

That was the beginning of friendship between Alexander Masko and Michael Zuckerman. Some time before it had been Masko who had fled from the Germans, carrying around his neck a piece of rope which had snapped.* Just like Zuckerman, Masko had seen death in the face. Perhaps because of that, the friendship between the two was so strong, so loyal. Under the difficult conditions of partisan life, Masko found time to take care of his friend. The doctor had done what he could, but the patient was in constant need of care plus a discerning eye and soothing hands. The throats of the hardy partisans constricted on seeing how Masko gathered red berries from the trees to feed his weakened friend; how he would walk, during the long marches, close to the sled that carried the sick man, covering him with his own fur coat, fluffing up the pillow under his head, carrying him to the campfire to bring warmth to him, and protecting his back from the cold.

At time a man may feel drawn to another not only because of the great responsibility involved in a cause, but because of the similarity of their trade. The friends lived in one earth hut. Once Zuckerman woke up upon hearing some knocking around the hut. Raising his head he saw Masko, his mouth full of nails, doing some some cobbling and, with the skill of a craftsman, taking out one nail after another and hammering it into the heel.

"Wait a minute," said Zuckerman with obvious excitement. "Who are you, really?"

Masko, thinking his friend to be dreaming out loud, replied, "Partisan Alexander Masko, of the Stalin company."

"And before that, who were you?"

"Before that I was a cobbler working in a village."

"And I am a tailor," said Zuckerman.

When working, Masko wore glasses. Now, greatly surprised, he shook his head, and his glasses fell over his nose. He strained his neck toward the sick man and looked straight at him for a long time.

"Swear to it!"

---

* An escape from hanging most likely, but this is unclear. (ed.)

"God is my witness."

Masko went over to his friend, shook him up, and burst out laughing.

"Here, I'm looking at you now and cannot think for one moment that you belong to our trade. Now the secret is out. Wy have you kept silent all this time? Now we can make something so all the other partisan companies will be filled with envy. Do you know how many cases of chrome uppers and sole leather we have taken out of German hands? They have been lying around here useless for so long ... "

When Zuckerman recovered completely the two friends began to work in their spare time, between battles and between the moving around from one place to another. Actually they did wonders, and accounts of their handiwork reached all the companies stationed in the Ukraine. When, for instance, partisans from other units met a fighter belonging to the company of Alexander Kamyensky, they did not ask him to what company he belonged, since his chrome leather boots simply gave him away.

One thing lay heavy on Zuckerman's soul. In battle he had to be separated from his friend. Zuckerman was a sharpshooter and Masko dealt with machine guns. His aide was a young fighter from the River Don region. Masko too was chagrined at having to operate separately. So the two talked it over and decided to bring the matter up to their commander, Alexander Kamyensky.

Upon receiving the fighters, Kamyensky sat down in a relaxed manner, took off his cap, pushed his hair back with his fingers, and asked them to take their seats. Masko and Zuckerman understood that they were about to start a cordial talk. Kamyensky called them the "Kozeshtrast" (leather producers association) and asked them about their businesses. "Are there shoes for all the men of the company?" he asked, adding some witticisms about cobblers in general, favorable remarks, until Masko found out that the commander himself considered cobblers the best people in the world. "It seems that he belongs to our trade ... "

"I don't understand your complaint and request," the commander said to Masko.

"I have no complaints at all," answered Masko, "but I'd like to explain to you that between me and Michael there is such strong friendship that to fight separately is so boring ..."

"There is a strong friendship between us," reiterated Zuckerman.

Alexander Kamyensky sank into deep thought. Friendship! Friendship was a frequent caller at his international company: A Cossak would befriend a Ukrainian, a Tartar, a Georgian, a Russian, a Beylorussian, a fighter from Tadzhikstan. These oft-recurring friendships did not appear only yesterday. Their roots went back to the historical days of the war for victory and the strengthening of Soviet rule. In the fire of the great war for the fatherland,* friendship was forged so strongly that it united men of different nationalities with close patriotic feelings. Through invisible cords this friendship was to continue deep into the partisan forests between one fighting company and another, so that when the Jew Kamyensky was in a tight spot, other commanders hurried to his aid, Salai the Ukrainian and Negriyev the Russian.**

"Too strong a friendship," Kamyensky whispered to himself, then said aloud: "Well, let it be as you wish!"

On the following day the two friends started to fight side by side, using the same machine gun. Soon word went round the company about the two cobblers, not only as good craftsmen but also as excellent sharp-shooters. Their friendship was to weather many a test. Then finally came the ultimate test, the test of blood.

After prolonged fighting the company had to encamp in the small forest of Kossyevsk where it was impossible to maneuver. The partisans were nearly exhausted from the demands of their struggle, and even the horses

---

* World War II. (ed.)

** Though acts of cooperation and friendship were numerous, the author does not mention the anti-Semitism and the tensions among ethnic groups that did exist. (ed.)

could not stand the hardships of having to move frequently from one place to another. The early days of
May were cold and chilling. The wounded groaned and
sighed. But it was impossible to rest to get some
warmth around the campfire, or even to eat. Night
came, and the scouts brought in the news that the
Germans were concentrating considerable forces,
bringing field guns, tanks, and armored vehicles. They
were in control of all the roads leading to the forest.
They had even called in the Luftwaffe.

The Kossyevsk Forest had an ill-fated reputation:
In it had been annihilated a local partisan company,
commanded by the secretary of the northern committee of
Dobryansk. It was necessary to get away from the trap.
Alexander Kamyensky urged the men toward further
effort. The company scouts found a path whereby it was
possible to bypass all the German roadblocks. To this
end the partisans began, under cover of darkness, to
leave the forest of Kossyevsk. The men were dreaming
of the forest of Topiechensk. toward which they
directed their steps, as a quiet home with a cozy
hearth; a place smelling of good cabbage soup, with
windows overlooking a quiet street. But how to reach
this forest where they could have some rest and also
continue striking at the Germans?

The path went by the village of Vladimirovka,
which held a German garrison and police forces. An
encounter with them meant a delay for the entire company in its forced march, a waste of precious time,
with the possibility that the Germans would use reinforcements of both men and material, artillery and
tanks. It was therefore necessary to divert the attention of the German garrison and police force from the
partisans' march until the fighters were far enough
from the village.

Before dawn, the two friends, Michael Zuckerman
and Alexander Masko, took upon themselves this difficult and dangerous task. Marshes surrounded the
village on three sides, and it turned out that to wade
through them was the best way to reach the place without being detected by the enemy. The men took their
machine gun and crossed the marshes, wading in the icy
water up to their hips. They walked into Vladimirovka,
reached the church belfry, and silently dispatched the
German sentry. They climbed into the tower and opened
fire with the machine gun. Pandemonium struck the
village: The partisans had taken hold of the church!

Firing their rifles and machine guns, the Germans hurried to the church. The soldiers and policemen surrounded the daring partisans. But high above, the partisan machine gun went into action, sowing death among the Germans. The faultless warriors naturally picked out the most coveted targets, and after half an hour's battle the ground around the church was littered with German bodies.

The belfry shook under the pounding of firing and explosions, and it was coming closer and closer. The bullets tore into the stone wall, and yellow brick dust spread into the air. But even through this cloud of yellow dust, one could see through binoculars how far away, in the vicinity of Vladimirovka, the company to which these two men belonged was fast slipping away from the neighborhood of the inferno which was raging in that previously quiet village. It was an encouraging spectacle which gave the warriors greater strength to carry on.

Another hour of fighting between greatly unequal forces had passed, and the Germans finally succeeded in setting fire to the church belfry. The fire spread fast, and the smoke made it hard for the partisans to breathe. Now it was possible to think of beating a retreat, since the company had fulfilled its task, having safely bypassed the village of Vladimirovka.

"Should we blast our way through?" asked Micheal Zuckerman.

The bursts of machine gun fire and the general noise were frightening. At first Zuckerman was not surprised to find his friend leaning toward him for the reply. But Masko kept leaning farther and farther. Suddenly Zuckerman saw blood coming out of his friend's mouth.

"Alexander," shouted Michael.

The Germans increased their pressure, and Zuckerman could not bandage his friend's wounds quickly. Masko passed out. In the meantime firing had ceased for a short while. Then Masko opened his eyes and turned his face toward his friend.

"I've been hit," he murmured with difficulty.

"What did you say?"

"I've been hit. Listen, Michael, run for your life. Try to shoot your way out, perhaps you can save your life. And please tell comrade Kamyensky ... please go, go, so long as you are alive ... "

The two friends usually spoke in low voices, called each other by their first names, smiling at each other. Masko's words now enraged Zuckerman. He shook his hands vehemently and said out loud:

"What is this, Masko, are you out of your mind? Shut up!"

Zuckerman carried his friend on his shoulder and started a fast descent from the belfry. It was quiet all around. Five Germans, the last remnants of the entire garrison, thought the partisans had reached a stage of exhaustion, and now, they, the Germans, crawled to the foot of the belfry. That was what Zuckerman had expected. He hurled two grenades at them, one after the other. He also had his rifle ready, but there was no need for it. The Germans were dead. In a nearby forest, a cart was waiting for the two friends. It brought them, after a trip of several hours, to the forest of Topichensk.

From now on Zuckerman was number one at the machine gun, and the man from the River Don region number two. Obviously, things began taking their normal course again, only the other way around. Now it was Zuckerman who took care of his wounded friend, Masko; now it was he who went along with the cart that carried the wounded man. Once again the two friends were dreaming of the day when they would not have to separate from each other again--not in battle, not at work, and not while resting.

* * * * *

This is the story of two rank and file partisans, but as the saying goes, one drop is enough to determine the quality of water in a well or a river. Deep friendship between people of different nationalities prevailed in the company. Life and struggle, hard as they were behind enemy lines, were permeated with a feeling of brotherliness which cemented together the entire company and urged its fighters on to battle. This feeling spread from the bottom upwards, and here, at the top, it was complemented by the friendly attitude of the company commander, Alexander Kamyensky, and his chief of staff, Konstantine Kossyenko.

The chief of staff began his military career in Kamyensky's company as an ordinary fighter. He was young, enthusiastic, and faultless. Alexander Kamyensky's sharp eye detected him in the early days when he joined the company and saw in him an extraordinary fighter. The company commander began to give him singularly responsible tasks, sending him to highly dangerous places, realizing fully that only fire could forge this unique young man. At that time we were engaged in continual fighting, one battle following hard upon the other. The company moved from the region of Chernigov to the regions of Bryansk, Kiev, and onward to the Poltava region. At the same time friendship also strengthened between Alexander Kamyensky and Konstantine Kossyenko.

Gradually the company commander began to call the young partisan "my son" and the latter called him "father." Friendship between these two men deepened from day to day. Official discussions ended with intimate and prolonged talks. Kamyensky not only imparted some of his experience to the man, but he also consulted him.

In the story of Kamyensky and Kossyenko we see them in our mind's eye in their spectacular exploits. We visualize Kamyensky, tall of stature, with his broad face, white hair, and narrowing eyes, sitting on the barrel of a field gun. Beside him a young man, with fresh and rosy cheeks. With a lofty military intonation, Konstantine Kossyenko is reporting to his company commander about the mission that has been carried out. His speech is interposed with pauses, hesitations; for he would rather fight from dawn to dusk and from night to dawn, than imagine, even for one single moment, that Kamyensky would not approve of his deeds. Kamyensky is satisfied; he pats his friend on the shoulder and says:

"Here, Konstantine Konstantinovich! It has been some time since I wanted to appoint you my chief of staff."

Chief of staff! This is really the "brain" of the unit. It should also be remembered that we are not speaking here of a regular army, but of a partisan company, in which the commander himself takes part in the fighting. Quite often Kossyenko had to leave his work at the staff office and join the fighters in the battle field. This is just what happened in the forest of Novobasansk in the Poltava region. The enemy had put around this forest a ring of steel and had every corner covered with tank-and-armored-vehicle fire, in addition to the Luftwaffe. The battle between these unequal forces continued for three hours, in the course of which the enemy closed and narrowed the encirclement. In the face of such a situation it was necessary to spread the forces out by concentrating them in different corners in order to break through the iron ring. Alexander Kamyensky gave the order to divide the company into two parts, each of which was to act independently of the other.

"I will take command of one company, and you of the other," said Kamyensky to his chief of staff. "Later on we shall meet and unite once again in the forest of Kobeshchansk. Good-bye!"

That was an unforgettable night because of the fierce battles that were fought. It was raining and darkness was complete. The flames bathed the woods in their eerie light. Huge trees fell with ear-shattering noise. Here and there the earth heaved and dirt flew up into the sky. In this flaming inferno the brave partisans blasted their way out. The carts and provisions were left behind. All the men, the women, and even the sick and the wounded who were in this convoy took up arms and prepared themselves for the decisive fight.

A close check of the enemy ring of encirclement revealed to Kamyensk's maneuvering company a suitable spot where it could deliver a resounding blow to the Germans. Both sides met in hand-to-hand combat a few times. A mine-thrower jammed, and its operator was killed. Under a hail of German bullets, Kamyensky repaired the mine-throuwer and began pouring fire into the fascists. We won the battle and broke the ring of encirclement. It was dark all around us, and, thus concealed, we could move on to the forest of Kobeshchansk. Suddenly Alexander came upon a wounded partisan from the company of Konstantine Kossyenko. The wounded man had miraculously escaped and his life depended on a hair. With great difficulty he told Alexander that the chief of staff had not succeeded in breaking through and that his company was under triple encirclement. Hearing this, Kamyensky, who had just come out of a ferocious battle, went back into the turmoil to save his friend Kossyenko. The battle was on once again. The forest blazed with the light of day. The "father" now himself wounded, was fighting to save his "son" and the "son", sensing this, summoned the remnants of his forces for the last battle of that night. The two parts of the company united again, the partisans were now hammering at one target from two directions ... In order to get an idea of that cruel battle, it should be borne in mind that the enemy threw into it a large force ot tanks, mine-throwers, and machine guns. But the brotherhood of the Soviet people was stronger than death. The fascists were smothered by the flames of their own tanks, and all of their overwhelming equipment was to no avail.

The night neared its end. The heavy raining did not cease. The reunited company wended its way to the forest of Kobeshchansk. In a cart drawn by horses newly captured from the Germans sat the two friends, Alexander Kamyensky and Konstantine Kossyenko. The young chief of staff supported the wounded commander. Around them were many friends, all members of one family: multinational, strong, and united. They marched along in the night, full of confidence in the battles to come, in victory which, like dawn, would overcome darkness; they marched along through the forests and the plains which had been drenched with so much blood, the blood of their brothers.

WITHOUT FIRE...

Shirka Gaman

In one small town the Germans did not leave any Jews alive, with the exception of a few craftsmen and invalids. They took out Ozer the blind man, put stones and wood stocks all around him, and shouted the command: "Jude, rechts! Jude, links!"* Ozer tripped anf fell down, rose to his feet, fell down again, saying, "Shema Yisrael!"**

The Germans went into the house of Zemach the tinsmith and dragged his wife Rachel from her bed, where she had been lying for years paralyzed in both feet. Two of them caught her under the armpits and the others shouted:

"Forward! You wife of a swine!"

One day Zemach found her lying injured on the floor. When he lifted her up and put her into her bed, she told him quietly: "Zemach, please have pity on me, give me the poison." Zemach had somehow gotten some poison. For about two months he had been keeping the powder, wrapped up in a piece of cloth, for her, but every time he fed Rachel with the spoon, he forgot to put the poison into the dish ... he stood at the entrance to his smithy, his hand in his pocket, his fingers holding the powder. He wanted to take out his smoking tobacco, but lately his hand had somehow been slipping to the poison powder ...

Today would be the end. He would redeem her, his own Rachel, "and they would no longer torture her," he dedided.

Suddenly he heard the sound of wheels outside. A drunken German had pushed a motorcycle into the smithy. Zemach at once saw that the sidecar was beyond repair.

---

* "Jews, right! Jews, left!" (ed.)

** Hebrew for "Hear, O Israel", a Jewish prayer, one sometimes reserved for imminent death. (ed.)

"What can I do for you, Sir?"

"The sidecar should be repaired by this evening."

"Please, sir," said Zemach, and went to the coal sack.

"No, no, you shouldn't use any fire. A Jewish tinsmith should know how to bend iron without using fire," the German said, sitting on a coal sack. He took out his pistol and asked: "Did you understand?"

"I understand quite well," said Zemach.

"Shut up, you cur," the Nazi retorted.

Zemach pretended that he did not hear; he looked around the smithy as if he were looking for something, went over to the wall, took down a wide piece of sheet iron, examined it with his hands, and bent down as if he were trying to pick up something.

"Sit up, Jude," the German shouted. "How long are you going to keep up this loitering!" He bent to take the piece of sheet iron from Zemach's hands.

Zemach raised his hands quickly and, letting out his breath as if he were bringing down the heavy hammer on the anvil of the smithy, threw the sheet iron around the soldier's head, and pulled it tightly with all his strength, as if he was winding a rope around his neck.

The German soldier groaned heavily. Zemach kept twisting the iron he held in his hands, pushing the German's head to the floor, then dragged him to the wall, threw a coal sack over him, and left the smithy, without closing the door behind him.

"Good morning, Zemach," greeted Hirsch the builder, who was passing by there by chance.

"Where have you come from, Hirsch?"

"From the forest of Yagila."

"How do the partisan boys feel there?"

"For the time being, very well. They are safe and sound."

"Come inside, please, I would like to show you something," said Zemach. He rolled back the coal sack from the dead German.

"Do you see, Hirsch?"

"I see. God bless the hands that did it! You will have to run away into the forest at once, to the partisans, to your 'sons'. Do you hear me?"

"Yes, I hear. Today there will be an end to all this. Today ... One moment, please ... " Hirsch looked at him in amazement. "Come on, Hirsch." He was ready to return to see his wife when they saw dark smoke rising in a thick column, and in the air hung the smell of tar.

"They have once again put the town on fire," said Hirsch. "It seems that your house also is on fire, Zemach!"

Upon reaching the place of the conflagration, they found, that of his house and his paralyzed wife Rachel, only a heap of cinders remained. For one moment they stood there in silence. Then Zemach turned in the direction of the forest, and went to greet his "sons", the partisans.

PARTISAN FRIENDSHIP

A.P. Feodorov
Hero of the Soviet Union, Major-General,
Former Commander of a Partisan Brigade

My brigade included fighters from various walks of life, different ages, men and women. Among them were Russians, Ukrainians, Uzbeks, Jews, Tartars, and Kirghizes. Within the partisan companies, with all the variegated nationalities, glowed all too brilliantly the brotherhood of nations, tempered by battles fought side by side, when our fatherland stood facing the danger of annihilation, when all had become brothers in the face of calamity ..

Shmuel Gottesban

He had been a student at the Leningrad Institute of Physical Culture. During the war with the Finns he volunteered to serve in the Tank Corps of the Red Army. In August, 1941, the Germans surrounded Gottesban's tank. Seriously wounded, he was taken prisoner. At the POW camp, which contained some twenty thousand prisoners, the Germans tortured our men with hunger and thirst. They even killed some of them. Gottesban managed to escape. He was later to escape from Kiev, where he had been living for some time, when the Germans led pogroms against the Jews. He was arrested and imprisoned in a cargo-train full of people. The carriage window was tightly closed and, inside, it was stifling. Under cover of darkness, when the train started to move, Gottesban succeeded in breaking open the window, and, together with some daring companions, jumped off the moving train. A woman who was passing by showed them the way to the partisans. And thus, Gottesban reached our group.

A battle was going on at the outskirts of the town of Kovel. Among the fighters in the partisan company was Shmuel Mordechai Gottesban. In this battle he accounted for twelve dead German soldiers and officers. In another battle around the tracks of the Kovel-Sarni railway, when a group of Germans tied to outflank us and attack us from the rear, the first to detect them was Gottesban, who shot six of them with his automatic rifle. Gottesban was not only a sharpshooter, but also an excellent saboteur. He took part in blowing up six

German transports, and, together with other partisans, destroyed six train engines and more than seventy train carriages loaded with military equipment.

In the Volyn area he worked intensively on organizing underground fighters. Gottesban had great authority among the men of his company as well as the entire battalion. For his exploits in battle, he was awarded the "Red Flag" medal.

Alexander Margalit

In the same company where Gottesban served, there was a platoon commander by the name of Alexander Mordechai Margalit. The partisans liked him very much and had a great deal of respect for him. He deserved it. He took active part in all the battles of the company. He himself accounted for the death of twelve German soldiers and officers. One of his remarkable exploits took place in the attack of the town of Bragin in 1943. Margalit's company had outflanked and attacked the German company in the rear, when the latter was engaged in providing aid for the garrison in the town. In this battle the Germans lost about thirty men and ran away. Among the partisans' booty were a field gun, two mortars, and two machine guns.

In the battle near Kovel, Margalit was at the head of his company, as usual. His fighters killed more than seventy Germans and took prisoner eighteen soldiers and officers. But Margalit himself fell in this battle. We all cherish his memory as a daring commander who instilled in his men love, hope, and sacrifice for their country.

Dossia Baskina

Mention must be made of one of our medical nurses --Dossia Baskina. There was virtually no battle in which she did not take part. She would bandage the wounded under a hail of enemy bullets and evacuate them from the field of battle. In this manner she saved the lives of forty-nine wounded fighters and officers. When on the move or while the force was camping, she would go around caring for those in need of medical treatment or giving a word of encouragement to someone who needed it.

Dossia Baskina was not only a medical nurse, but also a dauntless and expert saboteur. She took part in blowing up sixteen enemy convoys.

Some time before the war started, Baskina finished a course for midwives. She had occasion to use her knowledge while working with us. In the villages we visited, she came to the help of pregnant women about to give birth, at any time or hour, by day or night. She also had the opportunity to treat babies in enemy-occupied territory. Leaning her rifle against a wall and keeping an alert ear to any rustling sound, she worked fast, quietly, in a well-organized manner, as if she were in a hospital ward during peacetime. For her courage and daring exploits whe was awarded two medals.

Boris Baskin

A scout's work constantly involves self-reliance and courage. Death stalks him wherever he steps. The brother of Dossia, the medical nurse, was one of our best scouts. At the outskirts of Kovel he was ambushed by the enemy. In the exchange of fire that ensued, Baskin single-handedly accounted for four dead Germans. He was wounded, but he kept on firing until his partisan friends came to his aid.

Joshua Hirsch Baskin

Joshua Hirsch Baskin, who had the same surname as Boris, also proved to be a daring fighter. He would receive radio messages and set them in type for partisan announcements. His radio messages came from Russia.* He set them in print and distributed them among the partisans. The news items he provided were more vital to them than bread.

Yefim Litvinovsky

He fought the Germans with all his might. Without any hint of joking, he called himself "Denizen of the Next World." Actually Litvinovsky arrived at our camp as a survivor from the claws of death. When war broke

---

* In the original Russian, the term used was the "Great Land" or the "Big Land". (ed.)

out he was twenty years old, lived in Koibishev, was a student, and studied singing. He entered the Red Army as a volunteer. In one of the battles he was wounded and taken prisoner. The Germans sent him from one camp to another until he was eventually transported to Sobibor. Today everyone knows how the Germans killed people in such concentration camps as Auschwitz, Maidanek, or Sobibor. When Litvinovsky related to us, as early as 1943, the stunning atrocities perpetrated by the Germans, when he told us of the fires arising from human bodies, of the "bath houses" where they killed the inmates, of the mass murder of thousands of children--a shiver ran down our spines.

Litvinovsky "managed" to be among those in charge of burning the bodies of those killed by the Germans. This "privilege" made it possible for Litvinovsky and his friends to take active part in the revolt.* The day that the German guards went out for target practice, the inmates of Sobibor raised the banner of revolt. They broke into the armory and killed the Germans who had been left in the camp; but they could not break through the fences of the camp at the first attempt, as the gates were guarded by Germans with machine guns. Hatchets in hand, the rioters hacked out an opening in the barbed wire fences. Several were blown up by the German mines, but they had opened a safe path for the surviving escapees. The latter kept on firing, then ran for the woods. After hard and prolonged wandering, Litvinovsky arrived at our battalion together with his friend Tsadok Chaim Levin. Both had enough reasons to revenge themselves on the Germans.

And if patrol duty was a difficult and dangerous work, that of the runners, under the circumstances, was no less difficult and no less dangerous. We had runners both in the companies and in the villages directly under the noses of the enemy. They had to be continuously careful and on their guard. They did their duty at the risk of their lives.

---

*   On October 14, 1943, over 400 inmates of the Sobibor concentration camp led a revolt, killing ten SS men and thirty eight Ukrainian guards; nearly half of them survived, broke into six groups, and joined the Soviet partisans shortly afterwards. (ed.)

We had a group of runners, young boys. At their head was a boy of fourteen, Aaron, son of a partisan woman whom we called "Dossia the Linen Seamstress," to distinguish her from Dossia Baskina. Aaron was a daring, well-disciplined runner. At the head of his boys, he took upon himself the most responsible missions. No danger stood in the way of those boys; as young patriots they carried out each mission on time and with great devotion.

Among the Jewish commanders we may also mention the company chief of staff, Levin, who had remarkable resourcefulness and a knack for drawing up splendid plans for the fight against the German armies.

A filmmaker called Michael Moshe Glieder took part in a number of outstanding exploits of our brigade. His men were included in the picture "The Popular Avengers," for which he received the Stalin Award.* Twelve times he went out on sabotage missions. He took part in blowing up ten enemy convoys. Sometimes he would go into battle holding in one hand a movie camera and, in the other, a rifle. Another man who did a good job in our brigade was the photographer-reporter Yaakov Davidson. There were not many men in the brigade who did not take part in the battles themselves, but everyone contributed his own share, according to his occupation. Without these people our struggle would certainly have been a much more difficult task.

I have already mentioned the name of "Dossia, the Linen Seamstress," who sewed for our partisans. Nothing wears out clothes faster than the continual treks through the woods. Particular importance was thus attached to the work of the tailors. Tirelessly, tailor Shatzglovsky went on sewing clothes. Under our peculiar conditions he knew how to sew convenient, durable, and warm clothing.

The hatmaker Sorin had his hands full of work. He was an outstanding artisan, and knew how to let comfort

---

*   Another account of Glieder is given later in this book. The film mentioned is probably in the Lenin Library of Moscow. The editor is in the process of having this documentary released to the West. (ed.)

blend with warmth in the partisans' headgear, sometimes even pampering the idiosyncracies of individual fighters.

Our partisans also owe a debt of gratitude to artisan Godis, a specialist in leather work. Wearing one of his leather coats drove away one's fear of strong winds or snowstorms and made one think nothing of lying in ambush hour after hour under heaps of snow.

To my regret I do not remember the name of the partisan who made sausage for us. I only recall that they called him Isaac. He was excellent at making sausage. Not at every grocery store could one find sausages of such quality as those prepared by this man Isaac.

Mention should also be made of our pharmacist, Ziama Ahron Nesilevich. He was about sixty years old. His pharmacy he carried on one cart. Nesilevich managed it in a remarkable manner. Whenever we camped he would hand out medicine to the sick. Naturally enough our scouts would replenish his stock in the course of their patrol work.

The majority of our fighters were young men. Sometimes they would remember the old days, of peace, when they were free to enjoy themselves, to travel, to listen to music, to dance, to throw an improvised party. But these memories were not enough for them. In the calm hours when it was possible to relax and unwind, we also knew how to make merry. To tell the truth we had some very fine musicians. Violinists Gourari and Schwartz had an uncanny sense of when they were needed. From memory they would play our favorite tunes, songs and dances. They also played works by Tchaikovsky, Gelinka, Chopin, and Strauss.

Many Jews came to us along with their families. The men fought, but the elderly, the women, and the children worked in our rear lines. I remember well some of these families--Yakobovich, Karsik, Davidovich, Sirovsky, and others.

As partisans our duty was not only to fight the German invaders and their collaborators, but to do our best to help the local citizens by word and deed and, particularly, to save people, to free them from the hands of the fascist killers.

One day in the forest we came upon a group of people wearing tattered rags--old men, women, and hungry children. It was winter, and they were in danger of dying out there in the woods. We discussed the matter and decided to take them along with us. That was the genesis of our first civilian camp. As time went on two camps of this kind were set up. We took the sick and the weak to safe places. When they regained their strength, many of them joined our brigade as partisan fighters.

The inhabitants of the civilian camps did all they could to give us the help we needed. Each camp was attached to one of our battalions. When we were on the move, the people of the camp went along with our convoy under special guards. In sum, over five thousand Jews passed through our camps. They stayed with us for about ten months, and almost all of them were eventually taken to "The Great Land," namely--the Soviet Union.

When we freed populated areas our brigade would first release the prisoners. Thus on freeing Koriokovky (District of Chernigov) we released twenty-five Jews; in Sofeivka (District of Novozivkov) eighteen; in Leobishov, eight; and several Jewish people in other places.

* * * * *

I have a strong desire to mention one more friend. He did not belong to the partisans, nor did he belong to the civilian population, but meeting him was a great joy to all of us; in January, 1944, our men met for the first time scouts from the Red Army who had penetrated deep behind enemy lines. The commander of this group of Red soldiers was Leonid Leontiyevich Levitas, a native of the Ural Mountains. He was a fine man.

THE AVENGERS OF THE MINSK GHETTO

A. Chorny

The winter of 1941 was hard and forbidding. Already on the tenth of October the first snow started falling. Great and bitter suffering fell to the lot of those who happened to be in the region swept by the German attack ... had lost contact with the Soviet army.

It was also difficult for Israel Lapidot, in the region of Viasma, which had been encircled by the enemy. For several weeks he was to roam through the woods, seeking escape from the Germans. He did not succeed in finding the partisan nest and thus had to direct his steps towards Minsk, the town where he had grown up and worked and had concerned himself with public affairs. It was in this town that he joined the Red Army in the early days of the war.

Wearing a peasant winter coat and a yellowish beard, Israel Lapidot arrived at German-occupied Minsk. Barbed wire encircled like a belt the narrow and ancient streets of this old town. Death was beginning to be felt from behind the fence of the ghetto, where seventy thousand Jews were leading a life of desperation. Nonetheless Lapidot began to look for an opening into the ghetto. In those days Minsk came to a standstill as a town at five in the afternoon. Only intermittent firing and the monotonous marching of the German guards disturbed the eerie silence.

For quite a long time Lapidot kept looking for a way to get into the ghetto. Near the felt factory on Kolkhozniya Street he saw an empty lot and the pits that indicated the sites of former buildings which the Germans had burned down. He crawled a few scores of meters, crossed the ghetto boundaries, and was in.

Was there at least a single relative alive? How many citizens of the lively and boisterous Minsk region had Lapidot known? He reached the house of his relatives. They had survived. From them he heard the blood curdling account of the Germans' first pogrom against the Jews on November 7, 1941. His parents and son were among those killed by the Germans on that day. He hurried to look for his wife and found her, along with his surviving firstborn son.

Filled with a deep desire to avenge himself on the Germans, Lapidot decided to gather a partisan company, take it out of the ghetto, and add it to the forces engaged in the people's war against the fascists.

Lapidot also found his old friends: Davidson, Lussik, Gantman, Kravchinsky, and together they went about organizing the partisan company. It was diffificult to operate in the ghetto. But Lapidot found out that the spirit of the ghetto people had not weakened and that their will to act had not died out. He looked deep through each and every one of them, trying to visualize how the man would act in the forest, under the singularly severe conditions of partisan life.

Many of Lapidot's friends, workers in Minsk, were now in the army. Most of the ghetto people had never held a gun before; but every one of them had had his own tragedy, and the all-consuming fire of hatred for the Germans kindled in their hearts. Everyone was dreaming of taking up arms. But Lapidot picked only those who were fired by the desire for revenge. He sought people known for their self-restraint and self-control. In his mind's eye he saw the interminable tests to which the partisans would be put.

Cautiously and with great care he enlisted men into the company. The ghetto abounded with spies and German agents, and it was necessary to make all the preparations in complete secrecy. Lapidot asked type-setters Oppenheim and Rappaport to get him the necessary equipment for a printing press. They renewed their contacts with old friends living outside the ghetto, and they helped them get the type they required. To smuggle all the equipment out of the ghetto could be done only by hiding the parts in one's pockets or concealing them under one's clothes. That was a tough and dangerous job, but by the end of winter the partisans had set up their own printing press, with a sizable stock of paper, ink and type.

The first bulletin put out by the national avengers was directed at the ghetto Jews. It called for resistance and planted in their hearts hope for the day when Minsk would once again be a liberated Soviet city. Those who read the bulletin felt the taste that a thirsty person has for water from which he is given only one sip.

* * * * *

Winter passed amid tense preparations. Smuggling arms into the ghetto became extremely difficult. It called for great effort to get the twelve grenades, three pistols, three rifles, and about five hundred cartridges they now had. They guarded them like the pupil of their eye.

The weather was still cold. The trees were still bare of leaves, but the winter was now over. With the help of the underground Bolshevik organization, Israel Lapidot was able to pick out forty-eight people for the partisan company. Then the decisive day arrived. On the morning of April 10, 1942, when the groups of workers leaving for their daily work outside the ghetto boundaries were lined up in neat rows, the forty-eight people met on Rakovsky Street at a predetermined spot. They could not be distinguished from the other inmates of the ghetto: the same yellow patches* on the chest and on the back, the same sacks with the work tools on their shoulders, but among the tools there were rifles, and in their pockets they had grenades.

With no hitches they made their way in the streets of Spalirni, Rispublikanskaya and Chorniya, turned up Novomoscovkaya Street and, from there, onto the road leading to Slotsk. They had hardly left the outskirts of the town when they tore off of each other's clothes the yellow patch that symbolized forced labor and slavery.

On the Slotsk road the group was divided into smaller groups of two or three persons walking ahead at some distance from each other. At the head of this small scale exodus walked Lapidot, his wife, and their firstborn son.

After they had covered some forty kilometers down the road, the would-be partisans gathered once again, only to find out that not all of them had made it to that spot and that the daring operation had taken its first toll.

Turning in the direction of the villages of Rodkovo and Kilodnia, the company tarried for some time in the forest. The peasants of these villages knew

---

* The yellow patch or star distinguished them as Jews. (ed.)

Lapidot well, and he realized right from the outset that the company would have a fighting chance only if it could establish close ties with the local population.

From a peasant woman, Marosya, in the village of Rodkovo, Lapidot learned all that he needed for the first leg of their march. This piece of information helped him to acquire the right orientation for the conditions prevailing in the woods. Marosya had her own intentions in relation with the ghetto people. Some weeks after the partisans had started their activities, she approached Lapidot with the request to admit her into his company. In the forest the partisans went about pitching tents for themselves, since it was too early to think about more permanent quarters. In the ghetto there still remained many people who wanted to go into the forests. Before long Lapidot sent over to them three partisan women, Patinet, Ducker, and Borzin. The peasant women dressed them in their traditional dress and gave them two carts loaded with potatoes: one for Borzin and the other for Patinet and Ducker. The women reached Minsk safely and once again slipped into the ghetto. Although they had never done any reconnaissance or intelligence work, they fulfilled their mission faultlessly. According to a list which had been prepared by Lapidot, work started on organizing a new group, which in turn succeeded in evading the German claws. The women led the ghetto people over the familiar road that brought them to the forest adjoining the village of Rodkovo.

Meantime the company had become larger, and a name had to be found for it: a name which would be close to the heart of everyone. Someone suggested they call the company after the great Russian commander Kotuzov. The suggestion was accepted unanimously. A few days passed, and to Minsk went once again two women partisans of the "Kotuzov" Company, Patinet and Ducker. They were dressed as peasant women and carried false identity cards.

Near Shatzk the two women were stopped and taken to the Gestapo, where they were interrogated for several days. The two women did not disclose the name of a single partisan. The Gestapo started torturing them, but still the Germans could not extract anything from the brave women, and they killed them. Lapidot then sent Asa Binder to the ghetto to bring out another group. With commendable courage she followed the path which had earlier brought death to her two friends. On reaching Minsk she carried out the dangerous task she had been entrusted with. On many occasions women from the Kotuzov Company continued slipping into the ghetto on vital and dangerous missions.

Here is an example of the self-sacrifice revealed by woman-partisan Leah Borzin, who was formally declared a ground scout within a short time of her joining the company. On one occasion, when the partisans were about to mount an attack on the small town of Ozliani, Leah Borzin succeeded in slipping into the local German command. There she got all the necessary information the partisans needed. But she was arrested after she had succeeded in getting out of the building, and was taken to the Rodansk station where she was subjected to torture for a long time. Still, she did not reveal anything. With unspeakable cruelty they stabbed her in the eyes and then hanged her in the town square.

As a result of the viable relations which were established with the aid of reliable friends, the Kotuzov Company received new fighters every day: men and women who had succeeded in escaping from the ghetto or from the surrounding villages, which were groaning under the German yoke. When the company numbered about one hundred partisans, Lapidot began combat operations. The first attack was launched on the village of Hotliani. In this village there were twelve policemen who lived off the peasants like leeches. The partisans attacked the village under cover of darkness, cut off the telephone line, and killed the traitorous policemen. They took possession of a German store and distributed among the peasants all that was in it: sickles, scythes, shoes, grinders, and the like.

The operation succeeded without any casualties and kindled the enthusiasm of our fighters. The partisans then asked to be taken on further operations. They mounted a sudden attack on the village of Doshchenko as they had done on Hotliani before, setting fire to all the documents of the local management which listed the debts of the peasants. In the estate of Samuelova, formerly a kolkhoz,* they shot the German manager, dispatched the policemen, captured twenty-six horses,

---

* A collective settlement in Russia. (ed.)

-97-

some thirty cows, and ten tons of seeds. The sheep, the goats, and the bread they distributed among the peasants.

* * * * *

Thus relations were strengthened between the partisans and the peasants. Often they would come to Lapidot with the request to be accepted into the company, which was multinational right from the start, one of the numerous companies whose name was to become a household word all over Beylorussia.

The company led a life of brotherhood: on dark nights the fighters would go out on combat missions. They were through marshes and through snow, dressed in camouflage coveralls, looking alike. They would meet in huts, where the burly Siberian Danila Stolvov listened to the stories of an old cobbler from Minsk, Wolf Lussik; and the Ukranian woman Galina Kreiko watched with unconcealed excitement Lapidot's son, Misha, growing into a brave partisan and acting out theatrical characters. All of them were drawn close together by their abysmal hatred for the enemy.

With dogged persistence the partisans learned how to use arms. They had to master not only the Russian rifle but also the other arms captured from the enemy. The blacksmith from Minsk, Tokarsky, set up a workshop in the forest, where he repaired the arms taken by the partisans. It was necessary to get explosives, and the partisans learned how to take the dangerous but vital material out of the dud shells they found in the woods. The company laid ambushes, destroyed railway tracks, attacked command posts, as well as regional and district garrisons which had been set up by the enemy.

During the first fifteen months the Kotuzov company derailed twenty-one trains full of German troops, laid fourteen ambushes, and accounted for hundreds of dead German soldiers. The company inflicted heavy casualties on the Germans, destroyed their bases, and put the Ossipovichi-Minsk railway tracks out of commission.

The partisans weathered hard battles. Those who had come from the ghetto were honed to a fine point in these battles. Student Misha Lapidot was doing a fine job destroying enemy vehicles: he would jump on the top of a vehicle and shoot straight at the Germans inside it. The boy Abraham Zhitlzhey was outstanding in throwing hand grenades. Lazar Lessin, the 16-year old boy, derailed about ten trains. Pima Schneider had many explosions to his credit. They all struck at the fascists. These boys had come from the ghetto and had been school children only a short while before. But the old did not lag behind: the company included sixty-year old Leib Strogatz, and the old cobbler Vorobeichick.

Fine yet strong ties stretched from the forest near Rodansk to numerous villages in Beylorussia. The partisans distributed among the peasants new from the Sovinformburo (Soviet News Agency) and held political discussions with them.

The contact between the company and the ghetto of Minsk was kept viable mostly through the daring spirits who escaped to join us. Thus the partisans were to admit into their lines the three brothers Gulov who had escaped from the ghetto on their own and who, in their first battles, proved to be dauntless fighters. One of them fell in battle with the enemy, and the remaining two kept on fighting until the final victory over fascist Germany.

The ray of hope emanating from the forest near Rodansk was so luminous that even small children used to run away from the ghetto in their search for the site of the partisan company. They had all undergone nightmarish experiences at the hands of the Germans, who had killed their parents in front of them. Desperation had made them faultless fighters, and sixteen boys and young men, ranging in age from seven to fourteen, eventually succeeded in slipping out of the ghetto, hungry and unclad. They wandered in the woods for a long time. Peasants took them into their homes, fed them, and brought them into the forest to the partisan camp.

The Kotuzov company saved all those that could be saved and supplied arms to all those who could fight. Thought it lost many fighters in the course of its numerous battles, many of these fighters, who had come from the ghetto of Minsk, eventually succeeded in seeing their hometown once again.

After the war these former partisans returned to their work in the factories; some even went back to resume their studies. Rolling up their sleeves, they began to work on rehabilitating the economic and cultural institutions of their capital. And today, in the rebuilt and revived town of Minsk, you may once again see old Leib Strogatz, or the invalid cobbler Schafsal Vorobeichick, and the Lussiks, both father and son, along with Israel Lapidot himself, who has in the meantime resumed (Communist) party work. The former partisans often remember the stormy nights, the long treks from one place to another, the battles, and the reconnaissance missions. These recollections are certainly of great help to Misha Lapidot, who has now become an actor in the Beylorussian theater, when he acts out on the stage real characters of the heroes of the fatherland's great war.

PART THREE:

PARTISAN SOCIETY

IN THE FORESTS OF BRYANSK

V. A. Andreyev
Major-General, Former Commander of a Partisan Unit

The Shachors Partisan Battalion, of which I was Chief of Staff, was composed of Communist party members, Red Army soldiers, Soviet workers, and ghetto survivors from the Bryansk region of Beylorussia. Our battalion consisted of two groups: one, the underground group, was active in the district of the town of Kolodnia under the command of Pilkovsky, the secretary of the party's regional committee, and the other, led by Vassili Risakov, had already begun its activities around the village of Orouchiya.

For a long time I had only heard of Pilkovsky through hearsay. It was impossible to get to see him or the other underground fighters because of the distances that separated us and the difficulties involved in conspiracy. This situation continued for a long time, but, as the saying goes, "happiness would not have come had it not been for disaster."

The Germans turned a crack punishment squad against us. This squad came upon the tracks of our unit. A group commanded by Pilkovsky engaged the enemy in battle. Twenty-five men fought off an entire German battalion. As the defensive operations were organized in the woods, it was possible for the underground fighters to hold their ground till the evening. Under cover of darkness they slipped away from the enemy and fought their way to our camp.

This was the first battle for the Pilkovsky group. Generally speaking he was no military man, but in this battle he proved to be a dauntless and ingenious commander. He made good use of the arms at his disposal--two machine guns, two automatic rifles, a few bolt-action rifles, and one mortar--giving the impression that a much larger military unit was fighting it out with the Germans.

The first engagement of the Pilkovsky group with the enemy cost the life of an outstanding fighter and

Communist, Yamlianov, the N.K.V.D.* representative. The Germans, however, suffered heavier losses—they had forty killed and many wounded. Among those killed was their battalion commander.

I first met Pilkovsky in his earth hut, which had been originally intended for thirty people but at the time provided shelter for over a hundred. He was about thirty-five, of medium height, and strongly built. His homely features indicated intelligence, and his chest-nut hair was combed back. His eyes, also hazel, had an aggressive, manly expression.

Pilkovsky was wearing a black woolen shirt tight-ened close to his body with a military belt, from which hung a Tat pistol. His woolen trousers, also black, were tucked into crafted peasant felt boots.

I was to learn later that during the short time that the underground movement had been active behind enemy lines under the leadership of Pilkovsky, it had undergone many trying experiences. As early as October, 1941, the Germans had destroyed the partisan base and spread rumors that the party leaders, together with the regional Soviet officials, including Pilkov-sky, had been caught and put to death. By so doing, the Germans wanted to spread confusion and demoraliza-tion among the people. The regional committee had thus to issue a declaration to the inhabitants of the region to the effect that the Soviet leaders and the party associations were still active in their region in the occupied areas and were continuing their fight against the Germans and their collaborators. The regional committee called upon all the inhabitants to join the fight. The proclamation was signed by Pilkovsky.

In our battalion Pilkovsky, who had been promoted to the rank of commissar, was treated with deep respect. He was my age. He had worked in a tailor shop at Bryansk and had been an active Communist party member for ten years. According to his friends he had done excellent work in the prewar days. Now behind enemy lines, he worked with great enthusiasm. But often he seemed uncommunicative and, at times, even irascible. In the beginning I could find no explana-tion for such streaks of character.

---

* N.K.V.D. is the Russian abbreviation for the "People's Commissariat of Internal Affairs." (ed.)

"What's wrong with him?" I once asked Mazukin, the chairman of the regional executive committee--and he recounted to me the tragedies of Pilkovsky's life. When war started Pilkovsky moved his family--his wife, three children and a female relative--eastward, a distance of only two hundred kilometers.   Being in a strange place was no easy matter: they had no home to live in and the children fell ill.   At the same time the Red Army stemmed the German advance at the Sodost river.   In Vigonichi, the people assumed that the Germans would not advance any farther, and they began to bring their families back.   On October 5, Pilkovsky's wife, children and female relative returned to their home, and on the sixth of the same month the Germans occupied the entire region.   The Germans began a search for Pilkovsky and his family.   As Pilkovsky was then busy organizing the underground movement, his friends took care of the members of his family, smuggling them from one village to another to hide them from the Germans.   With the approach of cold weather they were living temporarily at the small village of Pavlovka.   It was here that the Germans caught them and put them to death in a most atrocious manner.

Pilkovsky blamed himself for the loss of his family and had no peace of mind.   I did everything, together with some friends, to help him get over his grief and take his mind off his personal tragedy.   As head of the battalion staff, I always let Pilkovsky take part in drawing up the plans for all the fighting operations of the battalion. He would get down to work with enthusiasm, get the fighters ready for battle, provide the propagandists with the necessary instructions, write announcements and leaflets.   On such days he would forget his personal tragedy and change to such an extent that it was difficult to recognize him.

While continuing our raids on enemy garrisons, we carried out demoralizing operations on the railway tracks.   At the beginning of January, 1942, Pilkovsky gave two of his partisans, Glyevsky and Tishin, the task of sabotaging the railway tracks.   The demolishing charge was prepared in a very primitive manner--a box was made out of some boards, filled with mines, and put on the tracks.   The operation succeeded.   The train, which was filled with German soldiers heading for the front, advanced at a high speed, and about ten carriages were blown up.

This successful operation meant a great deal to the battalion.   Pilkovsky suggested holding courses in sabotage activities. At the same time we were joined by First-Lieutenant Vorobiov of the engineering corps, whose unit had been surrounded by enemy forces, but he had succeeded in escaping to our lines. It was he who began to impart to the partisans the know-how and skill involved in sabotage work. The comrades were highly elated at the beginning of their "studies." But Pilkovsky put an end to that premature joy.

"For the time being you are only acquiring know-how. But we have no demolition charges. What're you going to use for demolition work?"

Actually the lack of explosives made the situation difficult for us. But Vorobiov suggested that we take the tracks apart. A great number of our men, led by the commanding commissar, went out on this operation, which succeeded without the use of explosives.

"We now have something to report on to the partisan center," Pilkovsky informed his men, beaming with joy. On that very night he wrote a telegram and sent it through our transmitter to the frontline headquarters. Two days later we heard a summary of the news items broadcast by the Central Soviet Information Bureau which said, among other things, that "the partisan company led by R. and the secretary of the regional committee, acting in the woods of Bryansk (Bryansk Region), derailed an enemy convoy heading for the front and inflicted heavy casualties on the enemy forces."

Pilkovsky had great concern for the local population, which was gravely suffering from the occupation forces. He addressed the people constantly through encouraging leaflets written in a cordial style. These leaflets he wrote together with his propagandists. When we had freed some villages from the Germans, Pilkovsky would hold a general meeting of the inhabitants. The speeches and discussions usually ended with a general get-together party.

"Comrades, let's not be downhearted. Let's sing!" --thus would Pilkovsky address the gathering. "Out with your harmonica," he would call out to a member of his company, Gotorov, the harmonica man, who was also one of his propagandists.

And Gotorov would begin. He would sing "Kassian" and play the Yarmak. Pilkovsky would start singing. The multivoiced choir would follow suit. In the end Gotorov would play the music of Stradanya (agonies).

"Let's dance!" And taking off his coat, he would lead the dancers.

It could only be that this man had once been a first-class dancer. He stomped wonderfully with his feet and invited into the dancing circle one fighter after another. He then gave his place to the singing girls. To the tunes of the harmonica, one of them started:

"Germans came to our village,
My song died out.
They burned my house down, took my father away
And hanged my beloved........

The other singer answered her, in song too, improvising:

"In the Nazi claws
We led lives of imprisonment.
When the partisan came
Our spirit came to life as a miracle!"*

At the end of such get-together parties, the partisans would feel a great relief after the day-to-day hardships of living in the woods.

Month after month saw the growth of the partisan movement in our region (Bryansk Region). By the beginning of May, 1942, we had five companies fighting alongside us, numbering nearly two thousand men. I was appointed brigade chief of staff and commander of the Baumann company.

Our companies performed heroic deeds. Pilkovsky was a remarkable company instructor. In the summer of 1942 he was awarded a number of medals, including the Red Flag and the Red Star.

* * * * *

---

* This is a free translation of the song text. (ed.)

The activities of the Bryansk partisans caused much concern among the Germans. They started to bring punishment squads into the region, increased their patrol activities, and attempted to infiltrate our lines in order to cause us as much harassment as possible. I shall recount in detail one such fascist provocation: it happened in those days when the Pilkovsky group had not yet joined our battalion. A young woman by the name of Irena was brought into our camp. She told us about her Jewish descent, that she was born in Berdichev (Ukraine), that she had not been able to escape before the German occupation and had thus been driven out into the ghetto, together with her parents. She had succeeded in escaping to Vigonichi where she came under the German order for the registration of all Jews, without her being able to evade it. But owing to her mastery of the German language, the Germans had made her work as an interpreter for the Gestapo at the high command.

It may be pointed out that I had come across Irena's name before she arrived at our company. In December, 1941, one of our scouts, a villager from Kolodnia, delivered a secret message to the commander of Rissakov's group. The message read: "Dear comrade, a friend is writing to you. Conditions have forced me to work for the Germans, but you have to know that I have worked, am working, and will continue to work only for our country. I shall do all I can to cause harm to the Germans. Give me whatever mission you want, and I shall prove my loyalty."

"What do you make of it?" the commander asked me, showing me the note. "Isn't this a provocation?"

"It is not unlikely," I answered, then asked: "How did she find our runner? And who is he? Can we trust him?"

"He is no doubt one of our men," came the commander's confident reply.

As we came to learn later, the runner had gone on a mission for us to Vigonichi during a snow storm, and he could not leave the village for three days. One day at dusk, while he was crossing the railway tracks, a young woman he did not know came up to him and asked:

"Where do you come from?"

"What's the matter?"

"I'm asking you, where do you come from?" the young woman said firmly once again. Then she went on: "I work at the German High Command. Here are my certificates. Do you have documents? Let me see them!"

The runner was confused and showed her his passport, as a resident of Kolodnia.

"Are there any partisans there?" she asked, lowering her voice, and looking around her.

"No."

"There are," she insisted. "I know. Don't pretend to be naive. You are a party scout."

Surprise confused the runner, and the young woman said to him in a firm voice, pushing an envelope into his hand:

"Deliver this to the partisans. If it doesn't reach them, I'll know where to find you, and you'll have a bitter end. I remember your surname, and I am familiar with the village. I'll find you wherever you go. Is that clear? And if you should decide to come with this message to the German commander, I know what to say, and then--you--," and she pointed at the sky.

Afterwards the young woman told the runner that she was a Jewess and that there was nothing to worry about.

"Let's put her to the test," I suggested to the commander. "Let her kill the German commander."

After some consideration we decided to put her to the test by giving her a lighter mission. We suggested to her, through the same liaison man, that she establish contact with the workers of the hospital at Vigonichi and commandeer medicines and instruments for us and, later on, that she bring us doctors. Among the workers of this hospital, we had friends who had worked for the army and had been taken prisoner. Needless to say we did not tell the unknown young woman that we had already revealed our plans to the doctors who were waiting for an opportunity to come over to us.

Shortly after giving that mission to the unknown young woman, the women doctors were safely with us.

They were POW's Lydia Onkovskaya and Lyuba Todorziba, to be joined soon afterwards by Styra, the daughter of Moshe Tyomkin. They brought along with them a great many instruments and other hospital items. Two medical nurses came along with the doctors. The whole thing had been organized in the best manner. According to the doctors the young woman, who had won the confidence of the German commander, succeeded even in arranging transportation for the hospital equipment to our base.

We kept wondering at the zeal, courage, and ingenuity of the unknown young woman. We decided, however, to give her the mission to kill the German commander. We were told that she eagerly took it upon herself to carry out this task. She acquired a pistol without any difficulty and, at a convenient moment, shot the commander in the back and killed him.

As it now was dangerous for the unknown young woman to remain in Vigonichi, we helped her come over to stay with us. To our regret we found out a few days later that the German commander was still alive and that she had killed another Hitlerite. She had fired in the dark and had missed. The man she killed had a silhouette similar to that of the commander. "Well, to hell with the commander; the Germans would certainly have sent another one in his place. But one more dead fascist," Rissakov soothed her. "A woman of valor! It's good that you yourself managed to escape!"

Irena was an asset to our company. In that crowded and stifling earth hut, she cleaned, ironed the men's linen, laundered, mended, and patched. Systematically and thoroughly she learned to use all sorts of weapons, and she missed no opportunity to take part in the operations of the company. Owing to her contacts in Vigonichi she even succeeded in getting for the battalion about ten rifles, several pistols, flare rockets, and flare-gun cartridges of different colors. She made only one mistake, and that was when we were sitting around the camp fire. She was playing with some flares when one went off, a green one. It went up and exploded above the camp exactly when an unidentified plane was flying over the woods.

Irena was also an excellent interpreter. She had a good command of both German and Russian and helped us in translating German documents. Thus she was able to render a great service to the partisan forces. This young woman got on well with all the men, especially with a young man called Chibolsky, who was known for his courage in battle and gaiety in everyday life. He would play the violin, and Irena would sing, a fact which may have brought them closer together. He was active in the company, like his girlfriend, and showed an interest in everything.

However, we were lucky to learn that Chibolsky was a prominent German spy, who had been sent to our company by the Gestapo and by the head of the investigation department at the police station of Bryansk, Chibolsky's despicable brother. During his stay with our company, this spy succeeded in causing us great harm--he brought about the capture of many of our runners and liaison men. At the questioning, Chibolsky admitted all that had already been known to us.

After we had executed Chibolsky our men kept close watch on Irena. She sensed it and demanded from the commander that he sentence her to death if he did not have faith in her. "I cannot keep on living like this," she told him firmly.

Some time after that incident two new comrades arrived at our camp. One of them Dimitri Yamlotin, who was about thirty-five had a quick and nervous manner of speaking and was also a chain smoker. He was a representative of the sabotage department of the N.K.V.D. and had stayed on his mission behind enemy lines. The other, Isaac Benzionov, who was quite dexterous and also a heavy smoker, brought me and Rissakov the following message: "You have a woman spy in your company, who poses as Jewess in order to cover up her tracks, but who in fact is a German. She was born in Bessarabia, has a good command of the Russian language, graduated from an espionage school, and has come to you for her first performance."

We at once understood that he meant Irena. We called her in for questioning, and when she realized that everything was up, she revealed everything. The liaison man from Kolodnia, through whom she had made contact with us, was himself a distinguished spy. He had assumed the image of a Red Army soldier who had escaped encirclement and succeeded in winning the confidence of Rissakov. The entire store of his meeting with Irena and the delivery of the message was fictitious. The operation of bringing the doctors and hospital articles over to us had been approved by the Germans. They knew that the woman doctors Onkovskaya and Tyomkin were Jewesses and that they had been planning to cross over to our lines. But they decided not to kill them and not to interfere with their going over to the partisans. By keeping the doctors alive, the Germans aimed at giving their agent a status of authority among the partisans. Even the killing of the German by Irena had been the result of cool calculation. The murdered man had not been to the liking of the German commander, who was interested in liquidating him.

Besides a number of tasks, such as that of signaling to the enemy plane in order to expose the camp location, she had been given the task of finding and killing Pilkovsky, the singer, and the other members of the regional committee.

"Why Pilkovsky, of all people?" Rissakov asked the spy.

"You are naive, young man. Our task is to kill off the head, and without a head there won't be any spirit," answered this low creature cheekily.

Some time later I met Pilkovsky and told him the story about Irena.

"No wonder," he said. "The Germans are capable of committing any crime or provocation. There is only one conclusion: our fighters must always be on the alert."

Admittedly, the infiltration of German spies into our camp and our discovering them after some time had a bad effect on the general mood of the partisans. A recurring question at the time was: "Whom can we trust?" Our commander himself, a young enthusiastic man, was so affected by the stories about the spies that he turned into a morbidly suspicious man and decided not to admit into the company any new man in order to avoid future subversive acts. After one successful operation, when the inhabitants of a village we had freed expressed their desire to join us, Rissakov refused to have anything to do with them. On another occasion not only did he not admit a woman fighter into the company, but he also hurt her feelings in a cruel manner. This behavior on the part of Rissakov enraged Pilkovsky, and acts of this kind were likely, of course, to have an adverse effect on the authority of the partisans among the local population.

Pilkovsky gathered the company activists and told them: "Do we have the right to be suspicious of any Soviet man?" These were his first words. Though very angry he did not raise his voice. Calmly and with logical reasoning he expressed his opinion, and his conclusions influenced his listeners against anything that might give the battalion a bad name, since this might weaken the blood alliance between the partisan fighters and the local population. Turning to Rissakov, Pilkovsky said: "The Party has left you here in order to strengthen the spirit of the people when the going is hard to encourage their belief in our cause, and to put them on the way to fighting the fascists. And what are you doing now? You are raising your hand against the most precious of our possessions--the Soviet people. The enemy, taking advantage of our carelessness, threw a few spies your way, and you panicked and began doing the wrong thing. That's just what the enemy expects. He has proved to be highly cunning, though not to the extent you think he is. The Party will not allow any man to smear the name of the partisan movement, let alone to let it die out. Whom do you want to disown, your Soviet people?"

Rissakov was sitting on the front bench. His lean face showed his deep feeling of shame. He listened attentively to Pilkovsky's words, which were true at bottom, and when he spoke, he admitted his mistake.

Pilkovsky announced: "I believe that Rissakov, the courageous commander, will acquire the qualities he now lacks as a Bolshevik partisan who derives his strength from the masses and whose feelings run true to the thoughts, wishes, and desires of the people."

In his own manner our commissar Pilkovsky influenced the behavior of the partisan fighters.

Partisan Doctors

In February, 1942, when we were building up our company, we all lived in one single earth hut. As I have said, this hut was meant to house thirty people, but it served as a living place for over a hundred. At night it was so stifling there that the kerosene lamp and the candle butts blew out alone. Consequently, lice appeared in our camp and with them, typhus. The epidemic brought down one victim after another, and this had a bad effect on the partisans--much more than the German encirclement and their numerous punishment squads.

With the arrival of the women doctors who had been brought over to us by Irena, we at once began to organize the sanitary service. All three women doctors, Onkovskaya, Todorziba, and Tyomkina, who had formerly worked in military hospitals, adapted quickly to the hardships of partisan life and were not troubled by the way things were going on at the camp. Rather at times I even believed that the hard conditions of everyday life, the absence of an elementary sanitary system, provided an incentive for them to work harder. The doctors were assisted by two nurses and one sanitary worker. At the head of the sanitary service was Doctor Lydia Onkovskaya.

Our collective efforts in the fields of sanitation and medicine did not succeed in checking the typhus epidemic. The disease attacked one of the doctors, Lydia Onkovskaya, and with her, one of the nurses. The whole burden now fell on the shoulders of Lyuba Todorziba and Styra Tyomkina. It became evident that as long as we did not improve our everyday manner of living and prevent overcrowding, we had no chance of overcoming the typhus epidemic.

"We should start building new living quarters and an isolation room for the sick and also tear down the earth hut--this is the only way to stop the epidemic," said Todorziba and Tyomkina.

We knew that digging the foundations, even with the help of explosives, was no easy job. One week would not be enough for this task. And how many new victims would the typhus epidemic claim in the meantime? We thus decided to bring into the woods a number of houses from the neighboring village. But how would we go about moving houses? There were Germans and policemen in all the surrounding villages. We could think of only one way out--to drive away the Germans from the village of Orouchiya and from there to bring some houses into the woods.

Pilkovsky brought the matter up for discussion, and the staff command drew up the plan for the task. We discussed the details, issued orders to the attacking parties, and got down to work. At sunset we called up all the fighters who were in good physical condition--forty men in all--and went out. The women doctors joined us too. We came upon the village in a pincer movement from three sides, firing white flares at the same time. The enemy was taken totally by surprise. The Germans did not stay to fight and they fled along the Sosnovia-Bolota road--the only outlet we did not have enough men to block. Only a few rear-guard units showed any resistance. By five in the morning Orouchiya had been cleared of enemy forces. Our men found in the village a good supply of provisions, about nine thousand rounds of ammunition, and some fifteen rifles and machine guns. We decided to take out the houses on that same day. For this purpose we marked the large house of the village head--who was a traitor--the office of the kolkhoz management, the kolkhoz storehouse, and two uninhabited shacks.

In the dark and by the light of torches, professional housebuilders among the villagers were authorized to mark the boards of the houses to be moved over so that it would be easier to put them in place afterwards. Fifty carts were used to haul the boards to the woods. On the next day we started work on setting up a new camp, and a few days later we erected in the woods a new partisan village, with a main road, a sector called "The Prospect of the First Earth Hut," a hospital alley, a barracks courtyard named after "Taras Bulba," and a site for the bathhouse. The kolkhoz villagers gave us bricks and some folk medicines, such as herbs for the sick. To the convalescent, they donated butter, eggs, and milk.

The epidemic began to die out thanks to the doctors' effforts and the help offered by the people. Only one typhus patient died.

Often we had visitors from the nearby village, seeking our medical services. But more often it was our doctors who went out to the neighboring villages to heal the sick. It may be pointed out that a considerable number of the villagers suffered from bullet wounds caused by the enemy. The wounded were taken to the hospital by the doctors. For some time the hospital was stationed in the village of Gavan. With the approach of the Germans, however, it was moved back into the woods once again.

* * * * *

At the staff command of the partisan brigades active in the Bryansk area and numbering some twenty-five thousand fighters, worked Arkadi Eidlin, a surgeon. He was in charge of the sanitary platoon and had to travel from one company to another, supervising and instructing, providing the necessary help for the young doctors in their work.

Not far from the village of Smilij, in a thick forest, Eidlin set up an underground hospital. According to his instructions the partisans dug out the foundations and built a large hut, fifty square meters in area. Into this hut they brought homemade iron stoves. Windows were put into the ceiling for light. At night they used oil lamps. Parachute cloth taken from the enemy was used for covering the walls and the ceiling. The hospital was clean, warm, and pleasant. In it were grouped many severely wounded fighters who were on their way to the partisan center in Moscow.

The Correspondent of Partisan Pravda*

Aronov was on the editorial staff of Partisan Pravda. He had started out as a partisan fighter in the Voroshilov Company. On one of its raids the company caputred typesetting letters and an Amrikanka printing machine. In cooperation with Zeitziv, the company commissar, Aronov started publishing a small newspaper called Voroshilovich. It was a good paper as they go, a fighting paper, printed on a quarter sheet. Voroshilovich soon had a good circulation among both the partisans and the nonfighting population. Needless to say, the paper necessary for printing was "provided" by the enemy.

When the decision was made to put out a central newspaper by the battalion, an editorial staff was picked from among the fighters, Bondrinsk, Korotkov, Andriev, Aleishinki, and Aronov.

Under battle conditions the editors got down to work writing notes and articles, and they themselves set the type for the paper and printed it. In general Aronov wrote accounts of the operations in which he actually took part. In the course of a German attack, the editorial staff found themselves in a particularly dangerous situation. They managed to retreat under

---

* Pravda means "truth." (ed.)

fire. Nonetheless, the newspaper came out on the day of the retreat. In the fall of 1942, his assistant, Comrade Sidorenko, who was later to die a hero's death, set up a well-defended base for the editorial staff. Here the Partisan Pravda was to come out regularly for about one year.

Before they launched their attack in the direction of Orel-Kursk, the Germans decided to secure their rear lines against our raids. Amassing for this purpose a number of divisions and a great many tanks and planes, they renewed their attacks on the area held by the partisans. The partisans of Bryansk had to take part in a number of battles at which they were greatly outnumbered. They actually fought for every bush, destroying considerable numbers of enemy forces and equipment. The base serving the Partisan Pravda was itself used as a stronghold. It was located in a marshland, highly convenient for defensive operations. The access road to this base saw a number of ferocious battles, joined in by the "Rule-for-the-Soviets" battalion which had been sent in for reinforcement. The fight went on for several days, during which the editors pitched in every now and then. In the end we had to withdraw, but the newsppaer continued to come out regularly, as the printing type and machine had both been evacuated in time. Aronov continued to visit the fighting companies. He also kept on writing articles for the paper.

Lazar Bleichmann

I first met him during the months of March and April, 1942 in the village of Beiliya Kharpatch in the Nablin Region, where I had gone on a liaison and information-gathering mission. Lazar Bleichmann was in command of a company he had organized under the leadership of the Party regional committee.

The meeting was short. At that time Bleichmann was in control of an important section of the railway tracks in our region. The Germans launched several attacks to get hold of this section, throwing in the battle tanks and heavy artillery. But the partisans of the Nablin Region held out and repulsed all enemy attacks.

Before long Bleichmann was apopointed commander of the Fourmanov Company. He started out by training men for sabotage work. In early July the Fourmanov fighters succeeded in derailing a German train carrying soldiers and arms. Bleichmann himself conducted the battle.

Bleichmann's company was known for its defensive activities against the German attacks. In late June and early July the Germans attempted to drive the partisans out of the woods of Ramasoks and the steppes along the back of the Desna River (northeast of Kiev). The first enemy blows fell on the Fourmanov Company. At the same time there were two more partisan companies in the woods of Ramasoks. Bleichmann succeeded in establishing close contact with them for joint action against the Germans. The partisans repulsed all enemy attacks. The battalion chief of staff, Kapitan Gogoliok, and myself visited the company grounds and helped in organizing defense activities.

The Fourmanov Company acted for a long period as a well-knit, powerful unit against the Germans who fought at the outskirts of the woods. When the order for withdrawal was received, Bleichmann carried out an outstanding manoeuver: he slipped unnoticed through the enemy forces and, on his way out, destroyed the police forces in the steppe sector in the direction of Tropchvesk up to the Pogra Area. Bleichmann also carried out a number of large scale and spectacular operations along the Desna River.

For his military achievements, Bleichmann was awarded the Order of Lenin. The Order was awarded to him by Alexander Pavlovich Matviev, chief of staff of the partisan movement.

Hungarian Jews

In the winter toward the end of 1942, the Felix Djerjenski Company received orders to attack and oust the German garrison stationed around the village of Shilinka in the Bryansk Region. The commander of this garrison, which was composed of Germans and Magyars,*

---

* Term for Hungarian soldiers who fought at the side of the Germans. (ed.)

was a Hungarian fascist called Major Farag. One day we received information that the enemy forces were planning to mount an attack on the woods of Bryansk from the southeast and that Major Farag was preparing roads for the withdrawal of the German forces, using for this purpose a large work gang of Hungarian Jews.

In the partisan company was a Hungarian, Paul Paldash, interpreter, scout, and fighter. Through his help we succeeded in establishing contact with the Hungarian prisoners. Shortly afterwards the Djerjenski Company raided the enemy garrison and killed Farag, whereupon forty-one Jews joined the partisan forces, expressing their desire to fight the Germans.

Thus the Felix Djerjenski Company came to include a special Jewish force. The outstanding doctor, Kobash Reizieh not only healed the wounded but also struck at the Germans, weapon in hand. In one of the battles he was wounded and fell down near the enemy. But he managed to escape. After long suffering he found his way to the Beylorussian partisans and joined them to fight our common enemy.

It is worthwhile to mention Beibai Lashello, too, from Budapest, who held an LL.D. degree. Partisan Lashello also did propaganda work for us. He wrote leaflets in Hungarian to be distributed among enemy forces. In these leaflets the Germans were called upon to kill their commanding officers and join the partisans.

The group of Hungarian Jews fought the German occupation forces with spectacular courage and took part in numerous battles. These former prisoners of yesterday had turned into popular avengers worthy of their name and kept up the fight against the enemy till the end of the war. Many of them learned Russian and served as interpreters in the interrogation of German prisoners of war.

The Partisans in Moldavia

In March, 1943, when the partisans of Bryansk established contact with the Red Army, I was called to Moscow by the Center of Partisan Movement and ordered to provide assistance for the partisan fighters in Moldavia. I flew far into the rear of the enemy forces together with a group of officials belonging to the Communist party center in Moldavia.

At the same time a number of small underground units had been active in the Moldavia area. We landed in Beylorussia. Our group included my chief of staff, Makkar Kozjukhar, and a number of comrades from Moldavia. Our mission was to smuggle organized partisan companies from Beylorussia into Moldavia, where they were to serve as a core for the entire movement. Our unit was joined by many new fighters on the way, gained valuable fighting experience day after day, and eventually came to number three thousand fighters, comprising three brigades and one cavalry squadron.

The Moldavian unit contained many Jews who fought alongside fighters from other nations. I would like to make special mention of some of them.

During the "War of the Fatherland," Mark Shirokov, a Moldavian, joined the Red Army as a volunteer. He had been seriously wounded in the fight against the enemy. But when he heard of the formation of the Moldavian unit he expressed his wish to join the partisans, although his wounds had not yet healed properly. At first Mark was a company commander. In an especially ferocious encounter with the enemy while the company was still in the region of Polesye, Shirokov's men held their ground firmly against the German attacks. The fight went on for more than two hours, in the course of which Shirokov proved to be a gifted, faultless commander.

In Moldavia, Shirokov was put in command of a group of saboteurs. We had over one hundred groups of this kind in our unit. To give an example of the value of their work, suffice it to point out that more than two hundred enemy transports were put out of commission within six months. The Shirokov group had much to show for itself in these operations. Mark himself blew up five military trains. Along with his sabotage activities, Mark also took part in reconnaissance operations.

I must also mention 45-year old Michael Tchoban. He first went on patrol missions and at once proved to be a courageous fighter. In the fall of 1943, Tchoban was appointed my deputy in the technical platoon. Michael saw to it that the provisions and the fighting equipment of the unit were in tip-top condition. Like Shirokov, Michael Tchoban also was awarded two orders-- the Red Flag and the Red Star.

In conclusion, a few words about partisan Boris Rokhlin. He laid mines on roads which were in German hands, blew up several enemy transports, derailed enemy trains--duties he looked upon as simply "hobbies." He would often say: "We are partisans in order to blow up German trains." This was, in effect, the epitome of his military career.

MEETINGS AND EVENTS

A. P. Brinsky ("Dadya Petya")

Hero of the Soviet Union
Former Commander of a Partisan Unit

In White Russia

Our partisan company was first organized in the District of Vitebsk, in the region of Lake Loklomsk. Comrade Nailiyoubo, its commander, actually had a fighting unit composed mainly of peasants from the village of Ogoureyich.

In September, 1941, we succeeded in establishing contact with Jewish workers from the neighboring small towns. A month later we called a joint meeting with the representatives of these small towns to determine the future line of action, and it was decided to organize sabotage groups. Soon enough we had a number of such groups acting in that sector.

The Loklomsk group distinguished itself in sabotage work. It was under the command of Isaac, a cobbler by trade. I forget his surname to my regret. Besides the killing of two Hitlerite officers, a captain and a major, they systematically provided us with reconnaissance information, along with medicines and bandages.

Before long we were to lose contact with these groups as the company was forced to move to other regions. At that time we had quite a number of Jewish fighters among us. They had come from Lepyel, Bogomol and Stislebel. In those days we had begun to receive from the neighboring small towns a constant stream of refugees, including not only youth in good fighting condition, but also old men, women, and children, and thus we had no alternative but to set up a cililian camp.

To leave the small town was no easy matter. The Germans had driven the Jews out into the ghettos and threw barbed wire fences around them. Sentries were posted at regular intervals, with orders to let out only work groups accompanied by Ukrainian policemen or SS men. We often received news of killings already perpetrated or imminent. We did our best to get the

Jews out of the ghettos with all the means at our disposal.

During this period we were forced to engage the enemy in a difficult battle at the village of Neyshkovo. In this battle we lost twenty Jewish partisan fighters from our company. Their bodies, which had been left behind, were later hung high by the Germans in order to terrorize the surrounding inhabitants.

On our way to the region of Baranovichi, I met a group of some forty Jewish partisan fighters near the village of Svinitsa. The group had contacts with the ghetto at Baranovichi. We provided them with arms and suggested that they bring out from Baranovichi as many people as they could. The mission succeeded. The company, reinforced by young men who had been saved from the ghetto, grew to such proportions that it now had the strength to carry out military operations by itself. With our help they blew up two enemy transports and burned down a large bakery that provided bread for the Nazis.

In the Baranovichi region I met another group of Jewish partisans in August, 1942. We held consultation with the other companies which were active in our region. The largest of these companies was the one called "Shchors." Before long this unit had grown into an independent company and had joined the brigade; it was commanded by Comrade Komarov.

I owe it to myself to mention here a Jewish partisan commander who fell in battle near Baranovichi. His name was Seidelnikov. He had been a newsman before the war. He was in command of a company which distinguished itself by its military activities against the enemy, blew up scores of German transports, and wiped out enemy garrisons in the camps of Idritsa, Beylaya, and others. The Seidelnikov company was widely known among the surrounding population, and many came to join it. The company was soon to grow into a brigade. In one of his brilliant operations, Seidelnikov succeeded in releasing some two hundred and fifty Red Army POWs from enemy camps. But, as I had just said, he died a hero's death in the furious battle that raged near Baranovichi.

In the Ukraine

In September, 1942, we moved over to the western regions of the Ukraine. At the same time most of the Jewish inhabitants of these areas were being atrociously wiped out by the Germans. Here and there a few small ghettos survived. The few Jews who succeeded in escaping and had not fallen victim to German bullets had to wander through the woods, hiding from both German and Ukrainian police and murderers. With the approach of fall these people had only tatters on their backs, suffered from hunger, ate uncooked potatoes, were afraid of being seen on the roads, and avoided lighting camp fires.

It was necessary to start setting up civilian camps. The first camps of this kind were erected in the region of the villages Izouri and Swaricheyvich in the province of Wissotsky. Here was active the partisan group under the command of Misyura. His second in command was the Jew Bakalczuk, a dauntless young man, and his adjutant Moshe Bromberg. The Jews of this group numbered about ninety. I gave the order to set up a new camp for all the refugees from the neighboring woods who came to us singly or in groups and delegated the Misyura company to guard it. To all the able-bodied men, we gave arms.

We soon had a second camp in the vicinity. Again I issued an order, this time to the Korochkin-Obokhov group, then active in that region. The new camp, which was organized by Korochkin, comprised some two hundred persons. Out of his camp a fighting group was formed which was soon to grow into an independent partisan company. This in turn grew into a brigade, comprising about seven hundred men, mostly Jewish. The brigade systematically disrupted the telegraph lines of the Germans, occasionally raided their food storehouses, disarmed three police stations, and blew up enemy transports carrying soldiers and military equipment.

The partisans under the command of Korchiev, Misyura, and Bakalczuk began their military activities almost without any weapons, but were soon to supply the neighboring companies with military equipment out of the booty that fell into their hands in their battles against the enemy.

In the month of January and February, 1943, a number of daring raids were carried out in this area on police stations, ranches, and German administration buildings. In these raids the partisans took many horses, cows, and foodstuffs which they later distributed to the neighboring inhabitants. The raids were led by Nachman Silberpark, Bakalczuk, and Bromberg.

At the head of one company stood a daring commander, Boris Yaakoblivitz Bazikin. He carried out many daring raids on German garrisons. Bazikin's company was distinguished for its attack on the Strashievo station, where an armored train stood at the time. Bazikin's fighters dispatched the train guards and blew up or otherwise dismantled about 400 meters of railway tracks. In addition, this company blew up eight transports, destroyed three bridgeways, and wiped out a number of village administration offices. Bazikin himself fell in a battle which took place in the region of Vladimir-Valinsk.

In the Kruk Company

The Kruk company was active in the area of Volyn (western Ukraine). Kruk himself was a Ukrainian, his real name being Konishchuk. When the Hitlerite invaders occupied Volyn and began their murderous persecution of the Jews, Kruk went about organizing a partisan company. In the village of Gryva, where Kruk had been head of the village council until the outbreak of the war, there lived only six Jewish families. Kruk turned to these families, and the first to take up the challenge was the Zwiebel family--the 75-year-old man, his four sons, and his brother. From the neighboring village of Leishnivsky, eight men joined the company, headed by the brothers Hannan and Shimon Kobel.

There were also volunteers from the town of Manevichi.* In the beginning there were only seventeen men. The military equipment at their disposal was sufficient for eight men only, but this did not deter Kruk and his group from going into action. They headed for the woods and began assembling people who had gone there to hide from the German murderers. Occasionally Kruk would himself slip into the ghettos of the neighboring small towns, and release the prisoners who would

---

* This is the town where the editor and his parents grew up. A fuller account of the Kruk partisan group is given in a later chapter. (ed.)

later join the ranks of the partisans. Before long the company numbered one hundred and twenty men. Eventually it was to comprise about seven hundred fighters.

Kruk's company acquired its arms in the same manner as other partisan companies: at the expense of the enemy, by attacking small German groups and seizing their weapons. As the company added more fighters, it widened its field of activity. Its men were active in the areas of Volyn, Rovno, and Brest. The company was well known for its sabotage activities: it blew up more than one hundred military transports, burned down two sawing mills, and destroyed tens of kilometers of telegraph and telephone wires.

Many partisans belonging to this company sacrificed their lives for the fatherland.

The Civilian Camps

The civilian camps caused us much trouble, but they also brought us great benefits. In our unit there were four such camps, comprising over a thousand Jews. We also had camps for Ukrainians, to which were brought families which faced death, and one for Poles, who had fled the terror of German and Ukrainian fascists.

We stationed the camps in the heart of the woods, in faraway spots, and on islands in marshland country. When we moved to a new place, we took the camps along with us. With the approach of Nazi punishment squads, we moved the camps to a far-off safe place.

In the early days we sent to the civilian camps all those we could save from the German holocaust. Among them were men, women, children, and the elderly. Gradually, after our companies had acquired additional weapons and military equipment, all the young and middle-aged men and women joined our fighting companies. At the camps were only the old men and the children. But even they did not sit there doing nothing. The old women patched up the partisans' clothes, did the washing, and knitted socks and mufflers. The old men mended the shoes, did some tailoring, and a little furriers' work. The children tended the cattle and collected seeds which were essential to protect us against scurvy.

The Jewish camp of Kruk's company rendered us an invaluable service. They had a big farm. The civilians mowed, sowed, gathered wheat and barley. The camp grounds under Kruk's command included a flour mill and a bakery which provided the fighting company with bread. There were also a considerable number of cows, sheep, goats, and horses. The buildings also included a hospital for sick and wounded partisans. But the most important thing for us at this camp was the workshop which built military equipment. From German dud (unexploded) shells our men took out the explosive charge and prepared their own bombs and mines.

The workshop was located deep in the VolskayaValya forest (in the Western Ukraine). It provided us with more than fifteen tons of explosives. This work involved constant danger and was shared by men and women alike. Chief among them were Wolf Rabinovich, Abraham Goldes, Gershon Grunberg, Israel Hirsch Pals, Erika Kirchenbaum, and Friedel Melamed. In the course of preparing the mines we lost 16-year-old Peisi Reiter and 13-year-old Shlomo Biedermann, both from the small town of Manevichi.

At the head of this camp was Isaiah Zwiebel, a highly practical man, who organized the very complex life in this camp with remarkable wisdom and vigor.

Mention should also be made of two brothers who stayed at Kruk's camp, Liezer and Abraham Lissoksky. The latter was the company's chief technician. He was the man with the golden touch. He not only repaired rifles and pistols but also designed and built machine guns and automatic rifles.

Boris Gindin and Others

We had a great many courageous fighters and commanders who spared no effort in their fight against the enemies of our fatherland. It is impossible to recount the exploits of them all, but there were many unforgettable men among them. When the war broke out Boris Gindin was only a junior lieutenant who had just graduated from military college. He was nineteen years old, and under his command an infantry platoon engaged in defensive operations near the town of Grodno. He fought in the city streets of Minsk and, to escape encirclement, organized a partisan company in a very short time. At our camp he was in command of a Jewish platoon. At the head of this platoon, Gindin blew up eleven enemy trains and destroyed five bridges. One of his platoon fighters, Valodya Zwiebel, holding a string of hand grenades in his hands, threw himself under an approaching German train and blew it up at the price of his own life.

When our battalion moved to the Ukraine, Gindin's thirty-seven-man platoon spearheaded its movement. It was difficult to march through the woods and the marshes. Each fighter carried about twenty kilograms of explosives.* We went twenty days on this march, but in the end our orders were carried out in full. The men reached their prearranged point through the towns of Kovel, Shaftovka, Sarni, Lutsk, and VladimirVolinsk. Before long Gindin was made second-in-command to Kruk, and shortly afterwards he was appointed chief of staff in Loginov's company. Within eleven months of military activity, from April 15, 1943, to March 15, 1944, Loginov's company blew up about one hundred and fifty enemy trains, together with one hundred and fifty train engines, killing some twenty-two hundred German officers and soldiers and wounding about four thousand. It also destroyed many enemy tanks, vehicles, and a large quantity of fuel and provisions.

Many partisan Jews also fought in the "Max" company. I remember in particular the fighter Melamedik, from the small town of Manevichi. He blew up three enemy trains and died in a raid on a police station.

When the war broke out, another Jew, Minich, had been working as a bookkeeper in the town of Rafalovka. He was soon to turn into a fearless partisan and was held in great esteem by his comrades in the compnay. He took part in blowing up nine enemy trains and two bridges. Minich, too, fell in battle, in the vicinity of Rafalovka.

The commander of a Jewish platoon, Bronstein, blew up eleven German trains, three vehicles, a large bridge, and burned down a sawing mill.

Yeshayahu Segel, who came from the small town of Manevichi, was our instructor. He was a dauntless partisan who knew every square inch of the forest. He was good at sabotage and was credited with blowing up seven German trains.

---

* This is about 44 pounds. (ed.)

I would like to speak of another one of our partisans who was distinguished by his manners and deeds, Rabbi Liefa, the son of Toder Yosilevich, from the village of Lolineych. The partisans simply called him Liefa. One of his friends hit the nail right on the head when he called him "The God of Israel's Vengeance." He was of medium height, had a dark beard, wore a deerskin mantle, and a warm cap. Carrying an automatic rifle across his chest, and with a string of hand grenades hanging from his belt, he naturally did not look much like a rabbi. He had a good command of Russian, Polish, and German. At the beginning of the war he was thirty-five years old. In the ghetto of Lolineych he called upon the Jews to rise in revolt against the fascists. The Jews of Lolineych had no previous contacts with the surrounding population; they also had no weapons. The rabbi succeeded in escaping from the ghetto. After much wandering he established contact with the partisans, and with their help he released many of those who had been trapped within the ghetto walls. But he could not save his own family, since he was first and foremost concerned with saving others. His wife and children were killed by the Germans.

I appointed Liefa Yosileyvich platoon commander because of his courage, wisdom, and logical reasoning. The partisans were satisfied with this appointment. "Our Liefa won't betray us," they used to say. As a matter of fact, whenever he went out on a mission, he would first take every military detail into consideration, and during the fighting itself he provided a good personal example of fearlessness and coolness under fire.

Once, two German battalions engaged in battle with a partisan company which had Liefa among its fighters. The partisans were highly outnumbered, and the fighting was fierce. But the partisans pushed back the Germans and began to chase them. In order to run faster, Liefa threw off his boots. The fighters did the same, and, barefoot, continued their chase. The Germans suffered heavy losses, but Liefa was seriously injured in the pursuit. The partisans evacuated him from the battlefield and on the first plane had him flown to Moscow and to a hospital.

Women Partisans

Among the Jewish partisans in our unit were many women, especially young women, who, rifle and hand grenade in hand, fought shoulder to shoulder with the men and were among the first to distinguish themselves in battle. From the very beginning of our struggle in White Russia, we had among us an outstanding woman partisan, Liza Leanders of Minsk, who was fearless and full of life. She took part in all the battle operations, kindled by the desire to take revenge upon the enemy.

At the small town of Wizna in the region of Slotzk, the Germans had a storehouse of provisions. We decided to destroy it. The task was entrusted to Liza Leanders and a young partisan, Karbackenko from the Ukraine. We dressed them as bride and bridegroom and drove them to Wizna for their wedding ceremony. The Germans were surprised to see that their guard had been killed and the storehouse set on fire. They pursued the "newlyweds" for eight kilometers, but the young couple and their guests succeeded in eluding the pursuing enemy. Liza not only took part in the fighting, but she also killed two collaborators with her own hands. She did not shirk any kind of work: she sometimes even did the washing and worked in the kitchen.

Other outstanding women fighters were Rina Guz and Mussya Bernstein, together with the sisters Raya and Ida Bert of Manevichi, the elder only nineteen years old and the younger only sixteen.

A fearless partisan woman was Dora Gilbert. In the beginning she worked in the kitchen, then as a typist at the office of the chief of staff. But Dora could find no satisfaction in such jobs. Eventually she was to take part in the blowing up of four military trains, aside from a number of battles with the enemy. She fell in a battle near the town of Vladimir.

In battle also fell Raya from Fabourin. I forget her surname. She was an exceptionally fearless young woman and took part in several attacks on police stations.

Partisan life was not easy for all of us, but it was particularly difficult for the young women. Besides taking part in the fighting, they also treated the wounded and the sick and did the washing and the cooking. Occasionally we were short of food and wore "raffia" shoes and whatever clothing we could find.* The young women did not complain and stoically endured the shortage. One thing they would not tolerate, however: not to be given arms.

Here is a request I received from Rina Guz: "Dadya Petya! My military record shows four enemy trains destroyed. You know fully well that I have military privileges, and my privilege to get arms is not less than that of the others. Give me an automatic rifle, I hereby request you, dear Dadya Petya!"

The favorite of the entire partisan group was 14-year-old Luba Melamedik. She worked as a cook and at the same time tended the sick and the wounded. She would see one of our men walking around in a soiled shirt and would immediately have him take it off and wash it for him. Her cousin, Yuri (Jack) Melamedik, was a fighter in the "Max" partisan group under the general command of Anton Brinsky ("Dadya Petya").

Partisan Doctors

I owe it to myself to say a few words about our doctors. They were extremely remarkable partisans. Our hospitals were often located in far-off spots, constantly under guard. When on the move we would usually take the sick and the wounded along with us, or, if the circumstances so dictated, we would leave them behind in the woods. Despite the difficulties involved we saw to it that the hospitals received the best available foodstuffs. Medicines and bandages were acquired in our raids on the enemy, which is also how we got our weapons. In many places we were in contact with doctors, pharmacists, and nurses who would give us all that we needed. In the small town of Rozhitsa in the district of Volyn there worked a Jewish doctor who posed as a "Shick."** He did a great deal for us, keeping us supplied with medicines and instruments.

---

* Raffia shoes were shoes made of soft leather or rubber, somewhat like tennis shoes, for moving quietly through the forest. (ed.)

** A non-Jew. (ed.)

Another physician, Dr. Melchior, had run away from the ghetto. His entire family had been wiped out. He was a great doctor and an excellent organizer. He served as a doctor in one of our brigades. Our men started to come down with typhus and dysentery, and we also had the seriously wounded. Dr. Melchior had not a single death among all the cases he treated. He himself would go out to get medicines and other materials, serving not only the partisans, but also the local inhabitants. He also went out to visit the sick in the neighboring villages, thus enhancing the respect and authority our partisans had with the local population.

A great deal of love and appreciation went to Dr. Weiner of Lvov. He worked with Loginov's company. His family had also been wiped out. Wiener did not stop at simply providing medical treatment, but also insisted on taking part in military operations. He was a real "national avenger."* He was credited with scores of partisan survivors and scores of Germans dead.

The senior doctor of the second brigade was Dr. Rotter of Stolin, in the district of Pinsk. His wife worked for us as a dental surgeon. The companies of Magomet and Doroshenko had such experienced personnel as Dr. Kurtz and his wife.

Despite all the difficulties our doctors carried out the most complicated medical operations under fire. Young Dr. Marmelstein carried out a serious operation of this kind on partisan Nicolai Zayetz, and saved his life.

There is also much to say for our medical nurses. I would like to make special mention of only one: Rubinstein was her family name. She was an elderly woman who tended not only the partisans, but also the local population. Despite her age she worked tirelessly; innumerable fighters were brought back to health, thanks to her efforts.

* * * * *

---

* This term, "national avenger," is a direct translation--it simply meant those Russians who took revenge for their dead families and friends. (ed.)

I have not told the entire story. All of us, from the simplest fighter to the unit commander, fulfilled his duty to our country. We felt a special concern for Soviet citizens who had suffered from Nazi plunder. A great number of Jews were also saved from the murderous claws of the Hitlerite beasts, and they were in great need of our help. A great many inmates of German prisons, upon joining the family of partisans, soon became fearless fighters and commanders and fought with honor for their beloved country.

A CIVILIAN CAMP IN THE FOREST

Pavlo Vershigora

Introduction

Pavlo Vershigora was born in Moldavia in 1905. He was an actor and a stage-manager. In World War I he was a commander in one of the partisan battalions under Sidor Kovpak, the commander-in-chief of the entire Soviet partisan movement. For his outstanding service as a partisan commander, he was awarded the title: "Hero of the Soviet Union."

In 1946 Vershigora published a book under the title People with a Clear Conscience, which includes historical accounts of the exploits and battles of the battalion against the German fascist invaders, besides personal glimpses of gifted and capable commanders of partisan units.*

Here is an excerpt from his writings:

...It was only by a miracle that a Jewish ghetto had been left in Skalat (not far from Tarnopol) early in the summer of 1943. Behind the barbed wires were Jewish craftsmen--tailors, shoemakers, saddlers. The Germans had put off for them the day of their doom-- they forced the Jews to work from dawn and well into the night on a starvation diet. The partisans, the Karpenko fighters, released them from the ghetto, over three hundred people who later appeared in the forest, including old men, women, and children. They were a mass of tortured people wearing tattered clothes.

Their appearance in the forest in the midst of the partisan camp caused no little embarrassment. We understood quite well that if they were to remain in the town, the fascists would have killed them all on the following day. But we could not take these wretched people along with us since we were a military unit about to go out on difficult missions. "How could such a mass of weak old men and miserable women stand the rigors of combat operations?" we asked ourselves;

---

* From Binyamin West's original Hebrew introduction. (ed.)

but there was no way out. Commander Kovpak ordered one of his aides, Pavlovsky, to have the weak carried on carts while the strong were to walk behind the fighters' columns.

Among the fighters some Jews must be mentioned, such as Misha Tartakovsky, Vladya Lapopin, and others. Tartakovsky served as an interpreter in the interrogation of German prisoners of war.

Right at the beginning of the motley march, Kovpak brought into a single line all the Jewish men and women who had come from the ghetto of Skalat and told them: "Now I would like to have a serious talk with you. We are military men. Our aim is to do valuable military deeds. And though I much regret it, I cannot accept you all into the unit. So every one of you has to consider his abilities and adapt himself to this military life whether it suits his strength or not. The decision is in your hands. This is how I am presenting the question, straightforward and fair. Those who want and can carry arms will stay with us. Those who hate the fascists will stay with us. Those who have no fear of death and are ready to sacrifice themselves for our country will stay with us. And those who lack them? Thus will I say straight and to the point. Do not go! As for those who stay behind, we will send them to the villages and find accommodation for them with the peasants. We will leave some food supplies behind. But if you join the ranks of the unit, you will have to take the oath, and if then you find yourselves incapable of doing the job, don't take us to task. We have one law for all, no matter who he is; Russian, Ukrainian, or Jew. This is an agreement. Think it over till evening. Talk it over with the elders. I will send for your answer before evening."*

----

* To our regret, Vershigora does not tell us the decision of the survivors or what happened to them. (ed.)

PARTISAN ALEXANDER ABUGOV

A WITNESS

Alexander Abugov was a partisan in White Russia and the Ukraine in the years 1942-1944. He was in command of a reconnaissance company and accomplished many exploits as a Jewish fighter.*

Before the war he was a physical training instructor in Odessa. He was recruited into the Red Army at the beginning of the war between Russia and Germany in June, 1941, was taken prisoner and spent four months in POW camps--first in a deep ravine near the town of Oman (the Ukraine) and later in POW camps in Viniche (the Ukraine), Shepetovka (the Ukraine), Brest-Litovsk (Beylorussia), Kobrin (Beylorussia), and Kovel (the Ukraine). During this period many Jewish prisoners of war were killed. Abugov was not killed, because he had succeeded in concealing the fact that he was a Jew. After numerous attempts he escaped from the camp at Kovel to the neighboring forests. Through his wanderings in the woods he succeeded in reaching a partisan unit not far from Pinsk, led by the commander Dimitri Popov.

Here are excerpts from his testimony to the Yad Vashem-Memorial Authority:**

Upon reaching the village of Svarichivichi (near Pinsk), we decided to encamp in the forest for the night. Our ground scouts went out to reconnoiter the area as we were not familiar with it. I well remember that it was cloudy and that the falling snow was mixed with rain, so that it was both wet and cold. Not all the partisans had winter clothes.

End of November, 1942. At dawn our sentry heard the sound of someone working with an axe and decided to go in the direction of the noise. On approaching the spot, he saw two men dressed in tattered clothes and

---

* This section was added to this book later.

** The international Holocaust documentation center based in Jerusalem, Israel. (ed.)

unshaven. They were cutting dry pine wood. The sentry, who was a Siberian, could not form any idea as to who those two men were. When they saw him they began to run away. He was wearing a short German coat, and they thought him to be a German policeman. He ran after them, shouting in Russian that he would not do anything to them if only they would tell him who they were. Finally he caught one of them and began to shake him. The man would not utter a word for fear. At this moment the sentry saw at some distance some huts from which thick smoke was rising. In the meantime the man who had escaped noticed the red ribbon on the cap of the partisan, who told him: "Don't be afraid of me. I am a Soviet partisan." On hearing this the man told the partisan that he was a Jew.

Both went to the huts where the partisan sentry found many Jews. At first they were afraid to come near him, but after he had assured them that he would do them no harm, they came to him slowly and began to speak. He learned that these were Jews who had come from various villages from Serniki, Dobrovicha, Svarichivichi, Vichevka, Gorodonia and others.

The sentry told us of his discovery when he returned to the camp. Upon hearing that there were Jews in the forest, I went to see them. I may take this opportunity to point out that no one in the company knew anything about my nationality. They thought I was a Russian. On seeing the huts where these Jews were living, I was overwhelmed with deep emotion. I remembered my sufferings as a prisoner of war in the German camps and how the Jews were wiped out. I thought to myself that there was a chance that these Jews, who were dispersed in the woods, unorganized, would come out alive from this hard war and that they would not be able to defend themselves under such difficult conditions in those tattered clothes--a camp of four hundred people. They came around and asked hundreds of questions. I did not have the answers to all of them. Only then did I have a feeling that drew me close to my people. The "Jewish spot" was revived in me. Until the time I was taken prisoner and during my life in the forest I did not have such a feeling because all that time I had lived among Russians, studied with Russians, had Russian friends; and for this reason I did not find it difficult to conceal my nationality both in German prison camps and in the company of partisans.

Among the Jews we found in the woods, I saw many young men who had side-curls. I took out my razor and shaved them on the spot, for I always kept my razor with me.*

Upon returning to camp, the idea flashed in my mind to get these people organized. For this purpose I had either to stay with them or to persuade the commander not to continue our advance eastwards. This latter possibility was out of the question for two reasons: first, the entire company would fall into the hands of the Germans who were getting ready for an extensive combing operation in the woods, mainly because of those Jews hiding in the forest; second, the company was moving eastwards to join the Red Army and so it could not be delayed in the woods. Thus the order was given to get ready to pull out on the following day. One of our guides had to take us across the river Goryn, but I decided to desert my company in order to organize a new partisan company out of the Jews in the forest, out of those who could carry arms and fight. In my company there were friends who agreed to stay with me in order to continue the fight behind enemy lines. They were Anatoly Korochkin, Serge Korchev, Genia Vodobozov, and Feodor Nikonorov.

The company pulled out at night, and we went together to the village of Svarichivichi were we destroyed a German police command. Then the company continued its advance to the village of Ozyresk, which lies on the road to the river Goryn, and then to the village of Villion, where we deserted it quietly and went back to the Jewish camp in the woods. We were five Jews.

On the following day we began to set up a new company of fighters. We gathered more than twenty Jewish young men. They were: Y. Boris, Asher Mankovisky, Shmuel Purim, Nahum Zilberfarb, Zvi Liebherz, the brothers Moshe, Efraim and Anshel Landau, Leibel Fleischman, who was known as Zamorochenski, and others. (All of them are now in Israel.)

* * * * *

---

* These were, no doubt, Orthodox Jews, whose side-curls ("peyos") would have given them away. (ed.)

We lived in earth tunnels in winter and in huts in the summer. These we set up in the forest and camouflaged them as best we could--living two in each dwelling. They were covered either with snow or with moss so that even in daylight one could not tell that partisans lived there, as they looked like small mounds.

Serge Korchev was appointed commander of the new company, which expanded with the addition of new people, both from among the Jews and the local population. One of them was a peasant called Missyora. He was a daring fighter who brought a pistol along with him. In order to strengthen our company so that it could start its military operations, we admitted into our ranks every man who could carry arms; Ukrainians, Jews, escaped prisoners of war, and others. Among them also was a Jewish young man by the name of Bakalchuk.

Two weeks later a Jewish woman came to me and said that half an hour before two Jewish boys had come into their shed from Ozyresk, beaten up and terribly wounded. One of them was called Asher Turkenich; I forget the name of the other. The veins of both were cut, and on the bodies of both of them were many wounds. One of them was in critical shape. Asher had fewer wounds.

The two boys, who were about twelve or thirteen years old, had hidden in a shed not far from the village of Ozyresk. Two Ukrainians had detected them there. On a night in December, 1942, when the two boys had lit a small fire for themselves, a Ukrainian forced his way into the shed, caught one of the boys, and started to stab him wildly. When he thought that the boy was dead, he threw him away and rushed at the other, Asher. But Asher succeeded in freeing himself from the murderer before the latter could inflict heavy wounds on him and escaped. The Ukrainian removed the boots from the feet of the near-dead boy and returned to Ozyresk. When Asher returned to the shed about two hours later, he found it in shambles and saw his friend lying in a ditch, covered with snow. He pulled him out of the ditch and, with great effort, dragged himself and his friend to the Jewish camp in the forest.

The partisans badnaged the wounds of the two boys, but in the camp there was neither physician nor medicines. The seriously wounded boy suffered from blood poisoning and after lying unconscious all night, died in the morning. Asher Turkenich recovered, lived to see the day of victory, and today he is in Israel.

I decided to take revenge on the murderer. Leibel Fleischman and Moshe Landau said that they knew the man and were ready to go along with me to the village and show me where he lived.

On the following day, a Sunday, we set out in the direction of Ozyresk, a distance of six kilometers from our camp. We approached the village from the direction of the cemetery without being detected. The Ukrainian lived in the house before the last. All around it was quiet and empty because it was a Sunday, and the villagers had gone to the village center where the Sunday festivities were being held.

I left Fleischman and Landau at the entrance to the murderer's house and slipped quietly inside. I found his old mother and his sister sitting there. They were very frightened when they saw standing before them a partisan, armed with a rifle and a cartridge belt. I warned them not to shout or try to escape and asked them to answer my questions in a low voice, otherwise I would shoot. I asked where the son was. The old woman told me that he was celebrating in the village. I wanted to keep on interrogating her, but at this moment the sister opened a window, jumped out, and started running in the direction of the village center. I ordered her to stop, but she kept running. I realized that the entire operation would fail if I let her alert the villagers, for they would come after me and, upon catching me, would hang me by the foot, as they had done to a prisoner of war who had fallen into their hands, an event which was spoken of a great deal in the forest. I could not lose one single moment, so I shot her in the back. She fell to the ground. But the shot was heard all over the village, and to my ears came the tumult of the approaching crowd. It was then that I decided to set the house on fire. The old woman jumped outside and began to shout. From a distance I saw people running with buckets in their hands. I fired a shot in the air. When the house was in flames, we started running in the direction of the graveyard, about half a kilometer from Ozyresk. On the way we passed through a solitary farm belonging to a peasant, a father of ten. I ordered him to run to the flaming house, and if the old woman's son appeared there, to give me a sign by baring his head. He refused. I threatened that I would kill him together with the members of his family if he did not obey my orders. He agreed to do what I told him provided that the villagers did not learn of it.

From the graveyard we saw everything that was going on in the burning house. A lot of people gathered there in an attempt to put out the fire. Before five minutes had passed I saw the owner of the farm remove his cap from his head. The sign had been given. I stood up and started to run to where the fire was. Young boys and girls who had been placed by the peasants around the house to serve as lookouts and to inform them if they saw partisans coming out of the woods, began to shout: "Partisans!" The crowd dispersed at once. I ran to the farmowner and asked him where the murderer was. He pointed to a young man. I went after him, but the peasants came to his defense, and formed a barrier between us. I fired a few shots. The peasants around him dispersed. He ran into a backyard and hid inside a shed full of chaff, closing the door behind him. Apparently he thought I hadn't seen him. I ran to the shed and burst open the door. The young man stood near the wall and wanted to lunge at me; but I caught him in the chest, holding my loaded rifle in my right hand. He began to plead with me, begging for pardon, and assuring me that he was innocent. At that very moment Fleischman arrived, and I asked him if that was the murderer who had cut up two young boys. "Yes," he answered. At first I wanted to tie the murderer and take him into the forest so the Jews could kill him. But there was no rope around. In the meantime a lot of people had gathered outside. I was afraid that if I stayed there a little longer, I wouldn't be able to leave the place alive. I fired straight into his belly. He slumped to the ground, murmuring: "You have already killed me." But I answered: "No, now I'll kill you so that you will stop killing and robbing other people." I reloaded the rifle, brought the muzzle close to his neck, and, while he was lying there slumped against the wall, I fired again, and the bullet killed him.

Coming out of the shed, I noticed a crowd of peasants closing. I fired above their heads, and they dispersed. All three of us ran back to the forest. The farmowner caught up with me and gave me a bottle of Samogon (a home-made alcoholic drink) to express his thanks for killing that knave. Some time later this peasant was to become our liaison-man.

Next day we ordered the village head to call a gathering of all the local inhabitants to hear an address by the partisan commanders. I was the first to speak. In my speech I warned the villagers that if another murder took place, no matter whether the murdered man was a Jew, a Tartar, a Georgian, or a person of any other nationality, we would put the torch to the entire village and shoot all its inhabitants, irrespective of whether they were guilty or innocent. I ordered them to offer aid to all prisoners of war and to all Jews that happened to reach the village. In this manner I emphasized the national aspect of the Jews in particular.

Before long many Jews were to reach Ozyresk, and the peasants received them with marked hospitality: They fed them and hid them in their homes during the search raids of the German police. The Jews who hid in that village lived to see the day of victory.

Our company had by now grown to a force of eighty fighters, mostly Jewish young men. A short distance from the company, a Jewish family camp was set up in which were grouped all those Jews who could not carry arms. Earth huts were built for them. In order to obtain the necessary equipment, I went out with a number of fighters to the village of Gorodnia where we confiscated from the peasants the Jewish possessions they had looted, loaded them onto three carts, and brought them to the family camp. We also brought along two cows, one for the partisans and the other for the nonfighters.

Gradually our company started its combat operations. We destroyed police stations and killed local inhabitants who had collaborated with the Germans.

* * * * *

...At the beginning of March, 1943, we received the information that a large partisan unit under the command of Feodorov-Rubensky was about to reach our area. Our ground scouts had met theirs. Some time later we received a letter from Feodorov-Rubensky in which he invited the commanders of our company to go over to their camp for talks. The letter was worded almost like an order. Three of our commanders, including myself, went to his headquarters in Zolowa. Feodorov-Rubensky suggested that we join his unit, since, according to an order sent down from Moscow, all the small companies had to be united into one large unit. This union had its advantages. We were formally recognized as partisans, maintaining contact with Moscow and receiving from it arms and ammunition. However, it was agreed that we remain in our present place. From now on our company was to be called the "Voroshilov Company of the Feodorov-Rubensky Unit."

As a result of the union, some changes took place in the command of the company. Company commander Korchev was transferred to the unit headquarters, and his lieutenant, Missyora, was appointed company commander in his place.

Missyora was a local peasant. He was thoroughly familiar with the area, besides being a daring and aggressive partisan. I may point out here that he did not discriminate between his men on the basis of their nationality, and he helped numerous Jews.

As head of the company staff, I was appointed commander of its ground scouts. Korchev who, as already mentioned, was assigned to the unit headquarters, tried to persuade me to move to his quarters so that we could both work together. At that time I got married to the partisan Chaya Landor, and this marriage was not to the liking of Korchev, for he did not want me to get tied down to a family. A number of orders were even issued in connection with my transfer to the unit headquarters, provided that I would leave my wife with the company. For my part, not only did I not agree to be separated from my wife, but I also did not want to leave the Jewish family camp of which I had taken so much care for so long. If I were to accept the transfer to the unit headquarters, I would have been forced to leave for good. In the meantime, strong relations had formed between the Jews of the camp and myself. It took great efforts to stick to my original opinion, and I am happy to point out that the great majority of those Jews survived and are today living in Israel, the United States, and Canada.

Toward the middle of March the company resumed its military operations, now under the command of Missyora. We laid ambush to the Germans on the road running through Gorodnia-Bitovo-Vichevka-Serniky where they moved frequently. We stationed ourselves close to the entrance. At dawn we saw a great number of German soldiers outflanking us on the right and the left. It was clear that someone had warned them. One of my ground scouts, Baruch Menkovsky, who was stationed at the top of the fire-brigade tower in the village, noticed that the Germans were advancing straight to the village. When he informed me of that, I reported the news immediately to Missyora in Vichevka. He felt quite at home at this place and decided to engage the Germans in battle. That was absurd. The Germans had twenty times as many soldiers as we had. They were armed with sub-machine guns and mine throwers and were all around us. From my bitter experience I knew what such a pocket meant. I tried to persuade Missyora that all we had to do at the time was to hold a position near the bridge through which we could withdraw into the forest at any moment. But he would not hear of it, and ordered me to stay at the spot, together with my platoon, which comprised only twenty-five men. I refused to obey the order and moved to a place close to the bridge. Company commander Missyora was angry at me, but he had no choice other than to follow me.

We dug in at a convenient point. To our right and left were marshlands, and the Germans could not mount an attack on us from the rear. Soon we were engaged in a battle which continued all day long. Under cover of darkness we succeeded in withdrawing through the road running between Vichevka and Bitovo. On the way we saw from the direction of Bitovo rockets which lighted the way for the Germans who had been sent to reinforce their colleagues with whom we had been engaged in battle near Vichevka. Without undue delay we laid ambush to the Germans. We lay in the ditches on both sides of the road. When the German carts reached the spot where we were hiding, we opened up at them from a distance of ten meters. In our crossfire many Germans and horses fell. We could not continue the fighting as we were tired out and highly outnumbered; so we returned to the forest, where we stayed for the night. In the morning we went back to the point of the ambush where we found only dead horses, a few rifles, and a pistol. From the cart owners who returned from the battle, we learned that they had picked up twelve dead and twenty-two wounded soldiers.

We returned to base without any casualties, only to be informed by our liaison man in Bitovo that the Germans had returned to the village, grouped the peasants and their children in a circle, poured kerosene on them, and set them on fire. We at once jumped on our horses and galloped to the village. But we were late. The Germans were no longer in the village, and the peasants had turned into cinders. I saw only dismembered bodies. One woman was lying there with her child in her arms, both having been burned together. In this manner, about thirty-five people were burned alive.

In April, 1943, the Germans mounted a massive attack on the village of Svarichivichi, after they had bombed it from the air. We had warned the inhabitants in time of the danger that faced them, and they had succeeded in taking refuge in the forest. The Germans burned down their entire village.

Anti-Semitic Tendencies in the Company

After Feodorov had appointed a new chief of staff and a new commissar for our company, anti-Semitic winds began to blow in its rank. The company consisted, among others, of Jewish girls and Jewish partisans' wives. They were among the first partisans to join the company before its union with Feodorov's unit. The women mainly took care of the cooking and the washing and looked after the wounded.

One day an order was issued by both the chief of staff and the commissar to expel, within twenty-four hours, all the Jewish women and girls from the company. I went down to the staff command and tried to prove to them that the order was unjustified, that the work of the Jewish women was of great benefit for the company, that they were looking after the wounded, and, therefore, no one had the right to expel them from the partisan company and, by so doing, to expose them to certain death. To my regret I realized that my arguments did not make any impression at all. I therefore informed them that I was leaving the company too. The rumor spread at once among the partisans. My scouts joined me, along with some partisans. In all, I had around me twenty-seven people, including the women and the girls.

When night came we left the company, armed only with our rifles. We went deep into the forest. In the morning the company command found out that we had left, and they at once reported to Feodorov's headquarters that I had deserted, together with a group of partisans and had even taken rifles along with us, although they knew all too well that the rifles were our own property. The headquarters sentenced me to death and issued an order to the effect that any partisan could kill me on the spot. Since they knew where to find me, they used to send, day in and day out, a messenger whose task it was to persuade me to go back to the company. I told them that I would go back on the condition that the two anti-Semites who wanted to do me evil were removed. To stay at that place was of course dangerous, and so we left the forest to where the company of "Uncle Petya" was encamped.

The Company of "Uncle Petya"

"Uncle Petya" was a Russian polkovnik* by the name of A.A. Brinsky who was dropped behind enemy lines together with twelve men toward the end of 1942. He organized a partisan company out of escaped prisoners of war who had been hiding in the woods of Manevichi (Maniewicz) in the territory of Rafalofka-Manevichi (Western Ukraine). The entire company did sabotage and demolition operations.

Upon reaching the company of "Uncle Petya" who had heard a lot about me and my scouts, we were admitted into his company without delay. He assigned us to the various groups within his company. I was assigned to the group of Moshe Bromberg of Svarichivichi which specialized in dynamiting operations. The group consisted of twelve men. Within two weeks we succeeded in blowing up three trains carrying German troops and ammuniton on the railway tracks running between Rafalofka and Manevichi.

In May "Uncle Petya" was called back to Moscow to be awarded decorations for his partisans. But before he set out, he filled out a questionnaire concerning my combat operations, and upon his return he brought back a copy of the order to award me the medal "Zabobeya Zaslogy" (for military successes) which was presented to me in Moscow at the end of the war.

In the same month we accomplished a difficult task. We had been assigned the job of blowing up a bridge not far from Manevichi. We divided our men into

---

* Russian army rank equivalent to colonel. "Uncle Petya" is "Dadya Petya" in Russian. (ed.)

two small groups consisting of six fighters each. One of them was ordered to outflank the bridge from the left and the other from the right. The access from the left was covered with a tangle of shrubbery. When the group was within thirty meters from the bridge, it was met by a hail of bullets. The Germans had detected it. The group who had deployed to the right heard the firing and hurried to the bridge to support the other group. A pitched battle followed. The Germans suspected encirclement and withdrew immediately.

To their luck the night was dark, and we could not see the direction of their retreat. In this battle Moshe Bromberg was fatally wounded by a fragment of a hand grenade. When we put Moshe on the cart he was still alive, but he did not survive the rigors of the trip. He was awarded the Order of Lenin posthumously.

The first operation aimed at blowing up the bridge thus ended in failure. A few nights later, however, we repeated the operation and this time succeeded. We even had time to remove the railway tracks.

Some time later I was given a new assignment. "Uncle Petya" appointed me the commander of the guards at the village of Galosy, which was only one kilometer distant from the station of Manevichi. These guards were in charge of all the access roads leading to the company command. In June, 1943, I was asked to report to the command. In the courtyard I met many ground scouts whom I knew from Feodorov's company. I got off the horse and walked in the direction of the village. Here I met Major-General Begma who had arrived in April by plane from Moscow at the partisan landing strip in Lamachichi, bringing along with him many decorations and orders for the partisans in the Ukraine and Beylorussia. He had been appointed chief of staff of all partisan units in these areas.

At the headquarters building I also noticed Korchev, who was standing near "Uncle Petya." I trembled all over but regained my composure immediately, saluted, and informed the general of my arrival. As I was to learn later, Korchev could not reconcile himself to the fact that I had deserted the company for which I had been sentenced to death by the firing squad. However, he had maneuvered the general into coming here in order to get me back into his unit. In answer to the General's questions, I recounted to him all that had happened, pointing out that the expulsion of the Jewish women and girls from the company had resulted from the fact that they did not consent to be the mistresses of the commander. I added that both the commissar and the commander would often send the brothers and husbands of these women on highly dangerous missions. In this manner they endeavored to break their spirit and thus make the women surrender to them. General Begma chided me for not having reported the incident to him directly. To this day I remember the words he said: "I hereby annul the death sentence, and I order you to return to Feodorov's unit." After a talk with "Uncle Petya" I went back to the unit on horseback with my wife. They received me with much joy.

Vanka Moryak

Next morning I was asked to report to the commander at the general staff. Around the table sat Begma, Korchev, Feodorov, and Kysia, the unit commissar. They asked me for the assignment I preferred. My answer was: fighter. On the following day I was asked to fall out of line and, in front of all the fighters, was appointed commander of the ground scouts of the entire unit.

I reorganized the unit. Some of the scouts I transferred to a number of companies, and many men of these companies I took into my group. I made a special effort to transfer into my unit as many Jews as possible. Upon finishing the reorganization of my unit, I was given a new assignment: to go on a sabotage mission with a group of three hundred men under the command of Korchev to the vicinity of Pinsk. In this area I felt quite at home as I had operated there as a partisan in former years.

Upon reaching the place, we found an armed camp comprising eight hundred men. It was under the command of a Russian nicknamed Vanka Moryak. We didn't know what they did exactly. The "Zimlyankas" (dwelling units dug into the ground) they lived in were arranged in wide squares--with furniture and carpets. Among Moryak's men was a Jewish doctor and two Jewish girls who were the mistresses of the commanders. We had come to them in order to use their camp as a base for our operations. But Moryak was soon to inform us that he did not like the idea that in his vicinity partisans would start blowing up trains since the Germans would soon put him under siege. We answered that we had been sent there by a large partisan unit and that the only thing we could do under the circumstances was to move away from his camp.

We went in the direction of the village of Zavishcha. There I was familiar with all the trails, and thus I could lead our group directly through the forest. On reaching a distance of about one kilometer from Moryak's camp, we saw on the roadside a destroyed "Zimlyanka" among an assortment of old objects, groats which were spread all over the place, and a tablespoon. It was evident that no partisans had dwelt here. One could assume that Jews had dwelt in this place and that something had happened to them.

Upon returning from the mission I went up to the Jewish doctor to get from him details about the abandoned "Zimlyanka." At first he wouldn't say anything, but when I revealed to him that I too, was a Jew, he told me that Moryak's men had murdered the Jews who had been living in that deserted place, sparing only him and the two Jewish girls. He spoke in a whisper, as he feared Moryak's men, adding that not far from Zavishcha there still lived some Jews who were hiding from both the Germans and the "Moryaks." On that very day I went to the "Zimlyanka," dug into the ground, and found beside it bodies of men and women strewn all around. They were covered with moss and fresh snow. On the next day, on our way to perform another operation, we saw another "Zimlyanka" about five kilometers from Moryak's camp. At some distance stood a sentry, who began to run away on seeing us. I had four Jews with me, and they called out to him in Yiddish not to run away. He stopped and guided us to the "Zimlyanka" where we found a few men and women and a wounded man lying on the floor. Here is what the wounded men recounted to us: "In this 'Zimlyanka' which was near the camp of the 'Moryaks,' lived thirteen Jews--ten men and three young women. All of them were residents of Yanova. In order to obtain food, they used to wander to the neighboring villages. One day three Moryak men came to the 'Zimlyanka,' including Moustafa, the notorious bandit. They dragged out one Jew some distance from the 'Zimlyanka,' pushed him to the ground and stabbed him to death with their bayonets. In this manner they killed all the Jews who were in the 'Zimlyanka'--one after the other." Even he, the wounded man, they wanted to stab to death. But the bayonet which was aimed at his heart wounded him in the shoulder only, without touching his heart. When he came to, it was already dark. He crawled until he reached this "Zimlyanka," a distance of about five kilometers from the scene of the the murder. At this place lived the Leibovitz family, who took him into the "Zimlyanka," looked after him, and dressed his wounds. Some time later, when Feodorov sent one of his companies to this place under the command of Michael Nadalin, the wounded man was admitted into its ranks to fulfill various missions assigned to him by the company. He met Moustafa a number of times, but did not take revenge on him.

As I learned after the war, the doctor sued both Moryak and Moustafa. But they, in their defense, argued that the Jews had stood in their way on their combat missions. Moryak later worked for the N.K.V.D. (The Leibovitz woman who treated the wounded man and thus saved his life is now living in Israel.)

In the region of Minsk we blew up, on several occasions, the railway tracks running between Pinsk and Brest, attacked police stations, and laid ambushes on the roads. For these operations I received the commendation from the general staff.

The Struggle to Capture the Landing Strip

At that time the military operations centered on this landing strip, not far from the village of Lanchichi. Here landed the planes that brought the partisans arms, ammunition, and various other supplies, and took the wounded back with them. The Germans knew about this landing strip and attacked it, but we resurfaced it after each bombing attack, because it was so vital to us.

After we had returned from the vicinity of Pinsk, I was sent to the landing strip along with a company of ground scouts in order to protect the planes that were to be flying in a great deal of military equipment, including 76-mm field guns. Immediately after the planes had taken off with the wounded, the Germans started a combined operation against the landing strip, from the air and with tanks. The bombardment continued for twenty-four hours. The Germans then entered the village, but they found it in ruins. All the inhabitants had gone into the woods.

In retaliation Feodorov decided to strike at the German garrison in Rakitnoya, which, according to my knowledge, numbered three hundred men. We shelled them all night, but their positions were well fortified. At dawn we were severely attacked by German planes. We had to withdraw. Under a heavy barrage of fire we crossed the river Goryn in the direction of the village of Velyun, but here too we could find no rest. My ground scouts detected in the area Germans who had just arrived in four military trucks. We attacked them immediately and wiped them out, taking only three prisoners. After they had been interrogated through our interpreter, Melech Bakalchuk, all three were handed over to me to be shot. One of them pleaded with me not to kill him, because he had children. I asked him: "Then why do you throw Jewish children into a well alive? I killed them all on the spot.

After this battle we proceeded to Zolotoya, where we massacred a group of Banderavtzim.* The company of Missyora also fought against them. On one occasion, while my company was encamped in the village of Vichevka, it was attacked by the Banderavtzim who wanted to free two German prisoners of war. The partisans, who were taken by surprise in their sleep, ran away to save their lives. The Banderavtzim made a search of the houses and found a Jewish sanitary worker by the name of Matilda who had not had the time to hide. They cut off her breasts, engraved the Magen David sign with a knife on her chest, and hanged her on a stock of wood which had been lying on the ground. In this battle, thirteen partisans were killed. The Banderavtzim took back the two German prisoners, some carts and horses, ammunition and food supplies.

The partisans, for their part, took revenge on the Banderavtzim while the latter were asleep in the forest five kilometers from Gorodnia. The same scene occurred, only this time the partisans had the upper hand.

At this time we attacked an armored train on the railway tracks running between Kovel and Best. Our 45-mm gun succeeded in a second shot to set the train on fire, and this forced the Germans, about thirty soldiers, to jump off it. Being mounted, I attacked them with my ground scouts and finished them off.

---

* Ukrainian nationalists, often Nazi collaborators, who preyed on Soviet partisan and Jew alike. (ed.)

As a result of all these battles, all the German garrisons along the way to Rovno were wiped out.

When the war was over, General Begma offered that I stay on in Rovno and serve as chairman of the urban committee on physical culture. I went to Kiev, where I received the necessary certificate and started to work. About two months later I was invited to see Korchev, deputy chairman of the district committee. He confided to me that before long, all Jews would be removed from important positions. To his pleasant surprise, however, I showed him my identity card in which my registered name was Abugov, Alexander Layontievich, a Russian. Under Korchev's recommendation I was soon to be transfered to the district committee on physical culture. That had a real advantage in those days--the chairman of the district committee was excused from military service.

The conditions of the Jews went from bad to worse. Jews were dismissed from the postions of factory managers and from other enterprises. My wife's family and all my brothers-in-law, who had been with me in the partisan unit, began to talk me into leaving the Soviet Union, especially when it was possible to go to Poland as repatriates. In the beginning I was against the idea, but later on I decided to try my luck and leave Russia, for which I had done and fought so much.

After many wanderings through Poland, Czechoslovakia, Austria, and Italy, we finally arrived in Israel in 1949.

THE PARTISAN FILMMAKER

A. Savitch

For one entire year Michael Glieder fought in the partisan camps under the command of Major-General Alexei Feodorov and also at the camp of High Commander Sidor Kovpak.

In describing his life as a daring fighter, Feodorov wrote:

"Comrade Glieder, fighting shoulder-to-shoulder with other fighters behind enemy lines, accomplished his missions with great success, attacked enemy companies as a fighter while also fulfilling his duty as a photographer. In his active participation in blowing up railway tracks which served for German transportation, he sometimes came as close as fifty paces from the tracks and there lay in ambush for the German train and all the soldiers and ammunition it was carrying, in order to see with his own eyes its approach and explosion and to photograph the entire event at once."

Sidor Kovpak describes Michael Glieder both as a photographer and a fighter:

"Michael Glieder demonstrated extraordinary heroism at the camp. He also did a highly significant work by directing his camera at the combat activities of the camp, as well as at the acts of cruelty of the Germans against the peaceful population. Documentary evidence is attached to his work as a battlefield photographer. He was also a courageous fighter against the German enemy. On May 12, 1943, during one of the hardest battles, he stayed at the forefront all the time, organized the crossing of the camp over the river Pripet, and served as an example to the other comrades. At the same time fighter Glieder filmed with his movie camera the accomplishment of this difficult and dangerous task." (From Einekeit, June, 15, 1944)

* * * * *

The first year of the war of the fatherland and half of the second year were spent by Michael Glieder, a movie-technician, in the Red Navy. In March, 1943, he was called to Moscow to make a documentary film on the activities of the partisan movement. The man required for the job had to be deeply familiar with the Ukraine. Without asking many questions, Glieder agreed to drop over the combat area of a partisan company behind enemy lines. He did not reveal, however, that he had never dropped by parachute before and that he had only seen it done by others. Thus, Michael Glieder was to arrive in Sidor Kovpak's famous unit.

The unit was having a very hard time. The Germans had surrounded it and were endeavoring to drive it into the triangle between the Pripet and the Dnieper rivers. The partisans attempted a breakthrough by crossing the railway tracks. That was the first partisan battle in which Glieder took part. As he could not do any filming in the dark, he fought as an ordinary soldier. The breakthrough did not succeed. The partisan forces were heavily outnumbered. Kovpak decided to cross the Pripet, and the preparations for the crossing went on all through the night. At this point the width of the river was two hundred and forty meters. The current was so strong that a temporary bridge could not meet the requirements, as it had also to withstand the passage of fieldguns, vehicles, and food supplies. All went into the cold water. The bridge was almost ready, but the ropes did not hold. Then Glieder remembered how bridges of this kind were thrown over the River Amur, and he suggested that wedges be driven into the bottom of the river and fastened with wires so that each beam should have its own supporting point. After that had been accomplished, the bridge was ready by dawn. The partisans carried the loads and the field guns safely across. When the Germans eventually realized what was going on, the partisans had put some distance between them and the bridge.

A few days later Glieder filmed the historical discussions between the commanders and commissars of the five largest partisan brigades in the Ukraine, with the participation of the secretary of the Communist central comittee, D.S. Korochenko, and the chief of staff of the Ukrainian partisan movement, Major-General Strokach. Some time later Glieder was attached to the unit of A.P. Feodorov.

Feodorov's was a fastmoving unit. Its men marched for sixteen hours on end. On their way they saw villages which the Germans had put to the torch. Here it was not the local population that provided food supplies for the partisans. On the contrary. It was the partisans that gave the inhabitants food from their own provisions. After the unit had defeated a German garrison in a battle in which Glieder took part, both as fighter and cameraman, it proceeded to the region around the railway tracks running between Kovel and Sarni. It was necessary to disrupt in this region all German communication lines which carried troops and arms to the front. Once the partisans were encamped in the forest, they at once went out on sabotage missions.

Glieder wanted to film at any cost an actual blowing up of a train by the partisans. Twelve times he went out on missions which resulted in ten blown-up trains, but only once did he succeed in filming such an event. In the meantime he had turned into a remarkable photographer of sabotage activities under the guidance of such a skilled artist as Pavlov, hero of the Soviet Union. The explosions shot by Glieder from a distance of sixty meters from the embankment have remained unique in the annals of movie photography.*

Feodorov's men fulfilled their mission: they totally stopped all enemy movement in their region, and the Germans were thus forced to send reinforcements through Rumania. No night passed without demolition explosions. Feodorov was proud of his saboteurs. People used to say that German trains "run only with their wheels upwards." In the intervals between one sabotage operation and another, Glieder filmed the everyday life of the company. He succeeded in shooting some four thousand pictures.

With the approach of winter the partisans started digging pits for the camp earth huts. But the Germans surrounded the camp and forced them to leave the place, cross the river Styr, and engage in battle. The Germans bombed the surrounding woods in their search for Feodorov's people. Along with the unit fighters, there was a civilian camp made up of Ukrainians and Poles who had been saved from certain death.

In the meantime Glieder learned how to lay mines and to read traces; he learned everything: the tactics

---

* His films rest in the archives of the Lenin State Library in Moscow. (ed.)

of partisan warfare, reconnaissance work, how to build earth huts without using nails, and, also, the art of interrogating German prisioners.

* * * * *

Not everyone who took part in the prolonged events of the partisan war remembers all the details necesary for recreating a vivid picture of past happenings. The power of observation, a phenomenal memory, and the diary he kept helped Glieder in postwar days to write an excellent book on Feodorov's unit.* In this book he gives a detailed account of how the partisans celebrated at their camp on the 7th of November, 1943, the First of May, and Red Army Day; and how they received the new year, 1944. He describes the celebrations, the parades, the evening of "personal activities." In his book on the battles and the sabotage operations, Glieder does not forget to give the accounts of individual fighters who contributed their share toward the final victory. He delineated a pageant of vivid partisan characters, their commanders, and their commissars: Kovpak, Feodorov, Rodniyev, Drozhinin, and others. On roads, sabotage missions, and in newly liberated population centers, the partisans met many civilian citizens, rural and urban, old and very young, men and women. The great suffering that fell to the people's lot under the yoke of the German invaders did not destroy the belief in the victory to come. In each and every place young people and adults joined the partisan camp. The women were ready to give everything they had to feed the fighters, and the children did all they could to help along. When the Red Army front was approaching Feodorov's region of operations, it was decided to move the wounded across the front line, along with the sick and the "civilian camp." But it turned out that the wounded and the sick did not want to be separated from their companies. They had made fast friends among their comrades, and they had been dreaming of one ceaseless struggle until victory was achieved. Even some of the civilians found it difficult to be separated from the main force; they were leaving their saviors behind enemy lines.

---

* See his memoirs, <u>Skinoapparatom v tylu vraga</u> (With a Motion Picture Camera in the Rear of the Enemy), Moscow: Gosknoizdat, 1947. (ed.)

All these situations were captured by Glieder on his movie film.

Glieder succeeded in shooting a particularly spectacular event: In January, 1944, a Red Army patrol penetrated for the first time into Feodorov's region of activities in order to establish contact with the partisans. Naturally both the Red Army soldiers and the partisans were apprehensive of a possible mistaken identity and thus gingerly approached each other. But when the partisans saw the stars on the headgear of the strangers and recognized the Soviet automatic rifles, they fell into each other's arms shouting, "Comrades, dear comrades!" Then the Soviet troops embraced the partisans, and the latter hugged the welcome Red Army soldiers. Many wept. The tears disturbed Glieder the photorapher.

The Red Army soldiers and officers spent the night at the unit's headquarters. They were fed well. The partisan girls washed their underclothes. In the evening a concert was given in their honor.

However, it was not easy for Feodorov's men to be united with the Soviet army. The days of ordinary activities returned to the partisans: blowing up of railway tracks, roadside ambushes, insignificant skirmishes. Unexpected rains came in that season of the year. The earth huts were wet, and it was impossible to move along the roads. The last large-scale operation in which Glieder participated took place in 1944, on the twenty-sixth anniversary of the Soviet army. On that night the partisans noiselessly dispatched the front guards of the Germans and entered the village of Nesokoyzishieh where there was a great concentration of enemy forces. The battle was long and hard. The partisan ground scouts were heavily outnumbered by the Germans, some of whom were firing from stone-built houses and properly sited firing positions. Nevertheless, only a few scores of Germans came out alive. About one thousand German soldiers and officers were either killed or taken prisoner. Feodorov's men captured enemy storehouses full of military equipment.

Following that battle the partisans made a breakthrough to their camp, reaching it after twelve days. They marched only in the dark, covering about forty kilometers in a single night. The Germans tried to follow them, and enemy planes dropped bombs on the roads and forests lying on their path. But the partisans arrived safely back at their camp, bringing all their wounded along with them.

In March, 1944, Feodorov and unit commissar Drozhinin were called back to the center in Kiev. Glieder crossed the front line back to Moscow. His photographs were published in scores of movie journals. They were included in the movie on the Ukraine produced by Duzhenko and went into movies on the partisans which were produced by Beliyev.* But in Moscow Glieder was to hear of his great tragedy, his only son, his brother, and his son-in-law were among those who fell at the front.

Before long Glieder accepted an offer to go out to the Slovak Corps: Producer Kupalin was shooting a film on Czechoslovakia. Thus Glieder was to become the movie-technician of the second brigade of the paratrooper air force. He filmed the brigade in training and, later, its first battle near the Polish village of Pelniya. In this battle Glieder pulled out from under a hail of enemy fire eighteen wounded, a field gun, and four vehicles.

At the same time an insurrectin broke out in the Slovak army which had been set up by the Germans and its quisling government. A "liberated zone" was formed near the towns of Banska, Bistritza, and Zbulin. The front command thus sent the second brigade of the paratrooper air force to aid the insurgents.

The first group with which Glieder flew landed safely in the liberated zone. But owing to bad weather, there was som edelay in airlifting the entire brigade. In the meantime the situation of the insurgents was worsening. The area under their control was not large enough and the insurgents were still inexperienced soldiers under equally inexperienced commanders.

The German attack was not late in coming. The brigade was moved into battle one part at a time, and so its full force was not brought to bear on the enemy. In the first encounters the insurgents had the upper

---

* Again, it is a private hope of the editor that one day, these films will be available to Western audiences. (ed.)

hand, but the Germans received great reinforcement, including airplanes. A great panic spread among the insurgents, and gaps began to show in the front itself. Elements of the brigade and the partisans put up a heroic fight, but they did not have the strength to withstand the pressure exerted by the enemy. The Germans captured Bansky Stiyabnitza. It was then necessary to leave the "liberated zone."

All the roads were blocked with numberless troops and refugees who had escaped from the advancing Germans. The road was hard and mountainous. The Germans bombed the roads with singular ferocity and disrupted all communications between the units that stood in their way.

In the tumult of retreat, brigade commander Prikaril called Glieder to him and said: "Although I am a veteran soldier and have seen no few battles in my life, I am not familiar with partisan war tactics. We are now expecting a highly unusual war, far beyond our strength. You are the only one among with the necessary experience. There is no other way but for you to take part both in command and in tactical operations."

The brigade numbered only one hundred and twenty fighters at the time. It was mandatory to move them away from the battlefield at once as the Germans were by now close at their heels. Glieder buried his movie camera in the ground. A difficult forced march began over the mountainous terrain, but a heavy downpour saved our lives by making it difficult for the Germans to bomb the retreating forces. The going was singularly tough over those steep hills with the arms and food supplies. The horses fell down. On our way we met soldiers from other units. They joined the retreating column.

At long last, high up on some mountain peak, in the earth hut of the commander of the partisan company, a meeting was held between the brigade commanding staff and the headquarters of the partisan movement in Slovakia, with the participation of members of the Czechoslovak parliament. In the course of discussions it was decided that the brigade should serve as a combat unit. Its commander was advised to take in troops from other units, besides volunteers from the civilian population, and switch to partisan tactics. Glieder was appointed commissar of the brigade. There was no time for arguments. Glieder said: "Thanks for the honor and your faith in me" and went straight to work.

The brigade by now numbered five hundred and sixty fighters and thirty-two officers. Glieder addressed them briefly. In his speech he did not try to hide from them the difficulties of the struggle ahead and asked all those who had doubts, fears, or misgivings to fall out of line. No one budged.

Once again they headed for the mountains, which were now clothed in thick fog and swept by strong winds. The fighters slipped, fell down, rose to their feet, and later rested and warmed themselves by the fire. The Germans cordoned off all the villages that lay in the valleys to prevent the brigade from passing through them. One battalion was instructed to move in another direction. The partisans had to eat their remaining horses; and as they had almost run out of bread, each one was given only one hundred grams.

The only way out was through the high mountain of Khabenyech with its permanent cap of snow. They kept on the ascent under a hail of fire. Snow kept falling. Strong winds threw the marchers down as they walked. Their clothes were covered with sheets of ice. But they did not come down from the peaks. They let the wind erase their footsteps behind them.

Then the descent into the valley began. Even now the people would slip and fall. Glieder felt that he could not move one step farther. He was saved by a soldier called Sidor, who pushed a stick into the commissar's hands and pulled him behind him. They crossed a number of streams and rivulets. In the dark the people fell into icy water. Parliament member Schvirman was exhausted from the effort and passed away in the valley.

The main column suffered relatively few casualties, but out of the second group, which numbered one hundred and three persons, only twenty reached the valley. The rest froze on the way. All the survivors had their weapons with them.

The people stopped at a mine known by the name of Lum. Down below spread the villages of Dolniya and Gorniya Legota. The commander sent a group of partisans to these villages to fetch some food supplies, and the vilagers gave them generous amounts of food. The next day another partisan group blew up two tankers at the Lupei station, captured a seed storehouse in the village, and handed the stock to the villagers.

New groups of soldiers and volunteers from the nearby villages kept joining the brigade. Glieder held talks with representatives of the local authorities. All were on the side of the people. Armed battalions quickly formed in the villages. The local population provided the brigade with food supplies and gave its commanding staff valuable information.

On several occasions the Germans announced that the brigade had been beaten, that it had dispersed, but at the same time they put up a reward of half a million Kronen on the heads of commanders Prikrila and Glieder. Once, when all the battalions had gone out on missions in various directions and the brigade headquarters were left without cover, the Germans mounted a sudden attack on them. A fire exchange ensued. The Germans were only twenty meters from Glieder's earth hut, and so we had to escape into the forest. Luckily, we suffered no casualties.

On the following day the command staff succeeded in joining one of the battalions. But the joy was shortlived. The Germans repeated their attack, and once again we had to move away. A few officers tried to persuade the commander and the commissars to stop the struggle. The answer was a categorical "No!" To turn a regular army brigade into a partisan one is no easy matter. This was particularly difficult for the officers, who had been taught according to the old school of strategy and tactics. The brigade command staff demanded operations that were usually carried out behind enemy lines. To bring together dispersed, temporary units, with mostly incomplete cadres into one army unit at combat level, whose duty it was to spearhead the battle of the people in that region, was not easy.

The brigade headquarters were now stationed in an isolated hut high in the mountains. Communications were gradually established with all the units, and provisions were supplied regularly. The local inhabitants helped in everything. They succeeded in establishing contact with the patriots in the neighboring towns, including the people of Bratislava. The runners became everyday heroes in their devoted work. Many presents were received from the local population for Christmas.

In one village the presents were collected openly, ostensibly for the German troops, and then delivered to the brigade. The Germans were then told that the partisans had attacked the vehicle that was carrying the gifts to them.

With the help of the brigade, a resistance movement was organized against the Germans in various settlements. The headquarters had contacts with twenty-one local authorities and ten underground armed organizations. On the first of January, 1945, the brigade comprised three full battalions. There were enough arms for all the fighters.

The healing of the wounded was a serious problem. The brigade medic, Regach, went about in the mountains endeavoring to visit the huts of all the units. The wounded and the sick were sent to the hospital at Podbriozovo. Hospital doctor Robert Kristik, an enthusiastic patriot, hid the partisans and treated them as he did the local residents.

* * * * *

At the conference of party workers in the district of Brezhno, where reports were presented of the activities of the armed battalions, and a discussion was held of the ways to be followed for stepping up the resistance of the people and integrating it with that of the brigade, Glieder represented the fighting forces. The meeting was held in the forest, at a distance of two kilometers from the German guards. Among the delegates there was also the priest Bartel who fought the Germans with a rifle in his hand within the ranks of one of the brigade's battalions. On the day the conference was held, the brigade saboteurs derailed a German train, attacked another one, and thus disrupted train traffic at the station of Leovyetova.

In the meantime the Red Army was approaching the region of the brigade's operations. On quiet nights one could hear the rumblings of the field guns. The Germans were getting ready for evacuating the region. In early Febrary, 1945, the brigade was thrown into the battle front. The need for ground scouts and runners was so great that Regach, the medic, did runner missions. The same medic would write down a summary of the news items sent by the Sovinformburo (The Soviet News Agency) and duplicate them. On the first of February, 1945, the first battalion of the brigade engaged in battle a large German unit and succeeded in wiping them out. That was a battle to remember.*

Fearing that the brigade might strike at their rear, the Germans made several attempts to defeat it before it withdrew from this region. They failed in their efforts to do so and were forced to station there strong units of guards made up of frontline troops against the "town people." After the Soviet Army had advanced so close as to make possible a coordination of operations with the brigade, one battalion after the other joined the battle against the enemy.

Some time later an order was received from the commander of the Czechoslovak corps instructing us to cross the front line. The order was carried out without any special difficulties. The high command of the Soviet army and the Czechoslovak corps, which had no accurate information about the brigade, could not rely on the latter's fighting ability. It was therefore surprised to see before it a full-fledged combat brigade. General Sbovoda embraced both Prikila and Glieder and said: "Thank you, thank you! God bless you!" Glieder informed him with some excitement that the brigade command had promoted and demoted a few officers, perhaps without being authorized to do so. Answered the general: "I confirm all your orders!"

* * * * *

Glieder's mission had come to an end. The frequent treks throughout the mountains had affected his health. For a long time he lay ill; but on recovering, he went back and dug out his movie camera from its hiding place. It still contained the film with the pictures he had taken before he had gone back to the role of partisan.

His photographs were integrated into the movies: "The War Day," "Our Moscow," "Avengers of the People," "The Ukraine in Its Struggle," "Czechoslovakia." Together with the director, Glieder received an award for the the picture "Avengers of the People." A great honor was bestowed on him: he filmed the parade at Red Square.

---

* It was also in all likelihood one of their last, for the war was to end in several months. (Ed.)

Michael Glieder, the gifted movie-technician, daring and courageous partisan, justifiably carries on his chest a chain of orders and decorations, both Soviet and Czechoslovak.

WOMEN SPIES

Gregory Linkov ("Batya")

Hero of the Soviet Union, "Polkovnik,"*
Soviet Partisan Commander

On his way back from a combat mission, Commander
Anatoly Tsiganov brought along with him seven new
fighters, including two women. One was young and
beautiful, so everyone called her "The Bride." Tsiganov
said that the new fighters had helped his company raze
two farmsteads and a large alcohol factory with a
considerable stock of products for the invaders.

I had a great liking for Anatoly Tsiganov since
the time of our joint activities behind enemy lines. I
took his words serously. This time his company had
fulfilled with great success the combat mission which
had been assigned to it between Baranovich and Minsk,
with the active participation and daring acts of the
two women fighters. According to him "The Bride" had
done outstanding work. The other women had taken part
in disarming the guards on the farmstead in the region
of Nisvizh and proved to be quite a good fighter.

But I was not convinced by the proof that Tsiganov
adduced concerning the fighting ability of the two
women. The Hitlerites at that time were doing their
best to find out the partisan bases, and for that purpose they used mainly women. Women spies could reach
us only as members of partisan companies, where they
had been accepted as loyal members after they had concealed all their contacts with the Gestapo. The participation of women in razing a farmstead and an alcohol
factory which had already been in the hands of the
fascists was not proof enough of their loyalty to the
partisans. In order to gain full confidence, one had
to do something of great importance against the
invaders.

I gave orders that I wanted to see the papers that
the women had carried on them, if there were any such
papers at all, and also to check up on certain bio-
graphical details concerning them. In the evening two

---

* Russian equivalent of colonel. (ed.)

passports were brought to me, one bearing the name of Yelizavita Vassilevna Alexova and the other bearing the name of Vera Shamenskaya. The two passports had been issued in Minsk at the beginning of 1942, that is, seven months before they came to us. Alexova was registered as a Russian and Shamenskaya as a Pole. I also learned that both spoke good German. It was presumed that Alexova had worked as an interpreter for the Hitlerites.

I could not sleep all night for fear that women spies had come into our partisan base. In the morning I made up my mind that I should not have any suspicions concerning the validity of my doubts. Accompanied by a few handpicked young men, I went toward Alexandrov's position where all the "newcomers" were grouped together. I had decided to talk with them, interrogate them thoroughly before issuing the order to have them executed.

The first one to be called into the earth hut was Alexova. I asked her to tell me how she had found her way to the partisans. I listened to what she was saying every now and then. She spoke in a quiet, composed manner while she related to me the story of her life. She gave details of her work for the fascist commander in Minsk as an interpreter and how she had decided after a quarrel with him to run away to the partisans in the forest, a thing which she did at the first opportunity.

Her words gave me the impression that she was lying all along. I could not make up my mind. "To hell," I said to myself. "Doesn't this girl think that she is endangering herself by giving such evidence?" Perhaps all of this was a skilled move played by an accomplished woman spy who knew how to treat her own life with indifference?

While listening to Alexova I did not ask any questions and did my best to give her the impression that I was satisfied with the story she was relating to me.

"Well, you may go now and do whatever you like," I told her, and I let here leave my earth hut.

Alexova went out. I gave the order to bring in Shamenskaya. I also ordered that upon her entering the earth hut, Alexova was to be arrested at once.

Shamenskaya sat calmly in front of me as Alexova had done before her.

"Tell me, please, how did you get here," I asked her, looking straight into her eyes.

The woman was disturbed. I had the impression that she was considering what to say and what to hide. I waited with patience for everything she had to say:

"I am Shamenskaya, Vera Mikilovna, from Poland," the second woman started slowly. "Till the war broke out and during the war, I had been living in Minsk. When the Hitlerites came to our town I did not know where to go. Many Germans knew Polish, and I knew a little German, so I had no difficulty in finding a job as a waitress at a restaurant."

I listened to her without moving my eyes from her lips.

"Once," she went on, "I had a quarrel with the manager of the restaurant. Because of that I was fired. On the same night I ran away into the woods to the partisans."

"How long were you in the woods together with Alexova?" I asked.

The woman cast a frightened glance at me. "We... we...were together for about six months."

"Perhaps you could tell me something about this woman?"

Shamenskaya's tension mounted. To go on lying was dangerous. Feeling uncomfortable, she blushed and became increasingly excited.

"I don't know this woman at all, and I cannot tell you anything about her," said Shamenskaya, fighting her inner feelings.

"Well, then, it is all clear to me now. I'll have both of you shot," I said very quietly.

Shamenskaya stood up in consternation. The soldier who was standing at the entrance to the earth hut aimed his rifle at her. The woman paled and clung to the wall, her strength ebbing. I made a move to leave.

"Comrade Commander, allow me to add a few words to what I have just told you," Shamenskaya said calmly.

"Speak," I stopped, waiting for her confession and the self-incrimination of the spy who got caught in the cobweb of her lies.

"Pardon me, Comrade Commander, but all that I have told you is one big lie," she said and began to sob. "I...we...thought that everything would be all right as it has been so far...but now I realize that I shouldn't keep on doing this...both of us, this young woman and I, are Jewesses...."

Without realizing it, the soldier lowered his rifle.

"She is a distant relative of mine, and I can tell you a lot about her. Everything. All I have told you has been due to the fact that our passports are false."

This announcement made me mad. I wanted to curse her, but I restrained myself.

"And how can you prove that you are a Jewess?"

"Among your men are three Jews, and if you will allow me to talk to them, they will testify that both of us are Jewish women."

"How do you know that we have three Jewish comrades here?"

"Can't anyone tell that they are Jews?"

At the position commanded by Alexandrov there really were three Jewish fighters, but one couldn't tell by the looks of two of them that they were Jews. Only I knew that they were Jews.

"Well," I said, "let it be as you say."

Commander Shlikov was instructed accordingly. A few minutes later the three testified that the two women were Jewish and that they had run away from the ghetto of Minsk into the woods. This evidence, of course, did not assuage my suspicions. Indirectly we checked up on them in the ghetto of Minsk, including their deeds in the battlefield. The facts proved that they had told the truth.

PART FOUR:

PARTISAN WARFARE

DAVID KAIMACH

Gregory Linkov ("Batya")
Hero of the Soviet Union, "Polkovnik,"*
Former Commander of a Partisan Unit

I was appointed commander of a paratrooper company. Although this company had already undergone
special training, I still had a host of worries, chief
among which was the absence of a political commissar.

September, 1941. I am traveling by streetcar in
the blacked-out streets of Moscow. I am trying to
think of a man who would fit the role of commissar,
sifting and weighing the qualifications of Communists I
know. I was reviewing an imaginary list of names, but
the role of commissar, which is essentially a difficult
and responsible one, calls for specific traits and
qualities.

Suddenly I feel a piercing gaze directed at me,
and before I had time to look around, I heard a voice
saying: "Gregory Matvievich, why haven't we been
seeing you of late; where've you been hiding?"

A young, tall man with dark hair and black eyes
gives me a warm handshake.

"David, it's so good that we've met! How're
things going at our laboratory?"

David Kaimach and I were both engineers. Until
recently we had been working together in a science
laboratory. We both had a record of Party work too.

"What's this talk about the lab?" David said
sadly. It's still there. Nothing has changed much
with us. Even the enemy bombs are obligingly missing
us. But sitting home is no easy matter. I believe
that my place is at the front. I don't feel like
working at the lab these days."

I looked into David's face with great interest.
Like him, I had had the same feeling in the early days
of the war.

---

* Russian equivalent of colonel. (ed.)

"Is it correct, Gregory Matvievich, that you have been appointed commander of a paratrooper company?" Kaimach inquired in a low voice.

"It is correct!"

David looked at me, a hint of jealousy in his eyes, and said: "How lucky!"

Suddenly I had an idea! This is the man I've been looking for--our political commissar.

"David, would you join my company as commissar?"

"I?" For some time he was deep in thought. "You aren't joking?"

"Is there anything to joke about here?"

"Then I'd gladly accept the offer. Do I have to send in an application?"

"Questions of this kind cannot be solved on a streetcar. Here's my phone number, and if you don't change your mind, ring me up three days from now."

David called me three days later and told me that he was accepting the offer to join my company.

I notified my immediate superiors. I told them about David, the man, his traits and qualifications, and asked their permission to have him appointed political commissar of my company. A few days later David appeared at the company barracks, happy and proud of the confidence we had shown him. I, too, was glad of the fact that he had joined us--I was about to set out on a long and difficult road.

I had known David for a long time. He was the son of a tailor from Odessa. At sixteen he had joined the Komsomol, was active at the trade association, and, later was a delegate to the municipal council of Odessa. In 1929 he was admitted into the Party as a student at the Institute for Machinery and Construction in Moscow. On receiving his degree he did postgraduate studies at the Institute and later became scientific assistant at one of the faculties there. I knew his curriculum vitae as well as I knew my own. An excellent worker, a good and sensitive friend, an ideal family man. Now we were once again to work together under difficult conditions of war behind enemy lines. I could not have wished myself a better commissar.

On the night of September 17, 1941, our company was airlifted in seven cargo planes heading for the front. We didn't make it this time. Heavy rain and a strong head wind stood in our way. The paratroopers could not jump according to plan. Tens of kilometers apart, one from the other, many fell straight into the hands of the enemy punishment squads and, in their first encounter with them, died a hero's death. David Kaimach and I also landed a considerable distance from each other.

For twelve days I had to wander alone in the woods and the inhabited areas, looking for my men and my commissar. At the same time David was trying to locate me, accompanied by a small group of paratroopers.

With the approach of autumn, the trees lost their leaves and shrubbery became sparse. There were long spells of rain. Behind us, like a shadow, doggedly moved the German punishment squads. We made ceaseless efforts to locate the remainder of the men, sustained by boundless stubbornness and our belief in the rightness of our cause. One evening, while I was sitting in the hut of a Beylorussian farmer, the door flew wide open and Kaimach appeared. Wearing a tattered and soiled shirt, with a wild growth of hair, tired out, he fell into my arms, beaming with joy. Peering from behind him was a young man, a physical training instructor by the name of Sakharov.* We embraced each other warmly, shedding tears of joy. From that moment on we were together once again, now behind enemy lines. We had no contact with Moscow. Almost without any military equipment, we nonetheless were strong in spirit, as we had to keep up the fight against the enemy. We started organizing the company in the woods. At the spot to which Kaimach later took me, there were about ten people from Moscow and some thirty men, local inhabitants who had been recruited by the commissar in the course of his wanderings.

---

* Probably <u>no</u> relation to the Soviet dissident Andrei D. <u>S</u>akharov, the noted physicist and father of the Russian A-bomb. (ed.)

Many of the inhabitants of the neighboring villages wanted to join the company. But there were all around us people who had betrayed the motherland, who had sold themselves to the enemies of the partisans and had even begun to serve as their secret agents. It is no easy matter to look into the soul of a person and to know his true identity. But we had to know who was for us and who was against us. In those difficult days of getting the company organized, Kaimach fulfilled his job with an unusual sense of responsibility. He had an uncanny knack for looking through people and telling a great deal about their character and personal qualities. It was an easy matter for him to ferret out provocateurs and secret agents who attempted to infiltrate our lines. He never misjudged a new fighter who joined the company: "This man is on our side; you can trust him," he would say.

David Kaimach had a liking for youth. At the camp when he was resting, he would be surrounded by groups of young people who loved him too and confided their deepest secrets to him. He knew when to have a talk with a person and when to give encouragement. Among the youth he looked young himself, laughing unreservedly, his eyes beaming, his cheeks crimson with excitement.

In the fall and winter of 1941 the Germans pretended to be settling down for a prolonged period in the occupied territories. Our scouts came back from a neighboring village with the unsettling news that the Germans were building a schoolhouse there.

"A schoolhouse? Impossible!" said David. "Who told you they were building a schoolhouse?"

"All the people are talking about it. All the villagers," retorted the excited fighter. "Comrade Commissar! The Germans have announced that a school is to be built in the village so that our children will be taught the German language. The announcement has been officially made through the head of the village. They are building schools in other villages too. In the village of Rodnay (Beylorussia) the foundations have already been laid. It follows that these creeps intend to stay here for good."

"No, someone has misunderstood the facts," said Kaimach. "For the present the Germans cannot afford it. Their attack has caused them great difficulties."

Kaimach asked me for permission to go out to the village. Accompanied by the reconnaissance men who had brought the news, he went out to Rodnay under cover of darkness and returned quite pleased.

"Well, I knew it. It's not a school. Only a stronghold. That's what the Germans are building. In some places they are laying brick foundations for their heavy artillery--the Germans are unsure of their position in these places, and they are getting ready to defend themselves."

Kaimach sat down and wrote a leaflet to this effect. The men had it duplicated and distributed in the surrounding villages.

The days passed. We had succeeded in organizing a company made up of 120 fighters. We kept wandering in the woods from one base to another, harassing the Germans with our daring surprise attacks. So far these had been only small scale operations; however, we managed to saw through the beams of a bridge which fell apart under the weight of a German tank; here and there we assassinated a fascist mercenary, the head of a village or townlet or a collaborating policeman; we cut off the telegraph wires; we lay in ambush along a road. The blowing up of a large bridge on the River Essa, on the road between Lepel and Borisov (Vitebsk and Minsk regions) finally drew the Germans' attention to us. So they sent a battalion of field soldiers, heavily equipped with artillery and mortars. We now had to withdraw to a valley full of marshes. For hours on end we had to wade, waist-deep, in cold water, which was covered with a thin layer of ice, holding our weapons up in the air and carrying the wounded on our shoulders. Thoroughly wet and freezing with cold, we finally reached a dry island where we could make camp fires to get warm and dry.

The three of us--David, the local chief of staff, and myself--held a council of war and decided to divide the company into two parts: one would be led by me back to our former base in the woods of Koubaleibichi (Beylorussia) and the other would be led by David to a well-guarded point in an impassable terrain in the direction of Lake Falik (Beylorussia). After the decision was made, we hugged each other and said goodbye. Who knows, we might never see each other again.

I gave my men the order to set out on our way, and we were soon once again waist-deep in the icy marsh water. Evening came. David, the light of the campfire dancing eerily on his face, sat tense, staring in my direction. When he saw that he had caught my attention, he took off his hat. Again I wondered at the sublime patriotic feeling of this man, who had left behind a nice job, a loving wife, and beloved son--all that so he could go through freezing marshes to a cruel struggle and perhaps even get killed.

At the first village we reached after coming out of the marshes, the people told us that the entire region was full of German soldiers. Two divisions, one of them having been pulled back from the front to rest and regain its strength, were all over the place. It was beyond our power to fight them. As it was, the Germans had already cut us off from the men who had supplied us with useful bits of information, arms, military equipment, and provisions. We were surrounded by fascist forces bent on annihilating us at any price.

While wandering through the woods, I began sending runners to Kaimach's base. Two groups, each made up of five fighters, were killed on the way. Some days later, while patroling the area with my company, I came upon the body of fighter Sakharov, loved by one and all, who had fought it out with the Germans to his last breath. Beside him lay the body of Chappai, his closest friend.

The third group we sent out for reconnaissance came back to report that our base at Lake Falik had been destroyed and that bodies of partisans were strewn around it in the snow. The local villagers gave contradictory accounts about Kaimach. One said that he had been killed in a fight with the Germans, another asserted that, together with a handful of fighters, he had broken through the German encirclement and escaped through the front line.

It would be difficult to describe all the hardships of that first winter in the woods. Often it occurred to me that we had better cross over to our main forces and then drop once again behind enemy lines, reinforced by a new company, with a transmitter and new military equipment. However, I dismissed this idea. After every attack, which cost us some of our best men, we went out once again on the roads, blew up bridges, sniped at the "Fritzes,"* and cut telegraph wires.

Our base in the woods of Koubaleibichi was named "Vainkomat" (military center), on account of the great number of farmers who came to it wishing to join the company in the fight against the hated enemy. Despite the German atrocities (which were aimed at terrorizing the inhabitants), despite the deep snow and the ambushes along the roads, we continued our raids on enemy units, thanks to the splendid relations we had with the people in the surrounding villages, relations long since established by Commissar David Kaimach. In the meantime we were getting low on ammunition and were totally out of explosives to use for mining the access roads. Our raids on the Germans had to be cut down accordingly.

In March, 1942, our fighters came back from patrol duty to report that they had come across a group whose men were well dressed and equipped with automatic weapons. The men called themselves guerrilla fighters and expressed their desires to establish contact with our company. At first I suspected this to be a trap set by the Gestapo. A few days later, however, I found out that the people I had suspected had met the chairman of the local kolkhoz, a fellow by the name of Ozoronok, with whom we were on good terms and told him that they were underground fighters sent out by Moscow to look for the "Batya" company. They then demanded to be shown the way to our base. Ozoronok told them that he knew no one by the name of "Batya," thinking, as I had done before him, that they were Gestapo agents. He ran to the village head and told him about the paratroopers so that Germans themselves would search for and trap their own spies. But the head of the village caught on and said to Ozoronok: "You can catch the paratroopers yourselves. There's one under every bush!"

To my great surprise I was to learn some days later that I had been mistaken and that a new sabotage group had actually arrived commanded by Commissar Kaimach. Everything happened the way we read in fairy tales. On March 27, 1942, I once again had the chance to meet my old friend. Needless to say, we spent the whole night in friendly talk.

---

* Another term for the Germans. (ed.)

"How is it that you decided after all the bitter experience of last fall to drop in here again?" I asked David. "You must certainly have heard that we had all been wiped out and that I was dead."

"That you were killed--well, I heard that. But, how can I put it...I somehow knew that you were alive. You may have noticed that I'm not saying that I believed it. To say that I believed wouldn't be enough--I knew it."

"Well, suppose it was so, but what chance did you have to find me here, in this area crawling with German punishment squads?"

"Here we are! I did find you, and I would have found you under any circumstances. In the first attempt the people helped me, and now they have done so again. You see, I didn't go into the 'desert'--I went to the people. 'Here's the commissar,' the people said, 'the soul of the company.' How can a soul live without a body?" he joked. "A soul has no peace without a body. It is...unpleasant. I wanted all along to drop in on you from a plane, from the heavens down to earth..."

We soon resumed our partisan activities. David was once again at the head of the fighters.

The Germans committed a number of atrocities in the villages. In their attempt to put an end to partisan activities before the coming of spring, they kidnapped and shot every man they met who looked in the least suspicious to them.

The people flocked to our military "center." Tirelessly, David picked out new fighters. At the same time we held sabotage courses at our central base to teach the new recruits the ins and outs of this business, of blowing up trains and cutting railway tracks.

When the snows began to fall, we decided to hit the enemy's transportation lines. The first company, with its forty fighters, went out in the direction of the Vileyka-Polotsk line (Molodechno and Vitebsk regions) and were led by Scherbin and Kaimach. It was difficult for me to say goodbye to Kaimach, my closest friend, but we couldn't help it--on our most important operation we had to send our best men and Kaimach was one of our very best.

On the first of May, the Scharbin-Kaimach company sent in reports of having blown up three German trains full of soldiers heading for the eastern front. In these operations more than two hundred Germans were killed. The last of these three sabotage operations were carried out by Kaimach, accompanied by five fighters. After they had mined the railway track, they went back quietly into the woods. David did not know that after the second operation against the Germans, the latter had alerted a large number of forces and brought a punishment squad to comb the woods for us.

David and his men were in high spirits. They sat on a nearby hill covered with green bushes, overlooking the tracks. They watched while the train chugged its way along the tracks and directly onto our mines. They then saw pieces of the railroad carriages flying up into the air. They heard the groans of the Germans and saw huge columns of black smoke rising from a smashed-up tanker going up in flames.

Having enjoyed the results of his work, Kaimach ordered his men to move back. The fighters crawled down the hill, but when they reached the woods they started moving at a fast clip and covered a distance of about three kilometers. Afterwards they quietly made ready for some needed rest. They made a fire and took off their clothes and leggings in order to dry. The water in the field cauldron had started to boil when suddenly they heard the rustling of branches. The Germans had surrounded their camping site. Kaimach at once ordered them to get their hand grenades ready and move away to the other end of the forest. He also ordered that the camp fire should not be put out. When the branches moved in the nearby bushes, Kaimach commanded: "With the grenades, fire!" Six hand grenades were tossed into the bushes. The sounds of the explosions and the whine of the splinters stunned the "Fritzes" and forced them to "hit the dirt." Kaimach's men opened up with automatic fire and broke through the German encirclement.

Taken aback, the Germans did not fire at the partisans. They were afraid they would hit their own soldiers. Not waiting for them to recover their senses, Kaimach and his men put some distance between the Germans and themselves.

Only later did the fighters understand why the commissar had ordered them not to put out the fire when the Germans were advancing towards the partisans' camp. The reason was that the attention of the Germans was directed toward taking the partisans by surprise and wiping them out. To have put out the fire would have given the Germans a clue. That's what they thought, but they had guessed wrong. Some hours later, Kaimach and his men were back at the base. Only one fighter had been slightly scratched. After some time, when I moved with my company to another area, I saw to it that the Kaimach-Scherbin group would be attached to a special fighting company.

Kaimach did not want to be separated from Scherbin. His company began to assume large responsibilities, acting on a sector of hundreds of square kilometers in area. When Vassili Vassilivich Scherbin later fell in battle, David took over. He had by then become famous as the commander of an invincible partisan unit--a reputation which served as a banner for the local population in the fight against the Germans and their collaborators. The fatherland recognized Kaimach's military exploits by awarding him the Order of Lenin and the medal of "The War of the Fatherland, First Class."

David did not live to see the happy day that signified victory over Fascist Germany. The plane in which he was flying on his way back to Moscow, in September, 1943, was shot down by Germans in the region of Vilisky, and David died.

For me that marked the loss of my best friend; for the Soviet country, the loss of a loyal son and a brilliant defender.

His memory will live forever in the hearts of all those who met him, especially in the hearts of those who lived and worked with him.

THE PARTISANS OF THE KOVNA GHETTO

M. Yellin and D. Galperin

Men of the Underground

It was the fall of 1941, far behind enemy lines, and the whole of Lithuania was groaning under the yoke of the fascist invaders. Thirty thousand Jews, inhabitants of the town of Kovna, were behind barbed wire. Pogroms, arrests, imprisonment, and cruel trials had uprooted thousands of people. But the German oppressors demanded fresh sacrifices every day. The condition of the survivors was desperate.

But the Soviet people who were imprisoned in this fascist concentration camp did not fall victim to despair. Under the direction of the Communists, there appeared within the ghetto a number of underground groups, each one different from the other, all with the single aim of waging partisan warfare. The head of one such group was a young Jewish writer and Communist by the name of Haim Yellin. Under stringent conspiratorial conditions the individual groups united into one antifascist organization in the ghetto of Kovna. This organization was first headed by a committee of five comrades and, later, by a committee of seven.

The fighting organization initiated highly important underground work in the entire ghetto. The number of its members grew from day to day and so did its influence on the rank and file within the ghetto. A powerful transmitter was set up, and it was well camouflaged. Day in and day out, news summaries were received from the Soviet information bureau and were transcribed onto leaflets and distributed in the ghetto. Every Soviet victory at the front, every important event in occupied Lithuania, every Soviet celebration, was reported in articles and leaflets.

The underground started sabotage activities against enemy transports, storehouses, factories, buildings, and such places where Jews were brought from the ghetto for forced labor. To such places the underground sent members who had succeeded in carrying out a number of incendiary and demolition jobs. Every day had its act of sabotage, which, though small or insignificant, caused some trouble to the Germans: the partisans changed bills of lading on train carriages, mixed up cargo designations, sabotaged engines and machines, cut off telephone and telegraph wires, punctured tires.

The main task of the organization was to channel the able-bodied ghetto dwellers to the partisan companies. For this purpose scores of organization members slipped out of the ghetto and, at the risk of their lives, went out on reconnaissance missions to establish contact with others and to get arms. Communist members like Shmuelov, Milstein, and Yaffe, as well as Komsomol members such as Slavyanski, Teitel, Borodovka, Stern, Lipkovich, and Rachel Katz, were the first to give their lives in this highly dangerous work. At last the persistent efforts of the organization achieved its objective: contact was established with Gisya Glazierita, whose nickname was "Albina" and who had been sent to engage in underground activities behind enemy lines. "Albina" would often ask Haim Yellin to come over to her hiding place in Vilna, where she would put him in contact with the partisans active in the forest of Rodnitzki. The commander of the partisan brigade in this forest, Genzig Siemen, who was secretary of the southern committee of the Lithuanian Communist Party, issued instructions to send people from the ghetto of Kovna to the partisan company which was to be formed under the name "Death to the Invaders!"

Those who went over to the partisans were in need of arms. Thus the underground people broke into a German storehouse at the center of town, directly opposite the Gestapo building, took out rifles and military equipment, put them into sacks, loaded them onto a waiting truck, and brought them to a hiding place. In this way it was possible to obtain a considerable quantity of antiaircraft weapons from the German storehouse. Sometimes it was necessary to attack in the open. One such operation, which yielded sizeable booty, was carried out in the forest sector of Bakaishadorsk.

The path to the partisan base was a long and dangerous one. Forty-three out of the first hundred men who left the ghetto for the woods did not reach their destination. They were killed by the Gestapo. Eleven were caught and sent to "Position Nine," a death camp for people from Lithuania and other countries. They were ordered, together with other prisoners, to unearth the bodies of some seventy thousand people who had been killed in that place and to burn them. The eleven underground members who were taken there were later to initiate the great daring escape of the prisoners of "Position Nine" under cover of darkness, on the night of December 25, 1943.

In order to prevent the killing of ghetto fugitives on their way to the partisans, the underground organization brought fighters in trucks to predetermined spots. The usual practice was to have an organization member, dressed in German uniform, arrive in a truck at the ghetto gates and take out people for "night-shift work," using false documents. The truck would then take them some 120 kilometers away from Kovna where special guides would be waiting to take them to the partisan base. Among these guides was partisan Nechemia Endlin, who at the same time served also as liaison officer for the party underground. For five months on end it was possible to send partisan fighters right to the gates of the ghetto, but in the end the Gestapo discovered the trick and laid an ambush for the partisan truck. At a short distance from the ghetto, a bitter battle broke out between both sides. Only part of the group of fighters succeeded in shooting their way out and coming back; the others died in the fighting.

The preparation of one transport cost us the life of the organization leader in the ghetto, the brave fighter Haim Yellin, who insisted on supervising all the work involved in sending partisan companies to the ghetto to help in taking many ghetto prisoners out into the forest hideouts.

In the Forest

In the early days of November, 1943, Constantine Rodionov, following an order from the Northern Committee of the Communist party, began organizing the "Death to the Invaders" company, whose chief duty was to receive into its ranks the fighters from Kovna. The company was stationed in the woods of Rodnitzki under the command of the secretary of the regional committee of the Lithuanian underground, Genzig Siemen ("Yurigis"). He had the full respect and love of the partisans as well as the local inhabitants, who played an active role in helping the avengers of the people.

In the beginning the "Death to the Invaders" company suffered from serious shortage of arms and mili-

tary equipment. Besides the number of fighting men was
small. Before long, however, new partisans joined it
from among the fugitives of the ghetto of Kovna. They
brought along with them arms, equipment, medicines,
bandages, clothing, and other things they had received
from the underground while still in the ghetto. To
everybody's joy, a powerful radio-receiver set was
brought into the partisan base, and the people in the
woods could now listen to the voice of the Moscow
broadcasting station. They heard the voice of the head
of the Lithuanian communists and partisan fighers,
Comrade Antanas Shenitskosa. His calls of "To Arms!"
added much strength and alertness to us all.

The company, complemented with armed refugees from
the ghetto of Kovna, could now carry out highly complex
fighting tasks. This company from now on was to take
part in large-scale operations which were planned in
cooperation with other companies operating from the
woods of Rodnik.

In the village of Koniokhy, some thirty kilometers
from the partisan base, the Hitlerites had a stronghold. They ambushed our units and fired at them from
their hideouts. The "Death to the Invaders" company
was ordered to wipe out this source of harassment and
murder. Thus a partisan group crossed forests and
marshlands under cover of darkness, approaching the
village at dawn. All of a sudden a rocket flare poked
a finger at the gray sky. That was a sign for the
beginning of the attack. Twenty fighters of the "Death
to the Invaders" company, headed by their commander
Michael Troshin, stormed the village. The Germans took
shelter in the houses and returned fire with rifles and
machine guns. The partisans had to fight from house to
house and to use hand grenades and fire-torches in
order to drive the fascists away.

Partisans who had come from the ghetto of Kovna--
Tepfer, Ratner, Valbi and Tzadikov--headed the attack
on the fascists under a hail of enemy bullets. Leib
Zayatz, a burly young man, broke into one of the hosues
after he had run out of ammunition, forced a rifle out
of the hands of a Hitlerite, and opened up on the
enemy. The Germans were wiped out; this fascist nest
was put out of commission.

In their fighting missions, the partisans of the
"Death to the Invaders" company often had to go through
the village of Streiltse. The Germans used to station

guards in the village. They even provided arms for the villagers to help them in attacking the partisans. So the company sent a group of fighters to the villagers and asked them to hand in their arms. The peasants gladly did what the partisans requested, and German weapons were turned against the Germans themselves.

A reconnaissance group of the "Death to the Invaders" company reported unusual activity on the part of the Germans in the nearby village of Zhagarin. Our mounted scouts brought in more detailed information about the setting up of a reinforced siege garrison in Zhagarin. The "Death to the Invaders" company mounted an attack on the Germans in full force. Taken aback, the Germans began to run away from the village. The partisans put the barracks to the torch, blew up the water tower and the railway station, destroyed the railway engine garage, put two railway engines and a number of full and empty railway carriages out of commission, dismantled a considerable length of railway tracks, and threw the rails into the marshes. They also blew up two wooden bridges for good measure. The road back was cut off from the Germans.

On another occasion a partisan reconnaissance party reported that a great number of arms was to be found in the hands of the nationalist GermanLithuanians in the village of Godakeimis in the district of Onoshki. The partisans now faced the double task of beating the German force and getting the arms. Leib Zayatz, Leizer Silber, Israel Yoels, Solomon Abramovitch, and Abba Diskant had enough reason to revenge themselves on the Hitlerites. No wonder, then, that they covered the entire sixty kilometers in exceptionally high spirits. The skirmishes they engaged in on the way did not cost the partisans any losses. Upon arriving at the spot, they surrounded the house of the gang leader who was having a good time with his friends. The partisans had only a few rifles and pistols. Leib Zayatz ordered at the top of his voice: "Mount the machine guns; the sharpshooters, after me!" The gang leader and his friends ran down to the cellar, thinking that they were surrounded by a large company. A few hand grenades thrown into the cellar did the job. A great amount of booty was taken and carried on carts to our base: it included fourteen rifles, about forty thousand rounds of ammunition, a machine gun, a radio-receiver set, rockets, and other military equipment.

The Struggle Along the Railway Tracks

An everyday practice of the partisans was the blowing up of enemy transports. Leizer Tzadikov, the first partisan to arrive from the ghetto of Kovna, started out by sabotaging railway tracks. In the vicinity of Visovis, some eighty kilometers from our base, he derailed an enemy convoy carrying military and technical forces heading for the front. In the same area he blew up two more transports. The boy Meirov, who was among the first to join the company, blew up five enemy transports. He fell in the sixth attempt.

Boris Lupianski carried out four sabotage operations on the railway tracks between Vilna and Veivis. Shimon Bloch had four to his credit, two of which were a hundred kilometers from our base, on the way to Pravyenishkis on the Kovna-Kaishadoris line and near Gayzhonai on the Kovna-Yonava line. His permanent assistant for military operations was Moshe Pochikarnik. The woman partisan Chaya Shmoylova and partisans Gilbert, Eidelman, Feitelsohn, Villenchok, Ida Filovnik, Berger, and others blew up German transports and carried out with great success the fight along the railway tracks.

Along with three comrades Yaakov Ratner blew up an enemy transport driven by two engines. The fascists went after him. The valiant partisans kept running in an area swarming with Germans. On the way back to the base, the also had clashed with a large group of fascist policemen. Yaakov Ratner was wounded in the leg and in the left hand by a fragment from a hand grenade. He fell. It was already a dark. The Germans swept the area with search lights and found the wounded partisan. They began to advance toward him. Ratner let them come close to him and then, with all the strength he could still muster, threw two hand grenades and opened up with his rifle. The Germans were confused and ran away. With his last strength he reached a peasant shack, crawled in, and passed out. The peasants gave him first aid and dressed his wounds. On the following day he was picked up by the partisans and taken back to the base.

The destruction wrought by the partisans left a dent in the German war machine; several kilometers of dismantled railway tracks, the loss of scores of German transports full of soldiers, military equipment and fuel, kilometers of cut telephone and telegraph wires, and other losses. These were the blows that the partisans struck at the enemy in that most vital element: the communication lines between the front and the rear.

A Well-Knit Family

New forces were added to the company that was formed from refugees of the ghetto of Kovna. The "Death to the Invaders" company grew larger and larger. Under the supervision of Constantine Rodionov ("Smirnov"), two new Kovna companies were formed: on January 11, 1944 the Vladas Baronas company (commander, Karp Ivanov-Seimokov; commissar, Michael Balkin), and on March 13, 1944, the Vaparoid ("Forward") Company (commander, Captain Tziko; commissar, Haim David Ratner). The bases of all three companies were not far from each other, and in the first one was located the joint command. The construction workers of the brigade worked hard under the supervision of Moshe Sherman in setting up partisan camps. They built earth huts, a camp bakery, and a bathhouse.

It was only natural that partisan arms would always be kept in tiptop condition. Leib Sher set up a workshop for this purpose. In it he tested the weapons and repaired them. Among the partisans who came over from the ghetto of Kovna were other specialists. In their spare time the tailors made new clothes and mended the old ones; the cobblers were kept busy making boots and leggings. There were also excellent fitters. The two academic degrees that Chuna Kagan had received from two colleges did not stand in his way in proving that he was also a good mason. Israel Gittelman set up a printing press at the barracks of the "Free Lithuania" company. It served a useful purpose for putting out propaganda literature for the local population.

The underground organization in the Kovna ghetto sent over to us a number of experienced medical nurses. Ziva Tinet and Rina Epstein remained to look after the Kovna companies. Other nurses were received at the "For the Fatherland" company and the "Free Lithuania" company. The ghetto organization saw to it that Soviet planes dropped us ammunition, equipment, literature, provisions, and medicines.

At the base itself one could feel a true spirit of brotherhood. The Lithuanians, the Russians, the Jews, and the Poles came to each other's aid with unbounded warmth. They were ready to sacrifice their own lives in order to save their friends. Once, partisan Ivan Dushin volunteered for a dangerous mission in order to save a partisan group from encirclement. Chaim Valba saved the commander of the Guryachiva group from certain death: when a German was taking a bead at the commander, Valba sprang up from his hiding place, charged at the German, and killed him on the spot. On another occasion, Commander Guryachiv evacuated Valba (who was wounded at the time) from the field of battle under a hail of enemy bullets.

Moshe Milner and Sofroni Orlov were once surrounded by a German company while on a reconnaissance mission. In order to make it possible for his friend to escape and deliver the information they had obtained, Milner engaged the Germans in battle. Eventually he was left with only four bullets in the chamber of his pistol, which he had received as a present from the ghetto organization before he left for the woods. Milner shot three bullets into the enemy, the fourth he reserved for himself.

On the way back from a successful mission in December, 1943, a group of partisans were ambushed by the enemy near the village of Kaleintatsau. In their escape the partisans turned onto a river which had frozen over a short time before. Commander Truchin was in charge of the crossing. Enemy bullets kept whizzing past him. Pesach Gordon-Stein fell and was killed by the pursuing enemy. The remainder succeeded in crossing over to the other side of the river in order to hide in the woods. Sharpshooter Aaron Gapanovich covered the successful crossing. The commander brought up the rear, but the much trampled ice finally collapsed and he went under, up to his chin in the freezing water. Partisan Lupianski, who had been out of danger, ran back to save his commander. The ice broke under his weight. Above his head the bullets kept whizzing. Lupianski succeeded in catching the drowning commander by the hair, pulled him out of the water, and dragged him away from enemy fire.

Daring and Courage

Ten kilometers from the main base in Vichiorishky stood the nerve center of the Germans. At that spot several narrow-gauge railway tracks crossed the Vilna

Grodna road. Here also was the Forest Authority. A reinforced German garrison was stationed in the town.

The three Kovna companies--"Death to the Invaders," "Forward," and "Vladas Baronas"--decided to attack this fortified crossroads. They divided into small groups, set up ambush units along the way, and advanced in the direction of the garrison. A well-aimed bullet fired by the unit commander, Truchin, accounted for the German guard. It also indicated the beginning of the attack. Shouting "Hurrah," the partisans stormed the barracks area through a barbed wire fence. The Germans were held in a crossfire. Krakinovsky pounded at the German command with an antitank gun. Gapanovich, Nimiseir, and Pasternak fired at the Germans with machine guns. The surprised Nazis jumped out of the hosues in their underclothes; some ran about carrying suitcases, reluctant even at such a moment to be separated from their loot. The bodies of the murderers rolled on the ground and among them were six officers. Other Germans who showed any resistance were cut down.

Suddenly firing started from the direction of the barracks. Hirsch Shmulyakov was the first to throw a hand grenade at the German machine gun and lead an attack on the barracks. Fadisan, Tsadikov, and Bloch also charged at the head of their groups. The fighters of the Strum and Eidelman group surrounded the staff headquarters. Lupianski broke into the building through a window and killed the German machine-gunner with the butt of his rifle.

One by one the houses of the garrison fell into the hands of the partisans. At the same time a partisan group was in pursuit of the Germans, who had escaped in the direction of Rodnik. The effective fire power of our groups was cutting down the Germans when, all of a sudden, a truck appeared on the scene full of armed fascists who had been sent over from Vilna to help the forces under attack. The handful of partisans now had to fight it out with a large enemy company. The "avengers of the people" entered into this unequal battle in order to enable the main partisan forces to reach the base safely, together with the booty and the German prisoners they had taken. The partisan rearguard returned fire until the last round of their ammunition. One after another, the partisans fell. The last survivor was Teibel Vishiniskaya. She was wounded. Raising her hands she turned toward the Germans, who were overjoyed to have a partisan woman fall into their hands. When they came close to her, she released the grenade she had kept in her hand, killing herself and six Hitlerites surrounding her. Of the sixteen partisans who died a hero's death near Vichorishky, thirteen were members of the party underground of the Kovna ghetto. The partisans vowed to avenge the blood of their fallen comrades. On the day after the battle, a group of fighters followed a German truck on the way from Vichorishky to Vilna. In it were seven German officers who had been wounded in the previous day's battle. The partisans blew it up. They landed one blow after the other until this enemy garrison was taken out of Vichorishky.

While on one of their military operations, partisans belonging to the "Invaders" company caught concentration camp commander Nikoliaunas, a hangman who had killed numerous Soviet prisoners. They put him to death on ths spot.

Once six partisans of the "Death to the Invaders" company were on their way to the Kaishiadoris station. They stopped for a day's rest at the village of Zhalyon. Suddenly they were detected by a local hooligan who informed the Germans. Protected by a small tank, a car-full of armed fascists arrived at the village. The partisans put up a brave fight. They blew up the tank with a grenade. But they were surrounded and greatly outnumbered. All the partisans fell in the fighting. Toward evening the Germans were seen setting up a gallows in the small town of Anoshkis. The next day the inhabitants of the town saw six nude dead bodies on the gallows. Those were the bodies of the partisans who had fallen the day before.

The murder of these six brave fighters was a great loss to our company. When news of it came to the base, the commander of the "Death to the Invaders" company issued Order No. 39, which read:

1. While on a military mission, a group of six partisans, under the command of Comrade Lupianski, was surrounded by Hitlerite killers in one of the houses in the village of Zhalyon. After intensive fighting, all the members of the group fell.

2. Comrade Lupianski, who was born in 1921, was an exemplary partisan, who was recommend-

ed for a state decoration for his battle honors.

3. Partisan Shmuel Martovski, who was born in 1922; Leizer Tzadikov, born in 1916; Matis Goldberg, born in 1922; Solomon Abramovitch, born in 1914; Itsik Miklashevski, born in 1923--they too were fearless partisans, loyal to their fatherland.

The glory of victory to the fallen heroes!
(signed)
Company Commander Smirnov

For the First of May celebrations it was decided to mount an all-out attack on the Rodnik road junction. Peretz Kliachko, Frieda Rothstein, and Rachel Lifshitz slipped in the early morning over to the bridge going through the small town of Merechenko and blew it up, together with the guards who were on it. This operation served as a sign for the beginning of the operation. Fire was opened on the German garrison. Michael Pasternak, an excellent sharpshooter, sent seventeen discs into the enemy. Sarah and Moshe Robinson, together with Aaron Villenchok, kept firing for three hours or more at close range into the exit doors of the fascist barracks. At the same time the railway station went up in smoke and fire. Boris Stern, Solomon Breuer, and Vassily Zheporoshitz destroyed the telephone station. Other partisans laid mines on the roads which were to be used by the Germans to send in their reinforcements. Anton Bundar, Hannah Faddison, and Katriel Kobleintz blew up the munitions factory. The companies returned to their base without a single casualty.

Now, the First of May celebrations had a special flavor. The privileged partisans were singled out for state decorations, and offered the deep appreciation of the high command. Among the outstanding fighters to be so honored were forty-nine partisans from the ghetto of Kovna.

Shoulder-to-Shoulder with the Beylorussian Partisans

The "Vladas Baranas" company received orders to move over to the woods of August and to continue the fight there. On the way the fighters encountered a number of ambushes, and an intensive fight took place near the small town of Valkeninkay. The company, more experienced now in the fight against the enemy, passed through these ambushes without suffering any casualties. Aaron Gapanovich alone accounted for three fascists, took their arms, and added six more prisoners to those already taken. At the predetermined point the company carried out a series of operations: they destroyed a bridge on the River Marika in the vicinity of Kapchiamastis and the bridge on the road running between Kapchiamastis and Grodna. The blowing up of both bridges was credited to partisans Klichko, Yoels, Deutsch, Lifshitz, and Shilin.

The operations in central Lithuania were entrusted to a group of partisans from the "Death to the Invaders" company, under the command of Stephan Kilikov, a well-known partisan favorite whom they nicknamed "Leochik" ("flyer"), and two experienced partisans, Tepper and Goldblatt. The group was active in the district of Aukmerg in the vicinity of Pagayliagy, setting fire to a tractor loaded with arms. Together with the tractor, eight Germans also went up in flames. German guards from the nearby POW camp hurried to the aid of their colleagues. The partisans took advantage of this development and attacked the remaining guards. They released Soviet prisoners of war, who in turn joined the partisans. In Sasiskay the partisans set fire to large storehouses for bread, destroyed in several places a narrow-gauge railway track running between Yonava and Aukmerg, sawed off the telephone and telegraph poles, and took a great many head of cattle from the Germans. The commander of the Hitlerite police of the Aukmerg-Keitorag district was also shot and killed. The partisans later distributed Soviet publications in Lithuanian, together with the newspapers <u>Tass</u> (Truth) and <u>Ozesh Tarivo Litova</u> (For Soviet Lithuania).

When the Germans were on the run out of Lithuania, the partisans blew up a bridge on the road leading from Tausnay to Aukmerg, destroyed a fast tank and another small one, fired at enemy convoys, set ambushes, and prevented many Germans from getting out of Lithuania alive.

At the time the Soviet army mounted its devastating attack against the Germans, which brought freedom to White Russia and to the greater part of Lithuania, the Vaparoid ("Forward") Company, under the command of Captain Tziko and Leib Solomon (Pietrovich), went into the woods toward the southwest, which extended from Kazlo-Ruda up to the former German frontier. Partisan Nehemiah Endlin, who had trekked hundreds of kilometers of Lithuanian soil with his outstanding knowledge of the roads of the country, was entrusted with the task of serving as guide on this difficult march.

On their way out from the woods of Rodnik, the partisans faced many difficulties. The Vilna-Grodna railway tracks were under heavy guard every inch of the way. Dugouts and mine fields stretched along the entire length of the tracks. Endlin went out to reconnoiter the area. Close to Rodishkis, he led the company on purpose along a road which was heavily guarded by the Germans, counting on the assumption that they would not expect the partisans in this area. When the Germans eventually grasped what was happening, it was too late. In the meantime the company had succeeded in getting into the forest.

Now it was necessary to cross the river Neiman. Though there were a number of suitable points for crossing, Endlin found that we had better choose the same path once beaten by former partisans. And, indeed, the number of Germans here was greater than in other spots, but in such cases it was more important to count on the aid provided by the local inhabitants, who had already come in contact with the partisans and knew how to provide the necessary information. The high command accepted Endlin's suggestion. The peasants of that area brought out all the canoes they could find, even wooden boards and drinking troughs. The moon came out to light the way for this motley armada now floating on that languid river.

June nights are short. In order to make it to the company's destination, it was necessary to be on the move at dusk and at dawn. Not far from Mariampol, the partisans were ambushed. They at once flattened themselves on the ground and opened fire with machine guns and antitank weapons. Their bullets checked the enemy attack. The partisans then commenced crossing into the forest, but all of a sudden an order was given by Endlin: "Run back; follow me!" The partisans obeyed the order and started running back. Endlin's keen senses, which had been honed to a fine point under the trying conditions of partisan struggle, did not fail him. He had sensed that an ambush had been set. The partisans were soon to realize that he was right: from the forest, hundreds of Germans came out "on the double," followed by vehicle moving at great speed. Apparently, after intensive firing by the partisans, the fascists realized that they had come upon a large partisan unit, which was now about to attack them. It was only natural, after this incident, to expect an encounter with the enemy near the railway tracks running from Kovna to Mariampol, where the partisans were likely to cross. In this case, too, the local peasants reported heavy German guards along the tracks. The peasants also reported that the ambushes were called back at eight in the morning, and guards were stationed at two-hundred-meter intervals. This valuable information helped the partisans decide to make their crossing in broad daylight. Thus at ten in the morning, the company crossed the tracks. This move elicited amazement and admiration from the peasants. Days later, after a march of some 230 kilometers,* interspersed with occasional fighting, the company went into the forest allocated to us, and there it set up its new base.**

A short time before this operation, a number of fighting groups had been sent out to establish contact with the partisans of White Russia. These groups also reached their destinations after some fighting with the enemy. When the Red Army launched its June offensive, the Kovna partisans stayed behind in White Russia in order to fight shoulder-to-shoulder with their comrades, the Beylorussians. In the company commanded by Major Shostakovich, special distinction was accorded to Alter Feitelsohn. In the operation that took place near Molodichna, on June 21, 1944, he used a mine-layer to destroy the enemy's firing position, and the partisans succeeded in taking this area without casualties. Yaakov Koveh was among his Beylorussian comrades when, in the course of a single night, they destroyed the railway tracks over a distance of forty-five kilometers.

---

* Approximately, 144 miles, a long march by any standards. (ed.)

** By this time, some of the partisans were organized by the Soviet Army, and forests or regions within forests were "allocated" according to military needs, not by whim. (ed.)

The Freeing of Soviet Lithuania

The Soviet Army advanced quickly toward Vilna. The Germans made great efforts to ensure for themselves a "quiet" rear line at any price. They sent reinforced units into the forests: guns, mine-layers, and even called in air strikes. With calculated maneuvering the partisans avoided any premature encounter with the enemy, deploying their forces for the military operations that lay ahead. The "Death to the Invaders" company received instructions to drive the German forces out of the small town of Rodnik and its surrounding villages when the Red Army began its attack on Vilna. Armed gangs of Beylorussians and Poles collaborated with the Germans. They laid ambushes against the partisans on the roads leading to Rodnik and often attacked them. In one particularly intensive battle the partisans beat the gangs. The small town of Rodnik was later freed from enemy forces. Red flags were raised on the houses. Both liberated and liberators sat together in a joint meeting.

New missions were now given to the partisans. The Red Army surrounded Vilna with a ring of steel. Shoulder-to-shoulder with the army the partisans fought. The "Death to the Invaders" company, together with other companies, crossed the river Balton Wakai and fanned into the outskirts of Vilna. Near Aoushrus and Vartai the partisans engaged the enemy in violent fighting. The fascists had barricaded themselves inside the houses, but the partisans liberated one house after another, one street after the other. On July 13, 1944, Vilna was finally freed from the German invaders.

The partisans helped put out fires and establish order in the city. They stationed guards on the roads leading to the old capital of Lithuania. Woman partisan Bella Ganialina happened to be in charge of the Vilna checkpost at that time and had the privilege of supervising the passage of Lithuanian government leaders, under Premier Yustas Faletski, through the checkpost. Premier Faletski was also head of the Presidium of the Supreme Council in Soviet Lithuania.

After Vilna had been liberated from the Germans, the "Forward" company was still fighting it out with the Germans in the woods near Kazloroda. The partisans were in control of the railway tracks running between Kovna and Mariampol. A number of enemy convoys on their way to the front were ambushed and wiped out. Shimon Bloch and his group fired at the Germans during the latter's crossing of the Seredsschoss. The partisans destroyed enemy vehicles, blew up a tank, and captured, among others, four Gestapo men dressed as civilians who had run away from Vilna. Shaya Vershovsky, Boris Stern, and Pesach Sadovsky laid mines on the roads and set traps at vital crossings. One German tank fell into one of these traps.

In the course of the military operations of the "Forward" company, a number of its men died a hero's death, among them Chaim David Ratner and Yaakov Levi, fearless fighters and loyal sons of the Communist party. Chaim David Ratner belonged to the underground organization in Kovna right from the time it was founded; he stood out as a great fighter and was eventually appointed group commander. Up to the time he was sent out on a mission to White Russia, Ratner served as commander of the "Forward" company.

Yaakov Levi, who had begun his partisan life as an ordinary fighter, became well known for his exploits in the underground and was eventually to become one of the best liaison men in the ghetto organization. Levi was one of the closest comrades-in-arms of Haim Yellin.

The "Forward" company came in contact with Soviet paratroopers in the woods of Kazlo-Ruda. Together they reconnoitered the area of the German batteries and passed on information to the high command of the Soviet army. The partisans noted with satisfaction that the Soviet planes had accurately bombed the spots they had marked out for them. In the meantime the battles around Vilna were coming to a close. The "Forward" company advanced to the city of its origin, Kovna. The commander told Endlin: "You have been the guide for the company so far, so keep on showing us the way ahead too! Lead the company on to Kovna!"

Endlin led one hundred and thirty-seven fighters. Upon reaching the Nieman River, the partisans saw the towers and chimneys of Kovna. The liberated Soviet town lay there before them, ready to receive its fighting sons.

TALKING OF FRIENDS

Y. Zbanatzki
Hero of the Soviet Union
Former Commander of a Partisan Unit

When the war broke out I was a high-school teacher in the picturesque town of Ostir, on the Desna river. In the fall of 1941 I organized a partisan company behind enemy lines. The company operated in the vicinity of Kiev and gradually grew into a mighty partisan unit. I would like to relate something about the lives and exploits of a few fighters who belonged to the company named after Nikolai Shachors.

* * * * *

The first snow had fallen. It had been falling throughout the night, and we, three partisans, had been on our way to the village for a meeting with some comrades when dawn broke on a white world all around us. The comrades were Red Army soldiers who had escaped from a German hospital for prisoners of war located in Ostir. We met at dawn. All three of us were at the point of exhaustion and nearly frozen. We had to stay at the village till night so as not to draw the attention of the Germans.

We were put up in a hut at the edge of the village. Our new friends were good natured, and after some time they were to be made commanders of partisan companies.

One of them drew my attention in particular.

"Are you a Jew?" I asked him.

"Yes."

"Were you at the hospital?"

"Yes."

I began to take an interest in the destiny of this fellow.

Boris Pinhasovich had lived in Kiev. He was a Red Army soldier right from the first day of the war. His platoon was driven back to Kiev by the advancing

Germans. In the region of Ostir the platoon was engaged in defending the people who were leaving Kiev. In these battles Boris was seriously wounded. Bleeding, he lay in a foxhole for some days, and one night was found by the children of the village. An elderly woman took him to her house and nursed him. The village peasants treated many wounded fighters in this manner. The Germans issued an order to bring all the wounded to Ostir, where they had set up a hospital for them. Had the Germans known that Boris was a Jew, his life would have been in danger. But the doctors did not reveal his nationality. When Boris had enough strength to walk a little, the chief physician sent him out with the hospital cows, and he took advantage of this opportunity to escape.

On the first day of our meeting with the new partisans, they had to fight for their lives. The German police who had gone after the escaped soldiers from the hospital surrounded our hut. The situation was quite serious. We had many people, but not enough arms to go around, a total of three rifles, three pistols, and a few hand grenades. Nevertheless we opened fire. In the fighting, the commander of the police company was wounded and his men dispersed. We took the arms they threw down and returned safely to the company. In this encounter, Boris Pinhasovich proved to be a cool and fearless soldier. At once I had the feeling that this man would make a good partisan and bring us great benefit, both as a daring fighter and as a politically well-oriented man.

He had a phenomenal memory. After he had spent some time with the company, he began to lecture us on politics. In the course of these lectures he would cite accurate quotations from Marx, Engels, Lenin, and Stalin, all from memory. His words captured our attention, since in those days we had no Soviet books or newspapers. In battle, Pinhasovich acquitted himself as an outstanding fighter. On one occasion the Germans formed a brigade out of Soviet prisoners of war and sent them to fight the partisans.

The brigade soldiers approached the station of Yanov, where they learned about the hideouts of the partisans. Whereupon, they at once attacked and killed the Germans, took their arms, horses, and military equipment, and started coming in our direction. They reached the village of Sorokoshichi on the Dnieper. A group of our fighters, including Boris Pinhasovich,

were in the area. On hearing of the new arrivals, and
without knowing anything about them, twenty of our partisans went out beyond the village. The strangers sent
a delegation to us. We met at the outskirts of the
forest. Company Commissar Molochenko received the
delegates and held a lengthy conversation with them
but, of course, was not in a position to believe every
word they said. He suggested that they lay down their
arms. This proposal raised some doubts and anxiety in
the minds of the delegates. Sensing this, Boris
Pinhasovich and his friend Georgi Khachatourian volunteered to go out to the new arrivals in order to see
for themselves who they were. Despite the possibility
of a provocative action, Boris and Georgi ventured out
in the company of a delegate to the newcomers.

* * * * *

Pinhasovich was soon to be appointed director of
political affairs in a company of the new battalion
which included the new arrivals. The battalion was
stationed in a forest sector in the vicinity of
Karpilov.

This was a small town. Suddenly a large German
unit approached the place in a pincer movement. The
new partisans were flustered at first, but the veteran
partisans led the new ones in the attack on the
Germans. Boris lead the attack. The German major who
was in command of the enemy company was killed. Confusion prevailed among the enemy forces. The battlefield remained in our hands.

I well remember another battle with the German
garrison in the small town of Reibnov Krup, in the
vicinity of Chernigov, where the Germans had built
construction wood factories. The partisans occupied
the place and destroyed all the plants that the Germans
had built. The enemy garrison, numbering some five
hundred soldiers, was taken. About two hundred bodies
were left by the Germans on the battlefield. Boris and
his company were outstanding in this battle. Some time
later Boris Pinhasovich was appointed commissar of a
new company named Voroshilov. Boris succeeded in
setting up a fighting collective which was to justify
its existence in many a future large-scale military
operation.

Meantime the Soviet army had reached the Desna and
Dnieper rivers. The Soviet informtion bureau had

announced the liberation of Konotop and Bachmatz. So we decided to come to the aid of our fighting forces in their crossing of the rivers. After this decision had been taken, the Voroshilov company dug in at the southern outskirts of the village Maxim on the Desna, between Chernigov and Ostir. A German brigade, reinforced with heavy and medium tanks, moved along the shore of the Desna. The Voroshilov company was the first to engage the enemy in battle.

Greatly outnumbered, the company fighters were ordered to stand their ground at any price until the arrival of the other companies. Boris carried the battle into the center of the village and took charge of defending the positions that eventually repulsed all enemy charges. His understudy and close friend Michael Lokianovich Dirivianko, an excellent machine-gunner, inflicted heavy casualties on the enemy. The battlefield was littered with German bodies. Changing their tactics the surviving Hitlerites lay on the ground and sent their tanks forward. Dirivianko inserted a disk with incendiary bullets into this machine gun and engaged the enemy tanks single-handed. At the same time partisan antitank guns manned by the Shachors company and led by Gabriel Adamyenko started firing. This company had been moved to the battlefield to relieve the Voroshilov fighters. Boris arrived on the spot and urged his men to attack the enemy. The Germans retreated in their vehicles up to the small town of Sokolvka. A great number of Germans drowned in the Desna in their attempt to cross over to the other side.

A few days later the partisans established contact with the advancing Soviet soldiers. In the villages of Maxim, Genilosha, Smolin, and Morovsk, the Soviet armies were carried in the vehicles which had been prepared for them by the partisans and the inhabitants of these villages.

The Voroshilov company hurried to the Dnieper River. Around the villages of upper and lower Sibki and Zshari, as well as Nabozi, we made preparations for ferrying Soviet army units from one shore to the other. Boris Pinhasovich worked with remarkable zeal in ferrying the armies to the left-hand shore. In the meantime, the right-hand shore was strongly defended against any sudden attack on the part of the Germans. The Soviet army safety crossed the Dnieper. The partisans took part in the battles with the Germans on the right-hand shore.

Boris Pinhasovich was highly respected by the company fighters, who loved him and had faith in him. He was on particularly friendly terms with Georgi Khachatourian and machine-gunner Michael Dirivianko. The machine-gunner that Boris held so close to his heart was killed near the village of Maxim. His death brought great sadness to Boris. Michael was buried by his comrades in the village of his birth.

Comrade Pinhasovich was awarded three state medals, including the "Red Flag" decoration.

Rassya

Once, one of our partisan companies was on its way back to base after a military operation. A snowstorm was raging in the area. The front sled stopped; something had gone wrong with the harness. In the midst of that snowstorm, at dusk, a human figure was seen moving about, disappearing every now and then in the eerie light that preceded darkness. It was a woman. She was running. In her attempt to catch up with us, she often stumbled and fell in the gathering snow, only to rise and try again.

"Help, help, good people!"

"Where're you running in such weather?"

The woman replied:

"I've been saved from certain death. I'm a Jewess. I've been looking for you, partisans."

The partisans took her onto the sled, covered her with clothes, and fed her. All that time the woman was shivering with cold and excitement. After she had regained her calm, she told the partisans about her prolonged search for their camp.

Rassya was her name. Her Ukrainian husband, Trytiak, was in the Soviet army. When the Germans started their extermination of the Jews, she fled to the countryside, leaving her young daughter with her mother-in-law. The kolkhoz people hid Rassya, but she began to miss her daughter terribly, and so decided to go back to her. On reaching her home she was told by her sobbing mother-in-law that the Germans had taken her daughter away in her nightgown, loaded her on to a cart and brought her to the cemetery, (and, presumably, shot her).

Rassya was badly shaken. At first she thought of committing suicide. Later on she decided to avenge the murder of her daughter. And now her wish had come true. She had never held a rifle in her hands, but when it was suggested that she join the partisans to do the housework, she firmly refused.

"Give me a rifle," she said. "Teach me how to use it. I want to kill at least one fascist. To take my revenge on the enemy; this is the wish of my life."

Rassya was admitted into a fighting company. She became a partisan. With alertness and loyalty she did her duty. She spent long hours lying in ambush along the roads, far from base. With great patience she bore the hardships involved in partisan life.

In the numerous battles against the Germans in which she took part, Rassya proved to be a daring and fearless fighter.

Paulina

I remember with good feeling the friendly old woman with the rosy, sunken cheeks, the tight mouth, and the dark eyes. She was neither sharpshooter nor scout, nor even a woman who fired a rifle in anger. She was merely the cook of a partisan company. The fighters simply called her "Mother," Aunt Paulina, or Paulina Abramovna.

I remember how Paulina received the weary fighters when they came in for lunch. She greeted them with love and motherly concern. Every now and then the restless cook would ask them if they were enjoying the food, if they wanted some more, or if they needed salt. When she saw that one of the fighters was not eating well or was preoccupied, Paulina Abramovna would go up to him like a worried mother, inquiring and carrying on a conversation to take his mind off his problems, even to the point of having him eat his food, ask for more, and leave the table in high spirits.

The events in the life of Paulina Abramovna ran similar to those that marked the life of Rassya Trytiak. She too lost relatives. Soviet people helped

her find the partisans. There, Paulina Abramovna found
a new family, respect, and love.

THEY WERE MANY

Nikolai Konishchuk
Commander of the "Kruk" Partisan Detachment

Until the war began I was the chairman of the Village Council in the district of Kameen-Kashirsky, in the Region of Volyn (Western Ukraine). On July 28, 1941, I began to form a group of partisans. Quickly I made connections with the Jews from the village of Gryva and the small town of Maniewicz. Our partisans succeeded in rescuing about two hundred Jews from the village and the nearby settlements—men and women who, afterwards, joined my unit. I will tell about several of them who especially excelled. The scout Avraham Blaustein came upon a group of twenty Germans. He fought against them until he fell with a severe wound. The Germans grabbed him and brought him, dripping blood, to the Gestapo headquarters in Kameen-Kashirsky. Here, they tortured him cruelly: they stripped his flesh and broke his ribs. The Germans demanded that he point out the location of our camp, "The Jewish Unit" as the fascists called my unit. But Avraham bore his suffering with supreme bravery and did not reveal anything to the Germans. He died a true partisan, a loyal and devoted son of his Soviet homeland. Avraham's brother, Hershel Blaustein, also fell in battle against the Germans.

Among other partisans there was Asher Flash from Maniewicz who was a guard at the partisan camp, as was Sender Lande, who was also a guard at the nearby civilian camp that was protected by the partisans. Susel Shepa also of Maniewicz went out on numerous missions and blew up train tracks and bridges.

Pinick Berman, who fought under the command of Anton Brinsky ("Dadya Petya") in other groups as well as mine, won many medals for his heroic deeds. The nephew of Asher Flash, Moshe Flash, was a brave fighter and also went out on many missions during his time in the partisans.*

---

* See Moshe Flash's partisan documents and medal in the appendix of the book. (ed.)

Volodia Zweibel was an excellent partisan saboteur. He died a hero's death. His murder cost the Germans dearly: in his last stand he wiped out six of the fascists.

Abba Klurman, along with his group, blew up eight trains, killing two hundred Germans who were heading toward the front. Aside from this he destroyed twelve tanks and no fewer cars. He was an alert scout and an excellent commander of his unit.

Joseph, the brother of Avraham and Hershel Blaustein who were both killed, blew up eleven German trains and destroyed eight cars and several tanks.

Itzik Kuperberg, along with his unit, blew up seven trains carrying military equipment and wiped out approximately eighty Germans.

Berl Lorber (called "Malenka) was the commander of a unit composed solely of Jewish partisans. This unit destroyed twenty four German trains, eighteen engines, forty coaches, four large bridges, and three hundred Germans. Lorber and his fighters also ruined twenty eight kilometers of telegraph and telephone lines.

Miriam Blaustein, a daring scout, took part in the partisan struggle from 1942 onwards. She helped carry out many acts of sabotage, blowing up German trains which were heading toward the front.

Itzik Zafron was born in 1928. This young partisan joined equally with all the rest in the attacks upon German garrisons and trains. He carried out the most difficult and most dangerous missions assigned to him.

Shaya Zarutsky was always in the most dangerous places during a battle. When an especially important mission had to be undertaken, a mission requiring extreme courage, Zarutsky was one of the first to come forth and volunteer. More than once he went out to scout three hundred kilometers away to check the places where we could capture arms and military equipment.

Isaac Avruch was one of my most devoted and loyal partisans. He accepted every difficult assignment no matter what it entailed and took part in many acts of sabotage against the German conquerors.

Vaveh Avruch was our mine technician. He emptied German bombs which did not explode in order to equip our unit with explosive material. He thus supplied us with a large quantity of explosives from the German booty we captured.

Israel Puchtik* (called "Zalonka") appeared in our unit with his own weapons. He killed several Germans with his own hands and took their rifles. He was appointed to lead one of our units and, along with his comrades-in-arms, he blew up eight German trains. Many times he went out on scouting missions, attacked German command posts, and destroyed bridges.

Hirsch Greenberg, like Vaveh Avruch, extracted caps from air bombs which didn't explode. In this way we obtained explosive material which was sorely needed. Greenberg invented an original method which simplified and speeded up this work. Many German bombs thus became the source of death for the Germans themselves.

Lena Blaustein also worked in our "mine factory." She prepared approximately one thousand mines, using very primitive methods. This courageous girl also went out on scouting missions armed with her weapon. She fell during an air-attack on our brigade.

Luba Flaum was our radio broadcaster. He coordinated the communications with other partisan groups and also with central headquarters in Moscow. He also worked actively on making our mines and took part in many battle operations.

Joseph Zweibel was the leader of a division. Together with other partisans he blew up trains carrying Germans and destroyed bridges. Also, Yankel Zweibel led a unit which blew up ten German trains.

Shimon Wolper was one of the organizers of our unit. Once I assigned him a mission to go to Maniewicz to save the Jews who still remained there. Wolper returned with thirty-two men and three women. All of them became active fighters in our fighting force.

---

* This is the editor's father. He was awarded the "War of the Fatherland" medal, First Class. (ed.)

I have mentioned the names of a small number of the Jewish partisans--those who fought and headed my unit. This small list could be expanded tenfold. There were many like these "Avengers of the People." With entire families Jews escaped from the preying teeth of the enemy, penetrated into the forests, and fought a life-and-death struggle against the conquerors.*

---

* Konishchuk is correct: a great many other fighters, both men and women, all of them Jews, could have been added to his list. His group is significant because, as noted, it was even labeled by the Germans themselves as a "Jewish Unit"; this was unusual, because most Soviet partisan groups were mixed groups. (ed.)

IN THE TUNNELS OF ODESSA

Shmuel Persov

On October 16, 1941, Odessa came under German and Rumanian occupation. Soon after that, the remainder of the Jewish population, except those who did not succeed in escaping from the town in time, were gathered in the courtyard of the local prison, ostensibly for registration purposes. In this courtyard, hundreds of people were to die each day of cold, hunger, contamination, and disease. Many of these prisoners were shot at the whim of the German sentries.

On October 26, about twenty thousand Jewish prisoners were taken out of the prison courtyard to the storehouses of the artillery corps and burned alive. But in the course of this transfer, a small group of prisoners succeeded in slipping through the gate and disappearing. Among them was Hirsch Fuhrman and his family. Having been born in Kolyanik, Fuhrman went to this small town, to his former neighbor and boyhood friend, Vassili Ivanov. The latter had connections with the Party underground organization. After Fuhrman had recovered a little, he was asked by Ivanov to gather all those who would be willing to answer his call and to bring them to him.

Fuhrman succeeded in gathering about twenty-five persons who, like him, had escaped from the hands of the German and Rumanian murderers.

Not unlike the majority of the inhabitants of Kolyanik, Vassili Ivanov was a stonecutter, extracting "clamshells" from tunnels for the buildings of Odessa. Here, in Ivanov's backyard, was the opening into those tunnels and to the stone layer below. Ivanov used this entrance to hide the ghetto fugitives.

Even before Fuhrman had appeared at this place, Ivanov had hidden a few rifles and pistols in one of the underground recesses. The arms strengthened the morale of the people and encouraged them to join the ranks of the partisans. It was then decided to set up a fighting company. Fuhrman, a veteran of World War I, was chosen to command it. For his aides he chose the brothers David and Gregory Bobrovsky. Mogalivasky, a former corporal in the Czarist army, undertook to teach the would-be partisans how to use the firearms and to conduct battles. He was also appointed head of the guards. Before long Fuhrman's partisans joined the company of Badayev, which chose Yaakov Vassin for their aide. This company, too, found shelter in the tunnels of Odessa.

The new united company occupied only a small recess in the tunnels. Here they had a fireproof safe where documents were kept and, beside it, a barrel containing fuel. This barrel was guarded day and night, for, in the eternal darkness of the tunnel, even the person most familiar with its endless labyrinths was doomed if the light went out.

On the first night after the union of the two companies, the partisan group came out of the tunnels under the command of Vassin and staged an attack on German-Rumanian guards who had been stationed near the tunnels.*   The partisans were greatly outnumbered, but they took the unsuspecting guards by storm and forced them to run for their lives. But reinforcements soon arrived, and the partisans had to fall back to the tunnels. Upon reaching the opening Vassin found out that one fighter, David Krassnostein, was missing. Under a hail of enemy bullets Vassin crawled back to look for his friend. He found him wounded and brought him back to the tunnels.

David Krassnostein belonged to the Badayev company right from the early days of its formation. Besides him, there were the fighters Elik Zassombsky and Haritun Liebensohn, a member of the Odessa Komsomol, who took part in the first partisan attack on the Rumanians on October 16, 1941. Danya Simberg was one of the best ground scouts of the company. On one occasion a Rumanian company surrounded four of our scouts, including Simberg. The stubborn and bitter fighting that ensued resulted in six dead Germans and the four partisans returned safely to the company.

* * * * *

---

* There were Rumanian collaborative police and army personnel working with the Germans. (ed.)

The former ghetto fugitives now turned into capable fighters and began to take part in combat missions of the united company. The brothers Bobrovsky, the members of the Fuhrman family, and others, proved to be daring fighters. Rita Fuhrman, the vivacious and intelligent 15-year-old girl who had in the meantime picked up some Rumanian, served as a runner. On many occasions she was called upon to carry out highly dangerous missions. She fulfilled them with flying colors.

Rita usually left the tunnels early in the morning. The partisan on duty accompanied her to the exit. Here he gave her the password. Late in the night, under cover of darkness, Rita returned. One of the comrades would be waiting for her at a predetermined spot.

At first the German and Rumanian invaders tried to let the people believe that all the stories about partisans hiding in the tunnels of Odessa were fictitious and that there were no partisans at all in these places. But after the enemy had come to realize that many of their soldiers and officers were falling under partisan bullets, they began to announce in the bulletins they distributed that, though there were actually partisans in the tunels, they were nevertheless, left there without any light, water, or air, and therefore, they were doomed to die.

In order to intimidate the local population, the German murderers killed forty-two people, forty men and two women, in the village of Nerobayesk, near Odessa. They then declared that these were the partisans they had caught inside the tunnels. The dead bodies were laid in a row on the street, and their burial was forbidden. Nevertheless, the villagers succeeded in burying them in secret, and now a tombstone stands at their mass grave.

The blows the partisans directed at the enmy became more frequent. The invaders did not succeed in stopping the partisan attacks. Out of blind rage, the Germans brought a field gun to the entrance of a tunnel and fired into it pointblank. In retaliation the partisans attacked the nearby enemy barracks and wiped out almost all the soldiers they could find.

The Hitlerites then decided to use gas for driving the partisans out of the tunnels. When this foul intention became known to the partisans, the latter mobilized all their manpower to collect stones and sand. Within a few hours an impregnable wall was put up at the tunnel entrance, which prevented the gas from getting into the tunnels. The invaders poisoned the wells that provided water for those who were hiding underground. But this, too, had no effect on the fighting spirit of the partisans. They dug two wells in the tunnels to a depth of thirty meters. This, of course, was no easy task, as they had to blow up a continuous stone layer. But nothing could make the Soviet patriots surrender to the invaders. The tunnels were connected to the surface by vertical shafts thirty to forty meters deep, from which stone had been quarried in former days. Now these shafts served as the only source of fresh air for the partisans. The invaders sealed off the shafts, and the patisans now were in dire danger of suffocation. But they opened the shafts once again. The Hitlerites then took a most stringent measure: they now used cement and mortar to seal off the shafts. The invaders sealed off about four hundred tunnel entrances. The partisans underneath walked scores of kilometers in the labyrinths in search of new exits. The extensive search was to bring about the desired result: exits were found at a distance of many kilometers from the main base. The partisans could now resume their combat oeprations.

Walking about with torches in their hands in the endless labyrinths, the partisans marked the walls with predetermined signs such as circles, lines, and letters which could be understood only by those who had been brought into their secret. These abstruse signs served as road markers.

* * * * *

On one occasion Badayev's fighters discovered on the walls signs which were unknown to them. This indicated that there were other people in the tunnels. Badayev's people decided to meet them. The meeting was set for March 14, 1942, at 12 o'clock Moscow time.

But they had to take precautions. The approaches to the base were walled up, and in the walls openings had been made for rifles and machine guns, together with an "eye" for observation. This barricade was connected by telephone with the underground command at a distance of two kilometers.

The task of holding the talks with the strangers was assigned to Yaakov Vassin, deputy commander of the company, and to partisan Pavel Postomalnikov. Behind them went a nine-man guard. The others were stationed behind the barricade.

For two days and nights the men of Badayev stayed at the predetermined spot and waited for the "guests." Finally on March 16, a flame was seen approaching in the dark. Some minutes later the newcomers stopped at a certain distance from the barricade. The "parliamentarians" among Badayev's men approached the newcomers. Toward them stepped out three of the strangers.

"How may are you?" asked Vassin.

"As many as may be required," echoed the reply.

"And who are you?"

"Same as you."

"A long time in the tunnels?"

"Not less than you..."

This diplomatic dialogue would certainly have gone on in this vein had not Pavel Postomalnikov cried out in jubilant excitement:

"Lazriyev! Simon! You...?" and they began to shake hands and kiss each other. In front of Postomalnikov stood Simon Lazriyev, accompanied by Nikolai Kryllyevsky and Leonid Gurbeil, secretaries of the underground provincial committee of the Party. Lazriyev was first secretary of the provincial committee and commissar of a partisan company. The commander was Nikolai Kryllyevsky. At that time the company numbered only seventy fighters.

After that exciting meeting Badayev's company united with the company of Lazriyev.

One day the ground scouts came back with the news that the Rumanians had laid mines at the tunnel exits. It was necessary to devote much time to unearthing those mines and then placing them close to the quarters of the Rumanian guards. When fighting started later that night between the two sides, many Rumanians were blown up by their own mines. But enemy reinforcements soon arrived, and the fighting went on til the morning. The Hitlerite forces suffered heavy casualties, but, still, they had the upper hand, and we had to withdraw. A number of partisans did not succeed in reaching the tunnels but they eventually found shelter with the local peasants. On that same day the Rumanians sealed off the entrance to the tunnels at the spot where the fighting had taken place. On the following night the fighters that had remained outside cleared the entrance, and before dawn they were once again with their comrades. The Germans tried to win the partisans over with sweet promises, inviting them to come out of the tunnels without any coercion and surrender to the German and Rumanian authorities. The partisans' reply to this "considerate" offer was to launch a number of new attacks. During the month of May, 1942, alone the partisans accounted for about forty-five dead and some sixty wounded enemy soldiers and officers.

The stock of food supplies in the tunnels began to run out, and in the end there was not enough food to go around. The partisans held a council of war and decided that under the prevailing conditions it was impossible to keep the fighters in the tunnels. So they decided to transfer part of Badayev's men to the partisans operating in the nearby forests of Saveran, and the remainder were to be sent into Odessa for underground work. Only the provincial committee stayed in the tunnels.

In the fall a group of "illegal workers" was captured by the German butchers. On September 9, 1942, twenty-three people were brought before a fascist court, of whom sixteen were sentenced to death. Among those executed were partisans David Krassnostein, Ivan Peterenko, Danya Simberg, Ilya Zasovsky, Yekaterina Vassina, Shaya Feldman, Haritun Liebensohn, Frieda Khayyat, and Zhenia Fuhrman.

For nine hundred and seven days the Germans and the Rumanians were in control of Odessa. During all this time, Simon Lazriyev and all the members of the provincial committee stayed in the underground tunnels and eventually survived the war.

With their exploits the partisans of the Odessa tunnels wrote a brilliant page in the annals of the Soviet patriots' struggle behind enemy lines.

SONYA GUTINA

S. Berkin

On a dark night in September, 1943, a runner came into the camp of the Shmiyakin company, then operating around the town of Vetka in White Russia. He was taken to the hut of the commander. Immediately the group commanders were called to a council of war.

Before long the entire company was alerted. The men were read the order for the impending combat mission, to attack the Hitlerites and the police forces that were about to enter a village for the purpose of kililng the Jews and the families of the partisans hiding there.

The partisans laid an ambush and massacred the Germans. One of the survivors of that village, a young woman, Sonya Gutina, expressed her desire to join the partisans. She was followed by others. Thus, Sonya, a former student at the Teacher's Institute, was to become a full-fledged partisan. She was soon to send a request to the commander to go out on a combat mission against the enemy.

Her baptism of fire was hard and grave. A partisan group that included Sonya Gutina went out on a ground patrol mission, but the Germans discovered and surrounded them. Six partisans engaged in battle an enemy force made up of thirty Germans. The exchange of fire lasted more than three hours. Sonya shot some enemy men, and when the Germans intensified their attack, she threw a number of grenades at them. They retreated, leaving behind thirteen killed and wounded. Out of the six partisans three were killed and one wounded.

A few days later Sonya once again went out on a combat mission, this time to blow up a troop train heading for the front. The partisans mined the rails and started to conceal their tracks. That was a hard task, as the Germans had intentionally leveled the embankment to such an extent that any trace would stand out on it. Every ten minutes German guards patrolled to check the embankment. Sonya said to the group commander: "Now you go along. I'll do the job myself." A short while later they heard the approaching train. An explosion followed, and a huge flame lighted the entire area around it. The partisans retreated fast. Over three hundred German soldiers and officers were killed or wounded.

The Germans did not let it stand at that. They brought two SS divisions into the region where the partisans operated. For three long months Shmiyakin's company fought it out with the Germans in the forest despite the shortage in equipment, medicines, and food supplies. The siege was intensified. Shmiyakin decided to make a breakthrough with his men. The attack started at dawn. Sonya went at the head of the attacking group. Our surprise charge carried us beyond the first German line of defense quite easily, but then the Germans opened up with their machine guns. These, however, could not stem the momentum of our attack, and the partisans scored direct hits at them. The company was safely out of enemy encirclement.

Then the fatal day came: Sonya went out with two fighters on a patrol mission. They were ambushed, and the two comrades were killed on the spot. Sonya hid behind a thick pine tree and kept firing while lying down until she ran out of ammunition. She started throwing hand grenades. After she had been hit by an enemy bullet, she lost consciousness.

Sonya was now in the hands of the Germans. They interrogated her for a long time, but she kept her mouth shut. They started to torture her. The fascist oppressors beat her up and smashed her hands. She groaned, but she did not answer their questions. For more than three days and nights they kept interrogating and torturing her. Finally they took her out to be executed.

On the way to the place where she was to be shot, the soldiers stopped at one of the houses to drink some water. With tears in her eyes, the housewife brought Sonya a glass of water.

"Don't cry, mother," said Sonya. "You shouldn't cry. They may kill me, but the people will triumph."

These were Sonya Gutina's last words.

THE DAVIDOVICH FAMILY

Mira Eisenstadt

When the Germans reached the outskirts of Novozivkov, recounts partisan Yaacov D., the Jewish population started to leave the place in a hurry. Only cart-owner Ziama Davidovich did not budge. His wife Hanna was bedridden with paralysis. "Go, Ziama," the invalid begged her husband. "Go and take the children, Dvora and Misha. Save their lives, Ziama!"

But Ziama answered: "I don't want to hear of it. Stop it, won't you?"

All the neighbors had left. The streets were empty. Sadness and boredom reigned all around them. One neighbor, a non-Jewish woman, Maria Stephanovna, offered to take the ailing Hanna into her home and to hide her there.

One night, when the German guns were booming all around the town, Ziama hitched his horse to the cart, took his daughter Dvora and son Misha on the cart, and left Novozivkov.

Where to? Of course, to the nearby forest. There, Ziama Davidovich met a partisan company and joined its ranks. In the partisan tents he found a nook for himself and his two children and thus stayed with them under the command of P.

Partisan Ziama of Novozivkov soon exchanged his whip for an automatic rifle and learned to use it quite well. But he was better at working with the axe. In pitched battles he would whirl his axe left and right, accompanying the movement with curses in Yiddish, without anyone being able to stop him.

His daughter Dvora, a young girl of sixteen, was called "Nurse" by the partisans. On quiet days she would cook and do the washing for the entire partisan company. But on battle days she served as a medical nurse. Crawling on the ground she would reach the arla where the fiercest fighting was taking place and drag back the wounded partisans whom she would later nurse back to health during the long nights.

Thirteen-year-old Misha also had something to do. He was a skillful, clever, resourceful boy who was soon to become the liaison runner of the partisan company. With remarkable daring the young boy went on dangerous missions and always brought back the necessary information concerning the enemy front positions. The partisans liked him for his quickness and readiness to run at all times to the flaming front. Between battles he was something of a musical entertainer. He would compose songs on the Germans, on Hitler and Goebbels, composing and singing, accompanying himself on the harmonica, and all the partisans, even those who were seriously wounded, would laugh and have a good time. It was enough for one of them to say "Quiet! Misha is performing for us!" and the partisans would at once get into a festive mood.

The company had for a long time known that the town of Novozivkov had fallen into the hands of the Germans, but it had not heard as yet of their atrocities. The partisans heard of that later through their connections with the nearby inhabitants who would come and tell them of the Germans' heinous crimes, which were talked about far and wide.

One day a man from Novozivkov came to the partisans with the news that the Germans had strangled Ziama Davidovich's wife in her bed at the house of her neighbor Maria Stephanovna. Even Maria they didn't spare. They hanged her, tying a small board to her chest with the words: "I have hidden a Jewish woman in my house; I am an enemy of Germany."

It is impossible to describe how the news was received by Ziama, Dvora, and Misha. They sat dazed, uttering not a single word. Suddenly Dvora asked:

"Where did they bury my mother? Together with the rest of them?"

"I think so," answered the man from Novozivkov. How could he tell the girl that they had burned the body of her mother, together with the others, and had thrown the bones onto a garbage heap?! It was enough to tell that to Ziama Davidovich.

In the evening, sitting around the fire near the tent, the Davidovich family--the father and the two children--vowed before commander P.:

"As long as I am alive, and my hand can bear arms and blood flows in my veins, I will not cease from taking revenge on the fascists for our mother, for all the murdered Jews, and for all the people who were killed in our country. I hereby vow that only the blood of the German hangmen shall bring comfort to my heart."

The Davidovich family went on the warpath. Dvora left her work as a nurse and, together with her father and brother, held a rifle in her hand. She vowed never to return to her former work until she had killed ten Germans with her own hands. Terrible and ominous was Ziama Davidovich, who worked his axe to the utmost. Since that time he had stopped counting the number of Germans who fell under his axe.

Hard times came upon the partisans. Thousands of Magyars (Hungarian fascists) encircled the company. The partisans engaged the enemy in fierce battles, until they finally succeeded in slipping through a narrow trail, while the Magyars kept firing at them from all directions. "The Death Trail" was the name that the surviving partisans attached to this path.

Dvora and Ziama Davidovich came out unscathed from these battles, but Misha, that clever and charming boy with the flaming dark eyes, died in horrible agony. A shell hit him in the belly, wounding him seriously. There was no chance to save his life, as no surgeon was to be found. The horses of the partisans galloped ahead in a storm in order to break away from that horrible front. "Shoot me," pleaded the seriously wounded boy. He repeated the words to every comrade who shot past him. Out of their great love for the boy, they could not raise a hand to finish him off. Nevertheless, someone quietly put a pistol beside the dying boy. The 13-year-old boy killed himself with his own hand, leaving behind his bereaved father and sister.

No smile came to their faces, and only occasionally could they utter a word. Even between themselves they used more sign language than words.

Partisans are known for their ability to observe how one of their comrades ceases to distinguish between life and death. That is what happened to the father and the daughter after the death of 13-year-old Misha.

Two years later the partisan company joined the Red Army. On that same day Ziama and his daughter filed a request to be accepted as combat soldiers into the fighting company. When they were offered a chance to go on a rest leave, they answered: "We haven't settled out account with the fascists yet..."

PART FIVE:

EPILOGUE

SOVIET JEWS DURING AND AFTER THE WAR OF THE FATHERLAND

L. Singer

A considerable part of the defense of the U.S.S.R. can be attributed to Soviet Jewry. It is a fact that 123,822 Jewish soldiers and officers were awarded military medals and titles, and 105 Jews received the very highest distinction, "Hero of the Soviet Union" for their bravery and heroism against the German invaders. Judging by the number of soldiers who were given awards, the Jews ranked fourth or fifth place, after the Russians, Ukrainians, and Beylorussians.

Among the heros of the Jewish people who distinguished themselves in battle were: David Dragonsky, a tailor's son who was twice awarded the title "Hero of the Soviet Union." From the rank of polkovnik (colonel) in the early days of the war, he became general-polkovnik toward the end. Of the same rank was Yaakov Kreiser, also a "Hero of the Soviet Union" and a member of the Jewish Anti-Fascist Committee; others include tank-commander David Katz, the daring pilot Michael Plotkin, submarine crew-members Israel Pissnovitch and Caesar Konikov, artillery commander Israel Baskin, the young Red Army soldier Hayim Diskin, the pilot Paulina Gellman, Alexander Matrossov, and the cart-industry worker in Birobidjan, Joseph Bomagin.*

Along with other Soviet patriots, Jews fought within the ranks of the partisans in great number. A great many of them provided examples of fearlessness and self-sacrifice. With deep respect and appreciation, twice "Hero of the Soviet Union" Major-General Sidor Kovpak, commander of the largest partisan detachment in the western USSR, writes in his memoirs about his highly esteemed tank commander, Abraham Friedman. With great love, twice "Hero of the Soviet Union" Major-General Alexsei Feodorov, commander of the Partisan Union, writes about Shmuel Gottesban, who, with his own hands, killed twelve German soldiers and officers on the Kovel (Ukrainian) front. Podpolkovnik (lieutenant-colonel) A. B. Brinski, another "Hero of the Soviet Union," (who fought under the nom de guerre

---

* It seems that even military support workers won medals as well. (ed.)

"Dadya Petya," Uncle Petya), recounts the heroic deeds of the Jew Sedlanikov, a commander of a partisan company. Sedlanikov was a household name among the local population and drew so many men to the company that within a short time it became a full-fledged brigade.

Furthermore, the commander of the "Boiboi" partisan detachment which operated in the district of Leningrad, was a Jew called Novkovsky, the son of a small-town manual worker. The company of Nikolai Konishchuk (called "Kruk"), which fought in the western Ukraine in the area of Rovno, consisted almost entirely of Jews from the surrounding countryside. Many were admitted along with their families.

In special independent units, as well as in mixed groups, Soviet Jews fought in the forests of the Ukraine, White Russia, Lithuania, Latvia, and Moldavia. Among them were outstanding fighters, commanders, political commissars, ground scouts, liaison men, nurses, doctors, and communication experts. Long is the list of Jews who distinguished themselves in the battles for the war of the Soviet fatherland. Their intrepid exploits can provide material for many books.

OUR PLACE

Ilya Ehrenburg

The Jewish people were not wiped out in Egypt, nor were they destroyed by the Romans, nor even by the zealots of the Spanish Inquisition. To destroy the Jewish people is also not within the power of Hitler, although human history has never known of such a brazen attempt to kill an entire people.

Hitler brought to Poland and Beylorussia Jews from Paris, Amsterdam, and Prague: professors, diamond-cutters, musicians, old men, and babies. The Nazis are killing them there every Sabbath. These Jews are being suffocated with gas after the modern achievements of German chemistry have been tested on them. They are killing them in full ceremony, against the background of an orchestra playing the tune of "Kol Nidre."

The Germans have razed to the ground those places they had temporarily occupied in Soviet Russia. Not a single Jew was left of those who did not escape in time or did not join the partisans--all the rest were wiped out. They were annihilated in Kiev, Minsk, Gomel, and Charkov, in the Crimea Peninsula, and in the Baltic States. For two years the German army fought against unarmed women, old men, and helpless children. Now, they have announced with arrogance that they have killed all the Jews, down to the very last one.

But the Jewish nation lives! Hitler the madman does not realize that it is impossible to destroy our people! True, there are fewer Jews today than there were before the war, but the value of each has risen in comparison with what it was before. It was not with laments alone that the Jews reacted to the despicable slaughter, but with arms. Every Jew vowed to himself, to his conscience, and to the ghosts of his murdered brethern: "We may die, but we shall annihilate those abominable murderers!"

The Jews are not over-zealous in fighting for its own sake. They do not enjoy displaying their "muscle" in order to show off. Despite the onrush of the forces of evil, they do not cease to believe in the power of human understanding. They are the People of the Book who illuminate the darkness with their brilliant con-tributions. When the terrrible days came these men of thought and toil, who had been tortured in the ghettos for hundreds of years, proved to be daring, unflinching soldiers.

Jews do not weep! Jews do not boast! Jews struggle and fight! I will not try to recount the number of heroes. Blood is not to be weighed on the balance wheel; heroic deeds are not material for statistics. I would like only to say that the Jews who fill the ranks of the Red Army and Red Navy are fulfilling a mission, a mission which every civilian, every patriotic fighter, must fulfill--they are killing the Nazi beasts!

Jews are fighting in tanks as if tanks were their natural home; in the midst of winter, Jews glide on skis; Jews are sailing in submarines; and Jews, who are known far and wide as experts in watchmaking, have now proved to be experts in warmaking. When I happen to speak with a German prisoner of war, I am eager to tell him: "Look, I am a Jew." I take great pleasure in seeing his dreadful look, the look of fear in the distorted face of the vaunted "Superman," now trembling in his boots...

Stalingrad, the river Don, North Africa--all this is only a beginning. The war will return to the place where it began. We, the Jews, understand only too well our rights: to sit in judgement of those who murdered the old and the young.

On the cobblestones of Victory Boulevard in Berlin, we shall engrave the names of Kiev, Vitebsk, Kyartz--the names of towns where the "brave" Germans buried alive thousands of children. These names shall cry out: "Let sleep never come to these hangmen and to their offspring. May they never know peace of mind!"

APPENDIX

SOURCES

For general background information the single most useful source for the English-speaking student and scholar is John A. Armstrong (ed.) Soviet Partisans in World War II, Madison, Wisconsin: University of Wisconsin Press, 1964. I have made use of this book in my introduction, especially in the sections dealing with the composition of the partisans and their social structure. It is invaluable, especially its index and excellent annotated bibliography of Russian books on partisan warfare. The Lenin Library of Moscow has by far the greatest collection of material on this subject. Other collections of memoirs and descriptions of Soviet partisan commanders (based on material found in the Armstrong book) are:*

V. A. Andreyev, The People's War, Moscow, 1952. Andreyev was a teacher of military history who later became a prominent commissar and partisan leader, eventually attaining the rank of major-general in the Bryansk Forest of Beylorussia.

G. Linkov, The War Behind Enemy Lines, Moscow, 1951, 1959. Linkov was an engineer and an important Communist party official before the war who organized and led one of the parachutist detachments that played a major role in reactivating the partisan movement in Beylorussia in 1941-1942.

A. Feodorov, The Underground Obkom in Action, two volumes, Moscow, 1947. There are also several other editions, including one in English called The Underground Committee Carries On, Moscow: Foreign Languages Publishing House, 1952. "Obkom" is a Communist party committee at the province level. Feodorov was not only a major partisan leader, but a high official in the Ukrainian Communist Party.

Anton P. Brinsky or Brinskii (known by his nom de guerre, "Dadya Petya" - "Uncle Petya", On That Side of the Front: Memoir of a Partisan, Moscow, 1958. An important document by one of the leaders of the orga-

---

* Unless otherwise specified these books are in Russian or Ukrainian and have not been translated into English; I am giving the English equivalent of the title only. (ed.)

nizing teams sent to West Beylorussia and later to the Western Ukraine to revive the partisan movement in those areas.

Nikolai Konischuk ("Kruk"), a leader of a nearly all-Jewish partisan brigade numbering about 300 fighters and support troops in the Volynia region of Western Ukraine, is mentioned in several books, among them Abraham Foxman, "Resistance: The Few Against the Many" in Judah Pilch (ed.) The Jewish Catastrophe in Europe, New York: American Association for Jewish Education, 1968, pp. 87-142, and Moshe Kaganovitch, Di Milchumeh fun di Yidishe Partizaner in Mizrach Europa, Buenos Aires: Central Union of Polish Jews in Argentina, 1956, Vol. One, pp. 217, 341, and 343, Vol. Two, pp. 283 and 358. Kruk was a village mayor as well as a partisan leader. He was killed by Ukrainian nationalists after the war in revenge for someone Kruk put to death during the war.

Michael (Mikhail) Glieder, the "underground" moviemaker and photographer, wrote his own book called With a Motion Picture Camera Behind Enemy Lines, Moscow: Goskinoizdat, 1947. Sheds some interesting light on partisan propaganda in the Ukraine.

Several other books should be mentioned. Vasilli Begma and Luka Kyzya, The Paths of the Unsubjugated, Kiev, Ukraine: Radyanskyi Pysmennyk, 1962. Begma was commander of one of the major roving bands in the Ukraine.

Sidor Kovpak, From Putivl to the Carpathians, E. Gerasimov, (ed.), Moscow, 1945. Several editions exist including one in English, Our Partisan Course, London: Hutchinson, 1947. Kovpak was one of the most famous partisan leaders, and his account is fairly accurate.

Timofei Strokach, The Partisans of the Ukraine, Moscow, 1943. Strokach, who is described in the Appendix, was a prominent NKVD official and chief of the Ukrainian Staff of the Partisan Movement, an extremely important figure.

Soviet Partisans: From the History of the Partisan Movement in the Years of the Great Patriotic War, Moscow: Gospolitizdat, 1960. This is, according to Sovietologist John Armstrong, the single most valuable volume on the partisan movement; it is a collection of sixteen very substantial monographs on many aspects of partisanship.

Sputnik Partizana, (The Partisan's Traveling Companion), Moscow, 1942. This was the semiofficial Soviet handbook for use by partisans and for partisan training. It was published by the Communist Youth League (Komsomol) Press early in the war.

Individual Chapters

The first version of the partisan oath is taken from a publication of the Der Emes Publishing House, Moscow, 1944; the second oath is taken from Armstrong, op. cit., p. 662, who, in turn, found a copy of it in the German Military Documents Section (GMDS), Federal Records Center, Departmental Records Branch, Alexandria, Virginia.

The tales of Shmuel Persov are taken from the Moscow-based Der Emes Publishing House, 1944, except for the last one which is found in Einekeit, March 15, 1943. For a description of Persov, refer to Alexander Pomerantz, De Sovietish Harugai-Malchut, -- (The Soviet Martyrs), Buenos Aires: YIVO-Yiddish Scientific Institute, 1962.

"The Partisan Mine and Abraham Hirschfeld, the Watchmaker" and "Women Spies" are taken from G. Linkov, The War Behind Enemy Lines, Moscow, 1959.

"The Davidovich Family"--from Einekeit, October 21, 1943.

"Remember!" by H. Orland from the publication To Victory ("Tzum Zig"), Moscow: Der Emes Publishing House, 1944, pp. 28-30.

"A Civilian Camp in the Forest" is from Pavlo P. Vershigora, People With a Clear Conscience, Moscow: Sovietskii Pisatel, 1953 (one of several editions.) Vershigora, a motion picture director in Kiev before the war, was an aide to partisan general Sidor Kovpak and later commanded a roving band himself in the Carpathian Mountains. See also his other book, The Raid on the San and the Vistula, Moscow, 1960, which deals with his independent operations in Volynia and Poland and is especially revealing on Soviet attitudes toward Communism in Poland.

"Without Fire" by Shirka Gaman is from To Victory, Moscow: Der Emes Publishing House, 1944.

"Soviet Jews During and After the War of the Fatherland" by L. Singer from The Resurrected People (Dos Oifgerichteh Folk), Moscow: Der Emes Publishing House, 1948.

"Our Place" by Ilya Ehrenburg, from Einekeit, June 25, 1943. Ehrenburg's works are well known, and his talents as a novelist and journalist were widely noted. He was an official correspondent for the Soviet army and traveled widely under its shield, culminating at the gates of Berlin. See S. L. Shneiderman, Ilya Ehrenburg, New York: Yiddisher Kemfer, 1968 for a biography of the man written in Yiddish.

Photographic Sources

Several of the photos are taken from the original Russian edition, Partizanska Druzhba, Moscow: Der Emes Publishing House, 1948 and from Binyamin West's Hebrew translation of the book plus other sources in his Heym Hayu Rabim (1968). The reader should forgive the sometimes grainy quality of some of the photos; they were taken under the most difficult conditions, and some have reproduced in less than excellent shape.

Other sources include two Soviet books, G.Deborin, Secrets of the Second World War, Moscow: Progress Publishers, 1971, pp. 144 and 256; and Soviet Ukraine, Kiev: Ukrainian Soviet Encyclopedia, Editorial Office, 1970, pp. 148-150 and 153.

Two photos are from Judah Pilch (ed.), The Jewish Catastrophe in Europe, New York: The American Association for Jewish Education; copyright 1968, pp. 105 and 111. Reprinted by permission of the AAJE.

Most of the photos, however, were contributed by various partisans that the editor interviewed, including Moishe Flash, Berl Lorber, and Irving Porter (Puchtik).

Map and Organizational Chart Sources

The maps of Eastern Europe are taken from Edgar M. Howell, The Soviet Partisan Movement, 1941-1944, Washington, D.C.: Department of the Army (Pamphlet 20-244, August 1956. The charts showing the organization of the partisan movement and of the partisan brigade are also from Howell, pp. 138 and 139. The charts of the other partisan organizations (the staff of the Ukrainian partisan movement, an operative group) are taken from John Armstrong (ed.), Soviet Partisans in World War II, pp. 99, 112, 119 and 343. Reprinted by permission of the Regents of the University of Wisconsin, Copyright 1964.

ANNOTATED BIBLIOGRAPHY

ON JEWISH RESISTANCE DURING THE HOLOCAUST

This bibliography is not meant to be complete, especially with regards to works on the history and sociology of Soviet Jewry or of Holocaust literature in general, but it does contain all major books in English on Jewish resistance. A great many other important books, originally written in Russian, Polish, Yiddish, Hebrew, or French, are still waiting to be translated for the benefit of Western readers.

The bibliography is geared specifically to cover Jewish resistance in four major areas: camps, ghettos, forests, and allied forces. The emphasis is on the Jews of Eastern Europe (Russia, Poland, Latvia, Ukraine) as opposed to, let us say, France, Holland or Greece. Most selections are in English, with a few titles in Russian, Yiddish, and Hebrew. There is also a special section on faith and values in the post-Nazi era, another that discusses Jewish "cowardice," and a third on Jews in the Soviet Union.

The Moshe Kahanovitch (or Kaganovich) books mentioned in the bibliography contain additional sources of partisan memoirs written in Russian, Yiddish, and Hebrew; and the comprehensive anthology edited by John A. Armstrong, Soviet Partisans in World War II, will direct the reader to original Russian memoirs of commanders and fighters, some of whom are also mentioned in this book: for example - Andreyev, Begma, Brinsky (Brinskii), Feodorov (Fyodorov), Moshe (Mikhail) Glieder, Kovpak, Linkov, Petrov, Saburov, Strokach, and Vershigora.

ANNOTATED BIBLIOGRAPHY

I. General References on the Holocaust and the Nazi Era

Apenszlak, Jakob. The Black Book of Polish Jewry. New York: American Federation of Polish Jews, 1943.

A "memorial book" containing photos, maps, and sources, this volume is one of the first accounts of the destruction of European Jewry and the Nazi occupation of Poland. It gives lie to the fact that the Allies and American Jewry did not know of the plight of the Jews.

Bloch, Sam E. (ed.) Holocaust and Rebirth: Bergen Belsen 1945-1965. New York and Tel Aviv: Bergen-Belsen Memorial Press and World Federation of Bergen-Belsen Associations, 1965.

An impressive and beautifully illustrated "Yizkor" (remembrance) book commemorating the 20th anniversary of the liberation of the Bergen-Belsen concentration camp--and a model for all "Yizkor" books. Written in English, Yiddish, and Hebrew.

Dawidowicz, Lucy S. "Toward a History of theHolo caust." Commentary, XLVII, 4 (April 1969), pp. 51-56.

A useful and critical survey of research perspectives and historical problems dealing with the Holocaust.

Dawidowicz, Lucy S. The War Against the Jews: 1939-1945. New York: Holt, Rinehart and Winston, 1975.

One of the most important histories of the Holocaust and clearly one of the best, but not without its biases.

Donat, Alexander. The Holocaust Kingdom. New York: Holt, Rinehart and Winston, 1965.

An exceptionally sensitive memoir by a Polish Jewish survivor and his wife, dealing, among other things, with the Warsaw Ghetto, the uprising, and the Maidanek concentration camp.

Esh, Shaul. "The Dignity of the Destroyed: Towards a
    Definition of the Period of the Holocaust."
    Judaism, XI, 2 (Spring 1962), pp. 99-111.

    A brief essay attempting to define the Holocaust
    as a subject of study.

Friedlander, Albert H. (ed.) Out of the Whirlwind. New
    York: Doubleday, 1968.

    A fine anthology of Holocaust literature, illus-
    trated in pen and ink by Jacob Landau.

Friedlander, Henry. On the Holocaust: A Critique of the
    Treatment of the Holocaust in History Textbooks
    Accompanied by an Annotated Bibliography. New York
    Anti-Defamation League of Bnai Brith, 1972, 1973.

    A short 30-page booklet with an excellent and very
    useful bibliography and guide to Holocaust mater-
    ial for both scholar and layman.

Glatstein, Jacob, Knox, Israel, and Margoshes, Samuel
    (eds.) Anthology of Holocaust Literature. Phila-
    delphia: Jewish Publication Society, 1968.

    One of the best anthologies in existence, with a
    solid section on Jewish resistance.

Hilberg, Raul. The Destruction of the Europoean Jews.
    New York: Quadrangle Books, 1961, 1971.

    A magnum opus based mainly on German sources and
    almost impertinently inadequate in the area of
    Jewish resistance.

Hilberg, Raul (ed.) Documents of Destruction, Germany
    and Jewry 1933-1945. New York: Quadrangle Books,
    1971.

    A compilation of official archival German docu-
    ments and autobiographical Jewish sources. Even
    after all the criticism heaped upon him, it still
    contains no documents on Jewish resistance.

The Holocaust and Resistance. Jerusalem: Yad Vashem
    Remembrance Authority. Israel, 1972.

    An illustrated 44-page booklet outlining the
    history of Nazi-occupied Europe, 1933-1945.
    Contains numerous photos and documents.

Jewish Black Book Committee. The Black Book: The Nazi
     Crime Against the Jewish People. New York: Duell,
     Sloan and Pearce, 1946.

     One of the earliest documents of the Holocaust,
     prepared by the Jewish Anti-Fascist Committee of
     the USSR, the World Jewish Congress Vaad Leumi,
     and the Palestine and American Committee of Jewish
     Writers, Artists, and Scientists. Contains valu-
     able documents and over 100 illustrations.

Katz, Jacob. "Was the Holocaust Predictable?" Comment-
     ary, 59, 5 (May 1975), pp. 41-48.

     A compelling essay that attempts to answer the
     question: how could people have been so foolish as
     not to have seen what was in store for them at the
     hands of Hitler? This question begs another...
     and what could they have done if they had known?

Katz, Shlomo. "6,000,000 and 5,000,000." Midstream, X,
     1 (March 1964), pp. 3-14.

     The numbers refer to the Jews living in the United
     States during the Holocaust and the number of Jews
     killed during the Holocaust. The introduction by
     Katz leads the reader to an article by Labor
     Zionist leader Hayim Greenberg and asks: what
     could the 5 million have done to save the 6
     million?

Levin, Nora. The Holocaust: The Destruction of European
     Jewry, 1933-1945. New York: Schocken, 1968, 1973.

     Well-written, well-researched, lively, compassion-
     ate, and moving. Fairly good section (pp. 317386)
     on Jewish resistance in the Warsaw Ghetto and in
     the forests.

Morse, Arthur D. While Six Million Died: A Chronicle of
     American Apathy. New York: Random House, 1967,
     1968.

     The shocking story of the appalling apathy and
     callousness of the United States government, par-
     ticularly the State Department, in the face of
     Nazi genocide.

Pilch, Judah (ed.) The Jewish Catastrophe in Europe.
     New York: American Association for Jewish
     Education, 1968.

An exceptionally well-written and conceived book,
especially useful for students and teachers. An
excellent section (pp. 87-142) on Jewish resistance which can serve as a useful model for other
textbook writers.

Reitlinger, Gerald. The Final Solution: The Attempt to
Exterminate the Jews of Europe 1939-1945. New
York: A.S. Barnes, 1953, 1961.

An important early work on the Nazi "final solution"; small sections (pp. 276-280, 288-292) on
resistance; they are essentially weak sections,
but no better or worse than most historical works
on the Nazi era, except for Nora Levin's book.

Robinson, Jacob (with the assistance of Ada Friedman).
The Holocaust and After: Sources and Literature in
English. (12th volume in the Yad-Vashem-YIVO
Documentary Projects Series.) New York and
Jerusalem: Yad Vashem and YIVO Institute for
Jewish Research, 1973.

The comprehensive bibliography of 6,637 items,
listed in this 354-page volume, deals with not
only the Holocaust, but also with political,
economic, historical and cultural life in the pre-
and post-Holocaust period.

Rutherford, Ward. Genocide: The Jews in Europe 1939-45.
New York: Ballantine Books Illustrated History of
the Violent Century, Human Conflict, No. 4, 1973.

A profusely illustrated, sensitively written
booklet.

Schoenberner, Gerhard. The Yellow Star: The Persecution
of the Jews in Europe, 1933-1945. New York: Bantam
Books, 1969, 1973.

An illustrated documentation of genocide with many
never-before published photographs. Includes a
chapter on Jewish resistance, mainly General
Stroop's report on the Warsaw Ghetto (pp. 209234).
Translated from the German by Susan Sweet.

Shirer, William L. The Rise and Fall of the Third
Reich: A History of Nazi Germany. New York: Simon
and Schuster, 1959.

A monumental work, probably <u>the</u> definitive work on Nazi Germany, but contains <u>very</u> little on Jewish resistance.

Trunk, Isaiah. <u>Judenrat: The Jewish Councils in Eastern Europe Under Nazi Occupation</u>. New York: Macmillan, 1972.

Winner of the National Book Award in 1973, this is the first scholarly attempt to analyze the Jewish Councils that presided over the ghettos of Eastern Europe. Massive and valuable footnotes.

Tsur, Muki and Yanai, Nathan (eds.) <u>The Holocaust</u>. New York: American Zionist Youth Foundation, 1970.

A surprisingly effective and useful paperback book with short, strong, forceful statements on various aspects of the Holocaust, including resistance (pp. 49-71).

Zack, Avraham and Razshansky, Shmuel (eds.) <u>Churban-Anthologia</u> (The Holocaust Anthology) Buenos Aires: Ateneo Literario En El Instituto Cientifico Judio, 1970.

In the original Yiddish, this is an excellent anthology of prose, poetry and drama, written by such renowned writers as Itzik Feffer, Chaim Grade, Avraham Reisen, Shmuel Halkin, Joseph Opotashu, and Jacob Glatstein.

1I. General References on Jewish Resistance

Ainsztein, Reuben. Jewish Resistance in Nazi-Occupied Eastern Europe. New York: Harper and Row, 1974.

One of the monumental works on Jewish defiance to appear in the English language. Containing nearly 1000 pages, it ranks with the works of Moshe Kahanovitch in magnitude.

Barkai, Meyer (ed.) The Fighting Ghettos. Philadelphia: J.B. Lippincott, 1962. (Available in paperback from Tower Books.)

A solid collection of essays on Jewish resistance in the ghettos of Warsaw, Vilna, and Cracow. Long out of print, now available in paperback. Also contains material on resistance in the camps and the forests. Translated from the Hebrew, this is an edited version of Seifer Milchamot Hagetaot, published in Tel Aviv by the Ghetto Fighters House and Kibbutz Hameuchad Association.

Bauer, Yehuda. They Chose Life. New York: American Jewish Committee, 1973. Illustrated.

A brief (68 pages) overview of Jewish resistance during the Holocaust, dealing with both unarmed and armed resistance, revolts in the ghettos, camps, and forests. Excellent for study groups and students. Bauer, head of the department of Holocaust studies at the Hebrew University in Jerusalem, is also the author of Flight and Rescue: Brichah.

Elkins, Michael. Forged in Fury. New York: Ballantine Books, 1971 (paperback).

Fast-paced, well-written account of Jewish heroism in Europe and the continued search for Nazi criminals after the war.

European Resistance Movements, 1939-1945. Oxford: Pergamon Press, 1960.

The proceedings of the First International Conference on the History of the Resistance movements, held in Belgium, September 14-17, 1958. Contains much valuable information including an article by

Philip Friedman on the role of the Jews in the Soviet partisans, entitled "Jewish Resistance to Nazism."

Extermination and Resistance. Israel: Ghetto Fighters House, Kibbutz Lochamei Haghetot, 1958.

Collection of essays published by a kibbutz among whose members are many partisans, including Yitzchak Zuckerman and Zivia Lubetkin, leaders of the Warsw Ghetto uprising.

Foxman, Abraham H. "Resistance: The Few Against the Many" in Judah Pilch (ed.) **The Jewish Catastrophe in Europe**, pp. 87-145.

An excellent well-documented, and comprehensive overview of Jewish resistance.

Handlin, Oscar. "Jewish Resistance to the Nazis." **Commentary**, 34, 5 (November 1962), pp. 398-407.

The prize-winning Harvard historian criticizes the "sheep to slaughter" perspective of Hilberg and Bettelheim calling it "dangerous," "misleading," "uninformed," and a "defamation of the dead and their culture."

Jewish Heroism in Modern Times. Jerusalem: World Zionist Organization, 1965.

A propaganda book, dealing with Jewish bravery both in Europe and in Palestine. Contains articles by Cholavski, Blumenthal and Karmish, Galili, Yehudah Bauer, and M. Schwartz. Of uneven quality.

Knout, David. **Contribution a L'histoire de la Resistance Juive en France 1940-1944.** Paris: Editions du Centre, 1947.

This is monograph #3 in a series of studies produced by the Centre de Documentation Juive Contemporaine of Paris. It is 184 pages long and contains photos and documents.

Latour, Anny. **La Resistance Juive en France.** Paris: Stock, 1970.

A fine account of the French resistance, with outstanding photos, documents, and maps.

Nirenstein, Albert. A Tower from the Enemy: Contribu-
    tions to a History of Jewish Resistance in Poland.
    New York: Orion Press, 1959.

    A somewhat disorganized bookk, with heavy emphasis
    on the Warsaw, Vilna, Cracow and Bialystok
    ghettos. Contains photographs. Translated from
    Polish, Yiddish, and Hebrew by D. Neiman and from
    the Italian by M. Savilli.

Porter, Jack Nusan. "Jewish Resistance During the Holo-
    caust." Wisconsin Jewish Chronicle, four-part
    series (December 1, 15, 22 and 29) 1972.

    An impassioned analysis of the myths surrounding
    Jewish resistance and a description of the major
    areas of resistance. Also includes a short
    bibliography.

Schwarz, Leo (ed.) The Root and the Bough: The Epic of
    an Enduring People. New York: Holt, Rinehart and
    Winston, 1949.

    A fine collection of tales by a well-known antho-
    logizer of heroism in Warsaw, White Russia and the
    Western Ukraine as well as first person accounts
    of survivors living in Israel.

Sefer Ha-Partizanim Ha-Yehudim. (The Book of Jewish
    Partisans.) Merhaviya, Israel: Sifriat Poalim,
    Workers Book Guild, and Yad Veshem, 1958, two
    volumes.

    A massive, nicely produced compendium of Jewish
    resistance. Each volume is over 700 pages long
    and includes maps, documents, memorabilia, etc.
    Indexed.

Soviet Ukraine. Kiev, Ukraine, S.S.R.: Editorial Office
    of the Ukrainian Soviet Encyclopedia, Academy of
    Sciences, no date, but circa 1960.

    A beautifully illustrated, single volume compen-
    dium of the history and sociology of the Soviet
    Ukraine. The section on the role of the Ukrain-
    ians during World War II contains a section (pp.
    150-54) on partisan warfare that is typically
    heroic in style and makes no mention of Jews, but
    is valuable background to the general Soviet par-
    tisan role in the war.

Suhl, Yuri (ed. and trans.) They Fought Back: The Story of the Jewish Resistance in Nazi Europe. New York: Crown, 1967. AVailable also in paperback.

A wide-ranging collection of reprinted and originally translated pieces covering heroism in the ghettos, the camps, and the forests. The editor is also a well-known novelist (One Foot in America). Contains photographs.

Tartakower, Aryeh (ed.) Jewish Resistance During the Holocaust. Jerusalem: Yad Vashem Memorial, 1971.

Very valuable papers and commentary by world specialists in Holocaust literature; the proceedings of a conference on the subject held in Israel in April, 1968. Translated into English, with three papers in French.

Tenenbaum, Joseph. Underground: The Story of a People. Philosophical Library, 1952. Out of print.

III. Specific Areas of Jewish Resistance

A. The Ghettos

Barkai, Meyer. The Fighting Ghettos, pp. 9-128.

> The struggle of the Jews within the ghetto walls of Warsaw, Bialystok, Grodna, and Brodi.

Foxman, Abraham H. "Resistance" in Judah Pilch (ed.) The Jewish Catastrophe in Europe, pp. 95-114.

> Deals with the Warsaw and Vilna ghettos, the Glazman affair, and other aspects of resistance.

Friedman, Philip. Martyrs and Fighters: The Epic of the Warsaw Ghetto. New York: Praeger, 1954.

> Documents of the ghetto, with illustrations, 325 pp.

Goldstein, Bernard. The Stars Bear Witness. New York: Viking, 1949. (Dolphin paperback edition in 1961 entitled Five Years in the Warsaw Ghetto.)

> Translated from the Yiddish, this is an important account of life in the ghetto by the leader of the Jewish Socialist Bund.

Goldstein, Charles. The Bunker. New York: Atheneum and Jewish Publication Society, 1970.

> A moving memoir of a Warsaw ghetto survivor and French partisan activist. Translated from the French.

Kaczerginski, Shmuel. Khurban Vilne (The Destruction of Volna). New York: The United Vilner Relief Committee, 1947.

> An account, in Yiddish, of the destruction of the ghetto of Vilna, with rare woodcuts, photographs, and songs.

Katsh, Abraham I. (ed. and trans.) The Warsaw Diary of Chaim A. Kaplan (originally published under the title of The Scroll of Agony). New York: Macmillan, Collier Books, 1965, 1973.

A most compelling, first person account of the ghetto, written by a Hebrew scholar and teacher who perished in the Holocaust.

Lazar, Chaim. *Muranowska 7: The Warsaw Ghetto Uprising*. Tel Aviv: Massada-P.E.C. Press, 1966.

The role of the Betar Zionist Youth Movement in the ghetto. Translated from the Hebrew. Illustrated.

Reiss, Asher. "A Quarter Century of Books on the Warsaw Ghetto Battle." *Jewish Book Annual*, 26 (1968-69), pp. 23-33.

An excursion into the literature, 1943-1968, of the Warsaw Ghetto. Quite useful in its bibliography.

Ringelblum, Emanuel. *Notes from the Warsaw Ghetto*. New York: McGraw-Hill, 1958.

A poignant insider's account of life in the ghetto, written by its historian and archivist. Edited and translated by Jacob Sloan. Now also available in paperback from Schocken Books (New York, 1974).

Suhl, Yuri (ed. and trans.) *They Fought Back*, pp. 51-54, 69-127, 136-143, 148-159, 165-171, and 231-245.

Resistance memoirs, translated from the Yiddish, dealing with the ghettos of Warsaw, Bialystok, Vilna, Lachwa, and Minsk.

The Warsaw Ghetto Uprising. New York: Congress for Jewish Culture, 1974.

Short booklet that includes essays, poetry, ghetto songs, and photos. Useful for Passover service.

B.   The Partisans

Armstrong, John A. (ed.) *Soviet Partisans in World War II*. Madison, Wisconsin: University of Wisconsin Press, 1964.

A massive and comprehensive 800-page summation of "Soviet irregular warfare." Though not describing

Jewish participation in great detail, this excellent book does help the reader in understanding the over-all conditions of partisan life. Con tains useful annotated bibliography.

Bakalczuk-Felin, Meilech. Zikhroynes fun a Yidishn Partizan (Memoirs of a Jewish Partisan). Buenos Aires: Central Union of Polish Jews in Argentina, 1958.

The Central Union should be highly commended for its diligence and energy in gathering and publishing accounts of Jewish participation in World War II. These memoirs are from the regions of Volynia and Polesye in Western Ukraine.

Barkai, Meyer. The Fighting Ghettos, pp. 129-189.

Authentic description of accounts of guerilla warfare by Jews, written by Moshe Kahanovitch, Abba Kovner, Tuvia Belsky, and Mischa Gildenman, among others.

Deborin, G. Secrets of the Second World War. Moscow: Progress Publishers, 1971.

Translated from the Russian and published by the English branch of a Russian publishing house, this book contains material and rare photographs never before seen in Western countries. See especially the chapter on Soviet partisans (pp. 195-214, 234-237, and 274-277). No mention of the role of Jews, and the language is "heroic and propagandistic"; the question is - are the facts correct?

Foxman, Abraham H. "Resistance" in Judah Pilch (ed.) The Jewish Catastrophe in Europe, pp. 123-137.

An excellent and compact description of the obstacles facing the partisans, plus tales of individual heroes in the movement.

Heilbrunn, Otto. Partisan Warfare. New York: Praeger, 1962.

A theoretical discussion of partisan resistance with a useful bibliography dealing with cross-cultural and comparative guerilla operations. No stress on the Jewish component in partisanship.

Howell, Edgar M. The Soviet Partisan Movement, 1941-1944. Washington, D.C., Department of the Army (Pamphlet #20-244), August 1956.

Prepared after the war in the Office of the Chief of Military History under the chief of that division, Major Howell. This is a useful, though boring, account of the partisan movement in Eastern USSR. Contains maps and charts of partisan fighting zones and partisan chain of command.

Kahanovitch, Moshe. Di Milchumeh fun di Yidishe Partizaner in Mizrach Europe (The War of Jewish Partisans in Eastern Europe). Buenos Aires: Central Union of Polish Jews in Argentina, 1956, two volumes, with illustrations, maps, index, and bibliography.

Written in Yiddish, this is one of the monumental books on Jewish partisan resistance. Someone should translate this magnum opus into English. Its Spanish title is La Lucha de los Guerilleros Judios en la Europa Oriental.

Kahanovitch, Moshe. Milchemet Ha-Partizanim Ha-Yehudim Be-mizrach Eropah (The War of Jewish Partisans in Eastern Europe). Tel Aviv: Ayanot Press, 1954, 435 pages, with illustrations, maps, index and bibliography.

This is the Hebrew version; it is a condensed version of the two-volume Yiddish edition that was published in Buenos Aires. The Yiddish version tends to ramble; this one is more compact.

Kahanovitch, Moshe. Der Yidisher Unteil in ther Partizaner-Bevegung fun Soviet Russland (Jewish Participation in the Partisan Movement in Soviet Russia). Rome: 1948.

Kahanovitch admits that his Yiddish and/or Hebrew version of The War of Jewish Partisans in Eastern Europe is a better and more inclusive account of Jewish resistance than this account. This is not a particularly good source; it is incomplete in many ways.

Macksey, Kenneth, The Partisans of Europe in the Second World War, New York: Stein and Day, 1975.

An objective but rather dull study of partisan
activity. It comes to the conclusion, shocking to
some, that the partisans had only a marginal
impact on the basic military issues of the war and
on the final outcome of the war itself.

Osanka, Franklin M. (ed.) Modern Guerilla Warfare:
   Fighting Communist Guerilla Movements, New York:
   The Free Press, 1962.

   A most comprehensive collection of articles on
   contemporary partisanship, useful for comparative
   research. Contains articles of uneven quality on
   Soviet partisans. Useful bibliography of English
   language books and articles. Has a biased perspective, as the title implies.

Porter, Jack Nusan. "Zalonka: An Interview with a
   Jewish Partisan Leader." Davka, (UCLA Hillel
   Foundation), III, 2, 3 (Winter-Spring 1973), pp.
   14-20.

   A son interviews his father in order to discover
   his past.

Suhl, Yuri. They Fought Back, pp. 160-164, 176-181,
   226-230, 246-281.

   Original translated accounts of heroism in the
   forests. Includes for the first time in English
   the story of the brave acts of the Herbert Baum
   Group, German-Jewish "urban guerillas" who defied
   the Nazis in Berlin; plus accounts of resistance
   in Paris, Rome, and Brussels.

Suhl, Yuri. Uncle Misha's Partisans. New York: Four
   Winds Press, 1973.

   The editor of They Fought Back, a chronicle of
   Jewish resistance during the Holocaust, has written an outstanding children's book (best for ages
   10-14) about the adventures of a 12-year-old boy
   who joins the Jewish partisan brigade of Dadia
   Misha (Misha Gildenman), which battled the Nazis
   in the area of Zhitomer, Soviet Ukraine.

West, Benjamin (ed. and trans.) Heym Hayu Rabim: Partizaner Yehudim B'brit Hamoatzot B'milchemet Haolam
   Hashiniyah (They Were Many: Jewish Partisans in
   the Soviet Union During World War II). Tel Aviv:
   Labor Archives Press, 1968.

Translated from the Russian version, Partizanska
Druzhba (Partisan Brotherhood), Moscow: Der Emess
Government Publishing House, 1948. Personal
memoirs and commentary. Contains rare photographs
and additional material not found in the Russian
version.

C. The Concentration Camps

Adler H. G. "Ideas Toward a Sociology of the Concentration Camp." American Journal of Sociology, LXIII,
5 (March 1958), pp. 513-522.

One of the few sociological analyses probing
methodological problems regarding research into
camp life. The concentration camp is seen as the
most recent institution of oppression in which
prisoners live without rights.

Barkai, Meyer. The Fighting Ghettos, pp. 191-251.

Jewish resistance in the concentration camps of
Treblinka, Sobibor, Konin, Ponyatov, Trabnik,
Ponar, and others by Isaiah Trunk, Yankel Vyernik,
A. Petzorsky, leon Velitzker, and Shlomo Gul.

Foxman, Abraham H. "Resistance" in Judah Pilch (ed.)
The Jewish Catastrophe in Europe, pp. 114-120.

Compact descriptions of revolts in Auschwitz,
Sobibor, and Treblinka.

Levi, Primo. If This Be A Man. New York: Orion Press,
1959. Also in Collier paperback, as Survival in
Auschwitz, 1961.

Written by a most eloquent survivor, an Italian
Jewish chemist, this is one of the best eyewitness
accounts of the extermination camps.

Steiner, Jean-Francois. Treblinka. New York: Simon and
Shuster, 1967.

Translated from the French by Helen Weaver, this
is a powerful account of the revolt by camp
inmates. It is, however, not a very reliable
account. The book is basically fiction, though
based on a factual event.

Suhl, Yuri (ed.) They Fought Back, pp. 7-50, 128-135, 172-175, and 182-225.

Descriptions of the revolt in Auschwitz led by Josef Cyrankiewicz and Rosa Robota, as well as descriptions of other camp revolts, such as uprisings in Treblinka, Sobibor, and Koldyczewo.

Wells, Leon. The Janowska Road. New York: Macmillan, 1963.

Sensitive report of a young Jewish boy which deals with the genocide of Jews in Eastern Galicia and with the camp at Janowska Street in Lvov (Lemberg).

D. The Armed Forces

Ainstztein, Reuben. "The War Record of Soviet Jewry." Jewish Social Studies, XXVIII, 1 (January 1966), pp. 3-24.

More than 500,000 Jews fought in the Russian Army; 200,000 fell in battle; and about 150,000 of them were deocrated for valor and devotion to duty; more than 100 Jews were named "Hero of the Soviet Union," one of the Russian army's highest awards. Ainsztein describes the scope of this participa tion.

Foxman, Abraham H. "Resistance" in Judah Pilch (ed.) The Jewish Catastrophe in Europe, pp. 120-123.

Thousands of Jews participated in the armed forces of the Allied Forces; they too should be consid ered as part of the resistance forces, in a sense.

E. The Brichah (The Rescue of Jews)

Bauer, Yehuda. Flight and Rescue: Brichah. New York: Random House, 1970.

The gripping tale of the role of the Brichah, the movement for rescuing Jews during and after the war; written by the Hebrew University social ana- lyst and the author of They Chose Life, an account of Jewish resistance.

Masters, Anthony. The Summer That Bled: The Biography
of Hannah Senesh. New York: St. Martins Press and
Washington Square Press, 1973.

The short but remarkable life of a Jewish partisan
parachutist. Contains photographs.

Syrkin, Marie. Blessed is the Match: The Story of
Jewish Resistance. Philadelphia: Jewish Publica
tion Society, 1948.

One of the first accounts of Hannah Senesh's
bravery. Also contains examples of other acts of
resistance.

Senesh, Hannah. Her Life and Diary. New York: Schocken
Books, 1973.

A poignant story of one woman, a Jewish partisan
from Palestine. Her story is now legendary.

IV.   The Myth of Jewish Cowardice

Arendt, Hannah. Eichmann in Jerusalem: A Report on the
Banality of Evil. New York: Viking Press, 1964.

A brilliant and impulsive essay on the Eichmann
trial in Jerusalem and a controversial analysis
of the Judenrat (Jewish Councils) as unwilling
struments of the Nazis. Read with caution,
however,

Bettelheim, Bruno. The Informed Heart: Autonomy in a
Mass Age. New York: The Free Press, 1960 (Avon
paperbacks, 1971).

An eminent psychotherapist presents a psychological theory of the Jews, maintaining that they were
unwilling to realistically evaluate their predica-
ment, thereby becoming passive victims in their
own destruction. Again, this book must be read
with a critical eye because it too contains many
errors of both fact and interpretation.

De Pres, Terrence, The Survivor, New York: Oxford University Press, 1976.

A brilliant book and an excellent retort to
Bettelheim; an account of the sociology of the
death camps.

Donat, Alexander. _Jewish Resistance_. New York: Warsaw Ghetto Resistance Organization, 1964.

This short, 32-page booklet is, in essence, an answer to the post-Eichmann trial myth that all Jews were cowards and "sheep."

Hausner, Gideon. _Justice in Jerusalem_. New York: Schocken Books, 1968.

Survey of the Holocaust and the Eichmann trial by the Israeli prosecutor. Should be contrasted with Arendt's book.

Robinson, Jacob. _And the Crooked Shall Be Made Straight: The Eichmann Trial, the Jewish Catastrophe, and Hannah Arendt's Narrative_. New York: Macmillan, and Jewish Publication Society, 1965.

A powerful and persuasive attack on Hannah Arendt's book _Eichmann in Jerusalem_. Massive and valuable footnotes.

Robinson, Jacob. _Psychoanalysis in a Vacuum: Bruno Bettelheim and the Holocaust_. New York: YIVO Institute-Yad Vashem Documentary Projects, 1970.

A rebuttal to the Bettelheim book, _The Informed Heart_.

Schappes, Morris U. _The Strange World of Hannah Arendt_. New York: _A Jewish Currents Reprint_, 1963 (pamphlet).

Another well-reasoned rebuttal to Hannah Arendt's book on Eichmann.

Shabbetai, K. _As Sheep to the Slaughter? The Myth of Cowardice_. New York and Tel Aviv: World Association of the Bergen Belsen Survivors Associations, 1963. With a foreword by Gideon Hausner.

An impassioned and eloquent plea for understanding the sanity and madness of the Nazi Era and its victims. Written in response to Arendt, Bettelheim, and Hilberg.

Wiesel, Elie. "A Plea for the Dead" in his _Legends of Our Time_. New York: Holt, Rinehart and Winston, 1968. Also Avon, Bard Books, paperback, 1970.

Nearly all of Wiesel's writings are a defense of the victims of the Holocaust, but this article is one of the most eloquent of those pleas.

V. Faith and Despair in the Post-Holocaust Era

Berkovits, Eliezer. Faith After the Holocaust. New York: KTAV Publishing House, 1973.

A Talmudic scholar of reknown and a distinguished rabbi and educator, Berkovits intensely analyzes the theological aspects of man's response to God's "hiding of the face" and his affirmation of faith despite God's mystery.

Cohen, Arthur A. (ed.) Arguments and Doctrines: A Reader of Jewish Thinking in the Aftermath of the Holocaust. New York: Harper and Row, 1970.

Twenty-eight essays focus on the internal conflict and ferment of post-Holocaust Jewish religious thought.

Cohen, Elie A. Human Behavior in the Concentration Camp. New York: Norton, 1953.

A valuable study of psychological reactions to total institutions like the camps. Translated from the Dutch.

Frankl, Viktor. Man's Search for Meaning. New York: Pocket Books (Simon and Shuster), 1963. Originally published by Beacon Press, 1959.

A psychiatrist who spent three years in Auschwitz develops his theory of logotherapy, which focuses attention upon mankind's groping for a higher meaning in life. He suggests that love can be an effective means of coping with suffering.

Fackenheim, Emil L. God's Presence in History: Jewish Affirmation and Philosophic Reflections. New York: Harper and Row, 1972.

An eminent Jewish theologian from the University of Toronto inquires into the role of the Jewish people; their duty is to survive and prevail as a people and as a moral force.

Halpern, Irving. "Meaning and Despair in the Literature
    of the Survivors." Jewish Book Annual, 26 (1968
    69), pp. 7-22.

    Halpern examines this "depressing body of litera-
    ture" from Viktor Frankl to Elie Wiesel in order
    to answer some existential questions about death
    and hope.

Judaism, special section, "Jewish Values in the Post-
    Holocaust Future," 16, 3 (Summer 1967).

    A series of statements and responses that emerged
    during a symposium on the subject. The contribu-
    tors include Emil Fackenheim, George Steiner,
    Richard Popkin, and Elie Wiesel. It raised more
    questions than it answered.

Judaism, special section, "Jewish Faith After Nazism,"
    20, 3 (Summer 1971), pp. 263-294.

    Contributions by Charles Steckel, Seymour Cain,
    and Michael Wyschograd examine the Holocaust
    through the works of Emil Fackenheim and Richard
    Reubenstein.

Neusner, Jacob. "Implications of the Holocaust" in his
    anthology, Understanding Jewish Theology. New
    York: KTAV and ADL, 1973, pp. 177-193.

    Neusner examines the implications of the Holocaust
    on Jewish theology and especially its impact on
    youth. See also Emil Fackenheim's article "The
    Human Condition After Auschwitz", pp. 165-175 in
    this same anthology.

Reubenstein, Richard L. After Auschwitz: Radical Theol-
    ogy and Contemporary Judaism. Indianapolis:
    Bobbs-Merrill, 1966 (paperback).

    A leading Jewish rabbi confronts the dilemmas
    within contemporary religion in the post-Holocaust
    era.

Wiesel, Elie. "To a Young Jew of Today," in his One
    Generation After, New York: Random House, 1970.
    Also, Avon, Bard Boks, 1972.

    The themes of faith and despair appear in almost
    any Wiesel novel or essay: Night, The Gates of the

Forest, A Beggar in Jerusalem, and in this essay, addressed to youth of all religions.

VI. Jews in the Soviet Union

Cang, Joel. The Silent Millions: A History of the Jews in the Soviet Union. New York: Taplinger Publishing House, 1969.

An engrossing history of Soviet Jews from the Revolution of 1917 to Brezhnev. Contains a very useful bibliography.

Eliav, Arie. Between Hammer and Sickle. Philadelphia: Jewish Publication Society, 1967, 1969.

A prize-winning account of the tragedy of Soviet Jews written by a member of the Israeli parliament and author of other books including Eretz Ha-Tzvi and The Voyage of the Ulua.

Frumkin, Jacob, et al. (eds.) Russian Jewry 1860-1917 and Russian Jewry 1917-1967 (two volumes). New York: A.S. Barnes and Thomas Yoseloff, 1966 and 1969, respectively.

Collections of articles dealing with historical, sociological, political, and educational areas; also contain two chapters on the Holocaust and Soviet Jews. Sponsored by the Union of Soviet Jews of New York City.

Gilboa, Yehoshua. The Black Years of Soviet Jewry 1939-1953. Boston: Little Brown, 1971. Translated from the Hebrew.

A well-researched valuable book, dealing with a crucial period in Soviet Jewish affairs: the Jewish Anti-Fascist Committee, the Stalin purges and "doctor's plots." Written by a leading Israeli journalist.

Goldhagen, Erich (ed.) Ethnic Minorities in the Soviet Union. New York: Praeger, 1968.

Collected essays read at a symposium held in the fall of 1965 at the Institute of East European Jewish Studies of the Philip Lown School of Near Eastern and Judaic Studies at Brandeis University. Includes bibliographies.

Kochan, Lionel (ed.) The Jews in Soviet Russia Since
    1917. New York: Oxford University Press, 1970,
    1972.

    An excellent collection of scholarly articles on
    various aspects of Soviet Jewish life, written by
    16 American and British experts in their fields.

Korey, William. The Soviet Cage: Anti-Semitism in
    Russia. New York: Viking Press, 1973.

    A lucid factual account of Russian anti-Semitism,
    written by the leading U.S. expert on Soviet
    Jewish affairs.

Kuznetsov, Anatoly. Babi Yar. New York: Dial Press,
    1967.

    A moving account of the famed masacre of thousands
    of Jews in the Babi Yar ravine in the Ukraine near
    Kiev.

Meisel, Nachman. Dos Yidishe Shafen un der Yidisher
    Shrayber in Sovietfarband (Jewish Creativity and
    the Jewish Writer in the Soviet Union). New York:
    Yiddish Cultural Union-Farband (YKUF) Farlag,
    1959.

    A general overview of Jewish theater, literature
    and other arts in the USSR from the 1920s to the
    1950s.

Shneiderman, S.L. Ilya Ehrenburg. New York: Yiddisher
    Kemfer, 1968.

    Written in Yiddish soon after the death of this
    controversial Jewish-Communist novelist, poet, and
    journalist, this is a short biography by a noted
    expert in the area of Russian-Jewish affairs.

VII. Miscellaneous Material

Berman, Aaron, et al. Thinking About the Unthinkable:
    An Encounter with the Holocaust. Amherst, Massa-
    chusetts: Hampshire College, Social Science
    Division, 1972.

    An impressive course outline organized and carried
    out by students that included speakers and trips

to Holocaust sites in Europe. A model for any
college or university course in this area.

Breakstone, David. God in Search of Himself. Washington, D.C.: Bnai Brith Hillel Foundations, 1974.

Called "a passage of respect for the six million,"
this is the personal quest of a young student from
Boston, now living in Israel, which can serve as a
basis for further inquiry and is valuable as a
teaching and group discussion guide. This drama-
tic reading is available from the national Hillel
Foundations.

Gottlieb, Malke and Mlotek, Chana (compilers). Twenty-
Five Ghetto Songs with Music and Transliteration.
New York: Workmen's Circle, Educational
Department, 1968.

Good collection of ghetto songs, with music, from
the Yiddish.

Post, Albert. The Holocaust: A Case Study of Genocide:
A Teaching Guide. New York: American Association
for Jewish Education, 1973.

This is a teaching guide and lesson plan for
teenagers. Though edited by professionals it is
more superficial and inferior in many ways to the
Hampshire College outline done by Berman et al.
but this guide is geared toward younger ages.

Roskies, David G. Night Words. Washington, D.C.: Bnai
Brith Hillel Foundation, 1973.

Subtitled a "midrash on the Holocaust," this is a
very effective reading and commentary on an almost
inscrutable event. The author is a young Jewish
activist and Yiddishist from Canada.

Sartre, Jean-Paul. Anti-Semite and Jew. New York:
Schocken, 1948, 1965.

A classic portrait of anti-Semitism, written by a
great non-Jewish philosopher and social activist;
translated from the French by George J. Becker.

GLOSSARY

Brichah--Hebrew for "rescue"; the attempt by Israeli and Jewish leaders to rescue Jews in Europe both during and after the war.

Brigada--Brigades, three to four otryads.

Civilian Camps--Refers to those groups of civilians who were part of the partisan bands and were protected by them.

Commissar--Communist party official. Some commissars were also military commanders. At other times there was both a military commander and an ideological and political advisor. His purpose was to teach and enforce party principles and policy.

Diaspora--Greek for dispersion; the Hebrew equivalent is Galut, meaning all lands outside of Israel, the "lands of exile." Also refers to the Jews living in these lands and to their state of mind.

Einikeit--The house organ and newspaper of the Jewish Anti-Fascist Committee of the Soviet Union. The word means "unity" in Russian. The first issue appeared June 7, 1942; the last issue, November 20, 1948.

Folk-Shtimme--Yiddish for "People's Voice"; an impor tant Yiddish Communist newspaper in Warsaw.

Genocide--The systematic murder of an entire people, nation, or race. The word comes from two Latin roots: genus, people, and cide, killing. The word was first coined in 1944 by PolishJewish legal scholar Raphael Lemkin. It is a legal as well as a sociopolitical term. (See Holocaust.)

Hero of the Soviet Union--The title of the highest ranking military award given to Soviet citizens for valor in battle. Nearly 150 Jews received such an award.

Holocaust--Literally means "destruction" or being con sumed by flames." It is the term that Jews use to describe the genocide of the Jewish people and the obliteration of the Jewish community and culture(s) during World War II. In Hebrew the term is <u>Hashoah</u>, and in Yiddish it is the <u>Churban</u>. (See Genocide).

Kolkhoz--A Communist collective farm found in the USSR.

Oblast--Russian term for province; it is not the American equivalent of a state, but more like a large county.

Okrug--Russian term for district.

Otryad--A Company-size Red Army unit or a smaller size partisan detachment.

Podpolkovnik--Russian term for lieutenant-colonel.

Pogrom--An organized massacre of helpless people and the looting of property, usually with the tacit support of the local officials; specifically, a massacre of Jews, as originally occurred in Russia or Poland.

Politruk--Political officer attached to a Russian army unit or partisan group. (See Commissar.)

Polkovnik--A Russian military rank somewhat equivalent to the American rank of colonel. A "General-Polkovnik" is a colonel-general, which in the U.S. Army would be equivalent to the rank of general.

S.S.--Abbreviation of the German word "Shutzstaffel," meaning protection squads. These were paramilitary units responsible for guarding the Nazi leaders, terrorizing anti-Nazi individuals and groups, and operating the concentration (death) camps of Nazi Germany. At times they were used, in conjunction with other troops, for putting down resistance, most notably the Warsaw Ghetto uprising of Jews in April, 1943.

Soyedineniye--A brigade-size group about equal to a division by U.S. Army standards.

Zimlyanka--underground hut or cave where forest partisans or civilians lived.

INDEX

INDIVIDUAL FIGHTERS

Note: In some cases, only the last name is mentioned; in others only the first or the occupation. Such were the times.

Korochkin, Anatoly, 137
Korotkov, 115
Kossyenko, Konstantine, 79-82
Koveh, Yaakov, 193
Kovpak, Sidor, 134,152,153,220,227,231
Kozjukhar, Makkar, 119
Krakinovsky, 188
Krassnostein, David, 208
Kravshinsky, 94
Kreiko, Galina, 98
Kryllyersky, Nicolai, 211
Kuperberg, Itzik, 204
Kurtz the doctor, 130
Kysia, 147
Kyzya, Luka, 227

Landau, Efraim, Moshe, and Anshel, 137
Lande, Sender, 203
Landor, Chaya, 142
Lapidot, Israel, 93-100
Lapidot, Misha, 98-100
Lapopin, Vladya, 134
Lashello, Beibai, 118
Leanders, Liza, 129
Lessin, Lazar, 99
Levi, Yaakov, 195
Levin, Tsadok Chaim, 89
Levitas, Leonid, 92
Liebensohn, Haritun, 208,212
Liebherz, Zvi, 137
Liefa, Rabbi, 128
Lifshitz, Rachel, 190-191
Linkov, Gregory, 64,164,170-179,226,228,231
Lipkovich, 181
Lissoksky, Liezer and Abraham, 126
Litvinovsky, Yefim, 88
Lorber, Berl ("Malenka"), 204,229
Lupianski, Boris, 185,187,189-190
Lussik, Wolf, 94

Mankoviskey, Asher, 137
Margalit, Alexander, 87
Marmelstein the doctor, 130
Marosya the peasant woman, 96
Martovski, Shmuel, 190
Masko, Alexander, 73-79
Matrossov, Alexander, 220
Matviev, Alexander Pavlovich, 117
Meirov, 185

Risakov, Vassili, 102-112
Robinson, Sarah and Moshe, 191
Rodionov, Constantine ("Smirnov"), 186-187; (see also Smirnov)
Rokhlin, Boris, 119-120
Rothstein, Frieda, 191
Rotter the doctor, 131

Saburov, 231
Sadovsky, Pesach, 195
Sakharov, 172
Salai, 72
Savitch, A., 152
Scherbin, Vassili, 177,179
Schneider, Pima, 100
Schwartz the violinist, 91
Sedlanikov, 221
Segel, Yeshayahu, 127
Shamenskaya, Vera, 166-168
Shatzglovsky the tailor, 90
Shenitskosa, Antanas, 183
Shepa, Susel, 203
Sher, Leib, 186
Sherman, Moshe, 186
Shirokov, Mark, 119
Shlikov, Commander, 168
Shmoylova, Chaya, 185
Shmuelov, 181
Shmulyakov, Hirsch, 188
Shostakovitch, Major, 193
Siemen, Genzig, 181-182
Silber, Leizer, 184
Silberpark, Nachman, 124
Simberg, Danya, 207,212
Singer, L., 220,229
Sirovsky, 91
Slavyanski, 181
Smirnov, Commander, 186,191; (see also Constantine Rodionov)
Solomon, Leib, 191
Sorin the hatmaker, 90
Stern, Boris, 181,190,195
Stonov, D., 72
Strogatz, Leib, 99
Strokach, Timofei, 153,227,231

Tartakovsky, Misha, 134
Teitel, 181
Tepfer, 183

The editor of this book, aged six months, with his
parents, Irving and Faye Porter (Israel and Faye
Puchtik), after liberation, Rovno, Ukraine, June 1945.
The partisan medal awarded was the "War of the
Fatherland, First Class."

Sender (Sam) Lande.
Now lives in Milwaukee, Wisconsin.

Berl Lorber (nom de guerre: "Malenka"),
an assistant commander to Kruk.
Now lives in Seattle, Washington.

Asher Flash. Now lives in Israel.

Susel Shepa of the Kruk Division.
Now lives in Denver, Colorado.

Yuri (Jack) Melamedik of the Max Group
under "Dadya Petya."
Now lives in Montreal, Canada.

Pinick Berman, a young bemedaled Soviet fighter
in the Kruk Division which was under the command of
General A. Brinski ("Dadya Petya"-"Uncle Petya").

Partisan Puchtik (Jack Nusan Porter's father) and
Commander Konishchuk (right) of the Ukrainian
Kruk Detachment of partisans.

Nazi officers executing partisans.

David Kaimach

A partisan stronghold.
Note the "Cossack" style winter clothes
and the automatic weapons.

Partisan detachment commanded by O. Saburov,
fording a river. Enemy rear lines, 1942.

Commander of the Kovno partisans, Leib Solomon, (right),
and the leader of the "Vaparoid" ("Forward") Brigade, Tziko.

Michael (Mikhail) Glieder, the "underground" filmmaker.

Laying the mine...

Derailing the tracks...

The results....

A group of Kovno partisans after liberation:
(left to right) An unidentified woman, A. Pilovnik,
S. Rubenson, and Y. Ratner. Note the extreme youth
of these Jewish partisans. Kovno is Kaunas, Lithuania.

Leaders of the Party Unit of the "Death to the Invaders"
brigade: (left to right) M. Lane, D. Tepper, K. Rudionov
(the head of the brigade), M. Sherman, and A. Tepper.

The Nazi eagle in the dust. Soviet troops look on.

Victorious Soviet troops return home.

Partisan papers and partisan medal belonging to Moishe
Flash of the Kruk and Kachtuchin Otryad under the
overall command of A. Brinski ("Dadya Petya"). He
fought in the western Ukraine and western Beylorussia
from September 1942 to February 1944. The medal is
"The Partisan Medal, First Class". Without the
documents, the medal was useless. Flash, who now lives
in Toronto with his family, had a nom de guerre:
"Ivan." (See next two photos also.)

БОЕВАЯ ХАРАКТЕРИСТИКА.

На бойца партизана ххх партизанского соединения Героя Совет-
ского Союза полковника Б р и н с к о г о тов. Ф Л Я Ш А
М о й ш е А б р а м о в и ч а рождения 1909 года , п/ парт/
уроженец с. Лолонька Колковского района Волынской области ,
Тов. Ф л я ш з а время пребывания в партизанах с августа 1944 год
.... в организации крушении воинских эшелонов противника
7 раз, атак .... риве .... при 6 раз, жолдер водокачки на
ст. Камен Коширск, в засадах против немцев 4 раза, против националистов 3 раза. Учавствовал в бои против немцев 6 раз и
против националистов 7 раз где проявил себя смелым бойцом.
учавствовал при уничтожении комендатуры полицейской, а также
при разгроме масло-перегоночных заводов, в разгроме немецких
лавок, принимал участие в уничтожении националистических шпи-
онов. а также в достаче оружия сам лично достал 13 винтовок,
Кроме этого тов. Фляш выполн спецзадания командования.

себя как десциплинированого бойца партизана/ изапрояленою борбу
против немцев командованием партизанского отряда представлен
к Правительственной награде.

КОМАНДИР ОТРЯДА ПАРТИЗАНСКОГО
.... Ст. Л е й т е н а н т   /К о с т и н/

НАЧАЛЬНИК ШТАБА ПАРТИЗАНСКОЙ БРИГАДЫ № 1
         Ст. л е й т е н а н т   /Б у т к о ./

Moishe Flash's partisan documents.

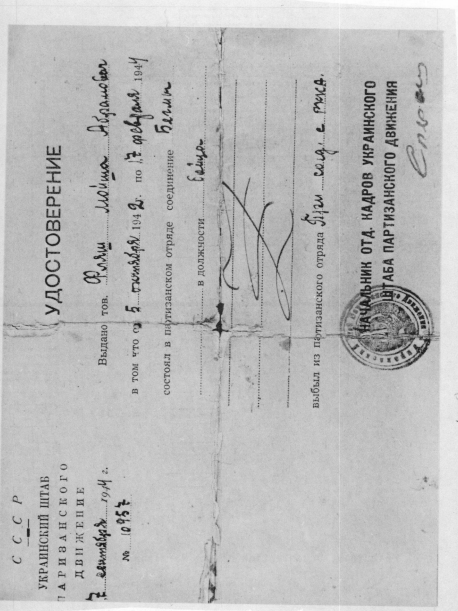

Moishe Flash's partisan documents.

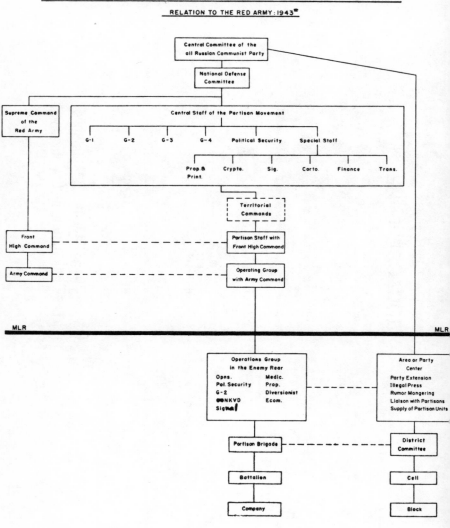

Figure 1. Organization of the Partisan Movement.

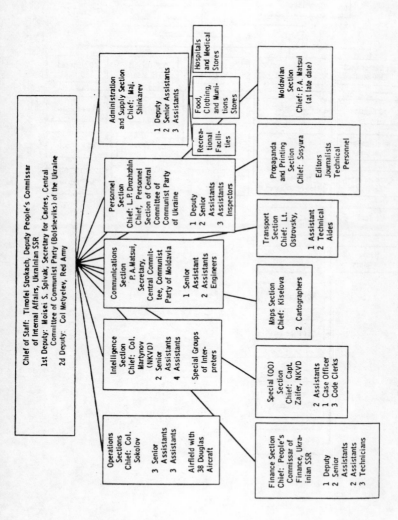

Figure 2. Staff of the Partisan Movement in the Ukraine.

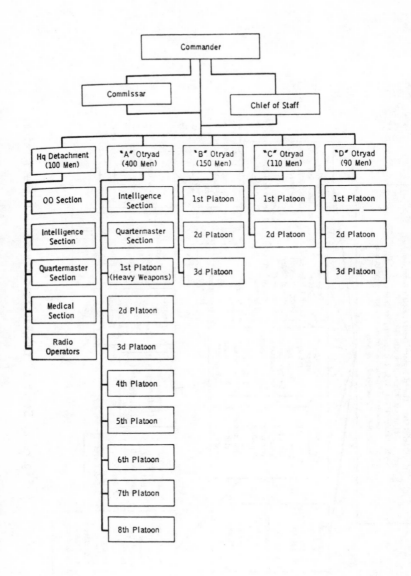

Figure 3. Generalized structure of a partisan brigade.

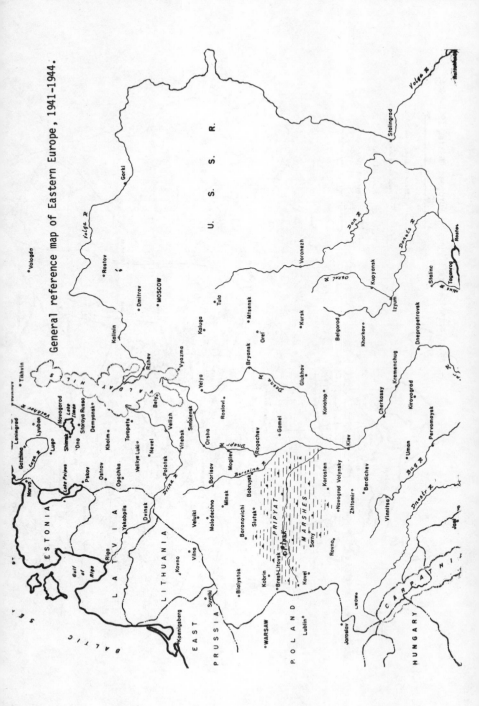

General reference map of Eastern Europe, 1941-1944.

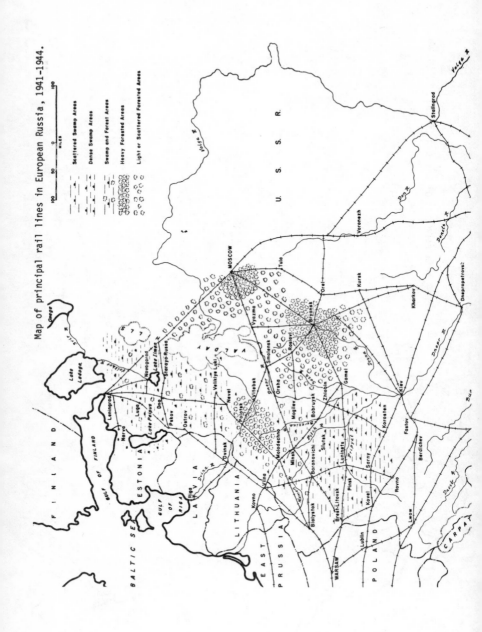

Map of principal rail lines in European Russia, 1941-1944.

ABOUT THE AUTHOR

JACK NUSAN PORTER is a sociologist, author, editor, and political activist. Born in the Ukraine and raised in Milwaukee, he graduated cum laude from the University of Wisconsin-Milwaukee and received his Ph.D. in sociology from Northwestern University in 1971.

He has published fifteen books and anthologies and nearly 150 articles, including Student Protest and the Technocratic Society, The Study of Society (contributing editor), Jewish Radicalism (with Peter Dreier), The Sociology of American Jews, The Jew as Outsider: Collected Essays, Kids in Cults (with Irvin Doress), Conflict and Conflict Resolution, Jewish Partisans (two volumes), and Genocide and Human Rights. He has contributed to many reference books and journals including the Encyclopedia Judaica, Encyclopedia of Sociology, Society, Midstream, and Writers Digest.

He is the founder of the Journal of the History of Sociology and the Sociology of Business Newsletter and the winner of the John Atherton Fellowship from the Breadloaf Writers Conference as well as fellowships from the Memorial Foundation for Jewish Culture and the World Jewish Congress. He is listed in Who's Who in the East, American Men and Women in Science, Who's Who in Israel, and Contemporary Authors.

Dr. Porter has lectured widely on American social problems and political/religious movements. He has testified before several government commissions including the White House Conference on Families and the National Peace Academy hearings. Long active in Israel and Jewish communal activities, he is considered one of the founders of the Jewish student movement in the USA and Canada in the late 1960s.

He lives in Boston with his wife Miriam and their son Gabriel, and is at present the Massachusetts representative of the American-Israel Securities Corporation.